POE DAMERON

STAR WARS

BLACK SQUADRON

BLACK SQUADRON

Writer	**CHARLES SOULE**
Artist	**PHIL NOTO**
Letterer	**VC's JOE CARAMAGNA**
Cover Art	**PHIL NOTO**

Assistant Editor	**HEATHER ANTOS**
Editor	**JORDAN D. WHITE**
Executive Editor	**C.B. CEBULSKI**

"SaBBotage"

Writer/Artist/Letterer	**CHRIS ELIOPOULOS**
Color Artist	**JORDIE BELLAIRE**

Editor in Chief	**AXEL ALONSO**
Chief Creative Officer	**JOE QUESADA**
Publisher	**DAN BUCKLEY**

For Lucasfilm:

Senior Editor	**FRANK PARISI**
Creative Director	**MICHAEL SIGLAIN**
Lucasfilm Story Group	**RAYNE ROBERTS, PABLO HIDALGO, LELAND CHEE, MATT MARTIN**

Collection Editor	JENNIFER GRUNWALD
Associate Managing Editor	KATERI WOODY
Associate Editor	SARAH BRUNSTAD
Editor, Special Projects	MARK D. BEAZLEY
VP Production & Special Projects	JEFF YOUNGQUIST
SVP Print, Sales & Marketing	DAVID GABRIEL
Book Designer	ADAM DEL RE

STAR WARS: POE DAMERON VOL. 1 — BLACK SQUADRON. Contains material originally published in magazine form as POE DAMERON #1-6. First printing 2016. ISBN# 978-1-302-90110-3. Published by MARVEL WORLDWIDE, INC., a subsidiary of MARVEL ENTERTAINMENT, LLC. OFFICE OF PUBLICATION: 135 West 50th Street, New York, NY 10020. STAR WARS and related text and illustrations are trademarks and/or copyrights, in the United States and other countries, of Lucasfilm Ltd. and/or its affiliates. © & TM Lucasfilm Ltd. No similarity between any of the names, characters, persons, and/or institutions in this magazine with those of any living or dead person or institution is intended, and any such similarity which may exist is purely coincidental. Marvel and its logos are TM Marvel Characters, Inc. Printed in the U.S.A. ALAN FINE, President, Marvel Entertainment; DAN BUCKLEY, President, TV, Publishing & Brand

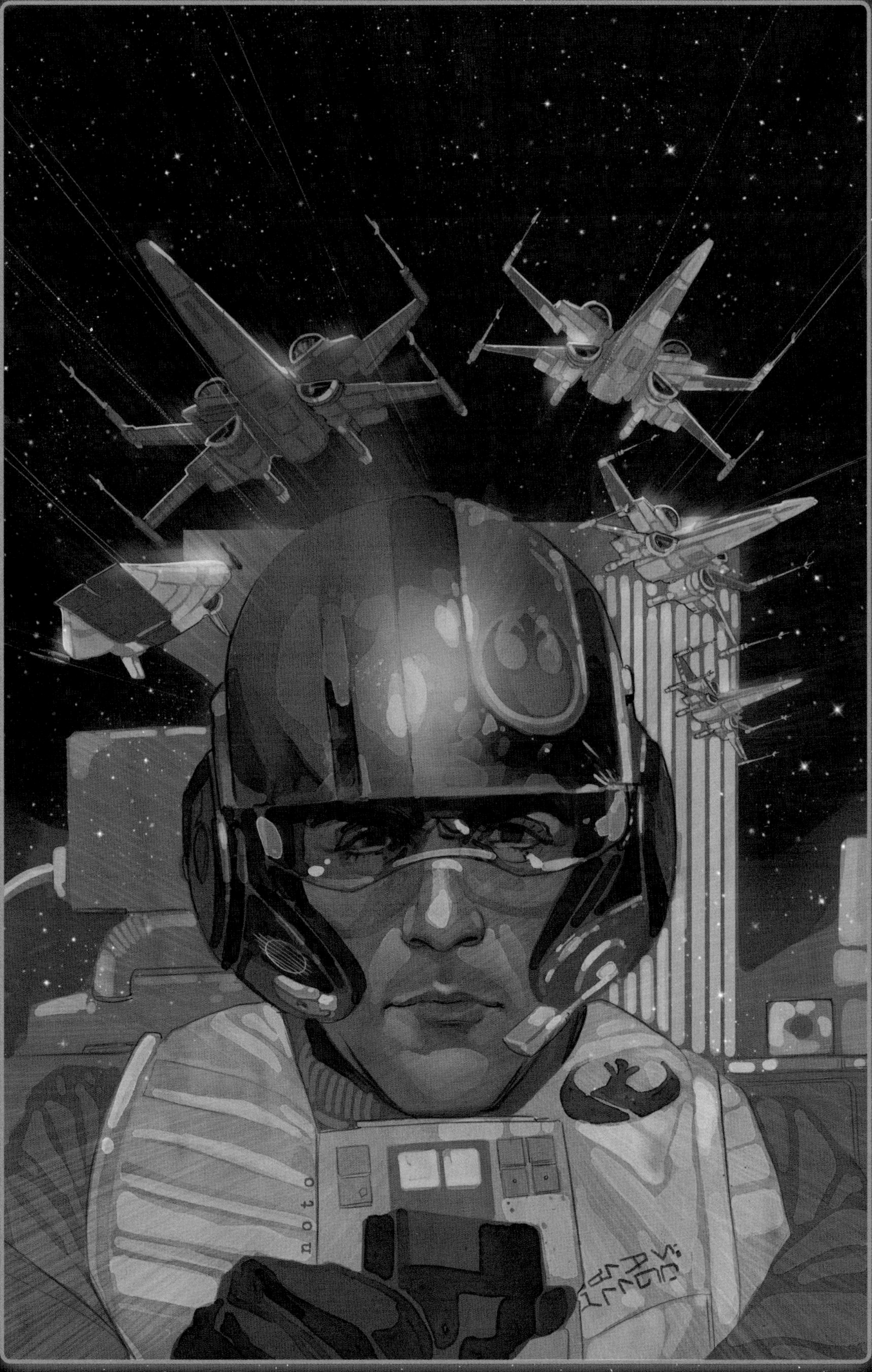

Book I

BLACK SQUADRON

Thirty years have passed since the defeat of the evil Galactic Empire, but threats of turmoil are rising.

To stem the tide of the First Order, a military force aiming in secret to overthrow the New Republic, General Leia Organa has founded the Resistance movement. Looking to expand her forces, Organa has recruited the best pilot in the galaxy – POE DAMERON.

Now, with the help of his droid BB-8 and squadron of fighter pilots, Poe must act quickly to defeat any threat to the Republic that comes his way, no matter how deadly the risks....

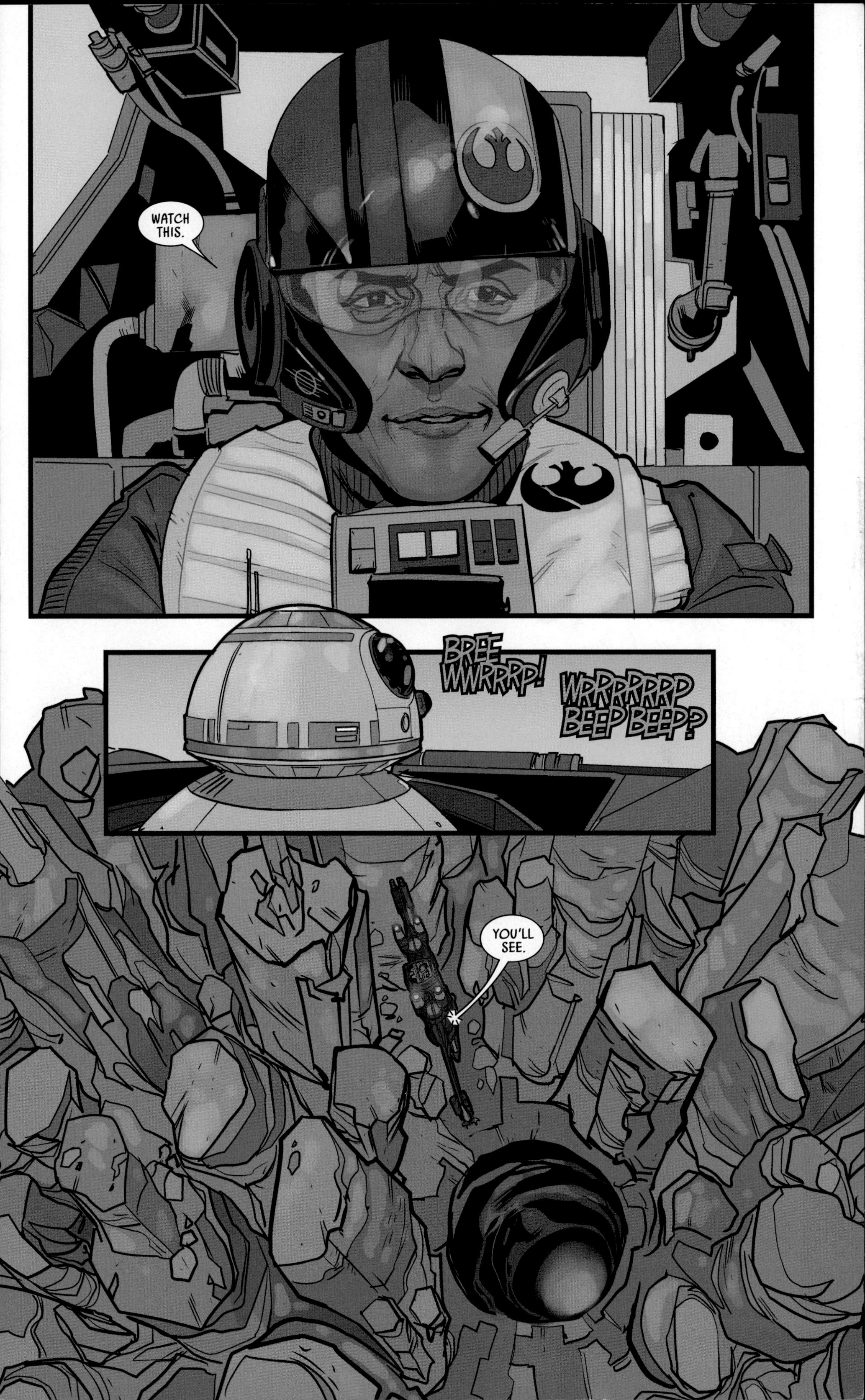
WATCH THIS.
BREE WWRRRP!
WRRRRRRP BEEP BEEP?
YOU'LL SEE.

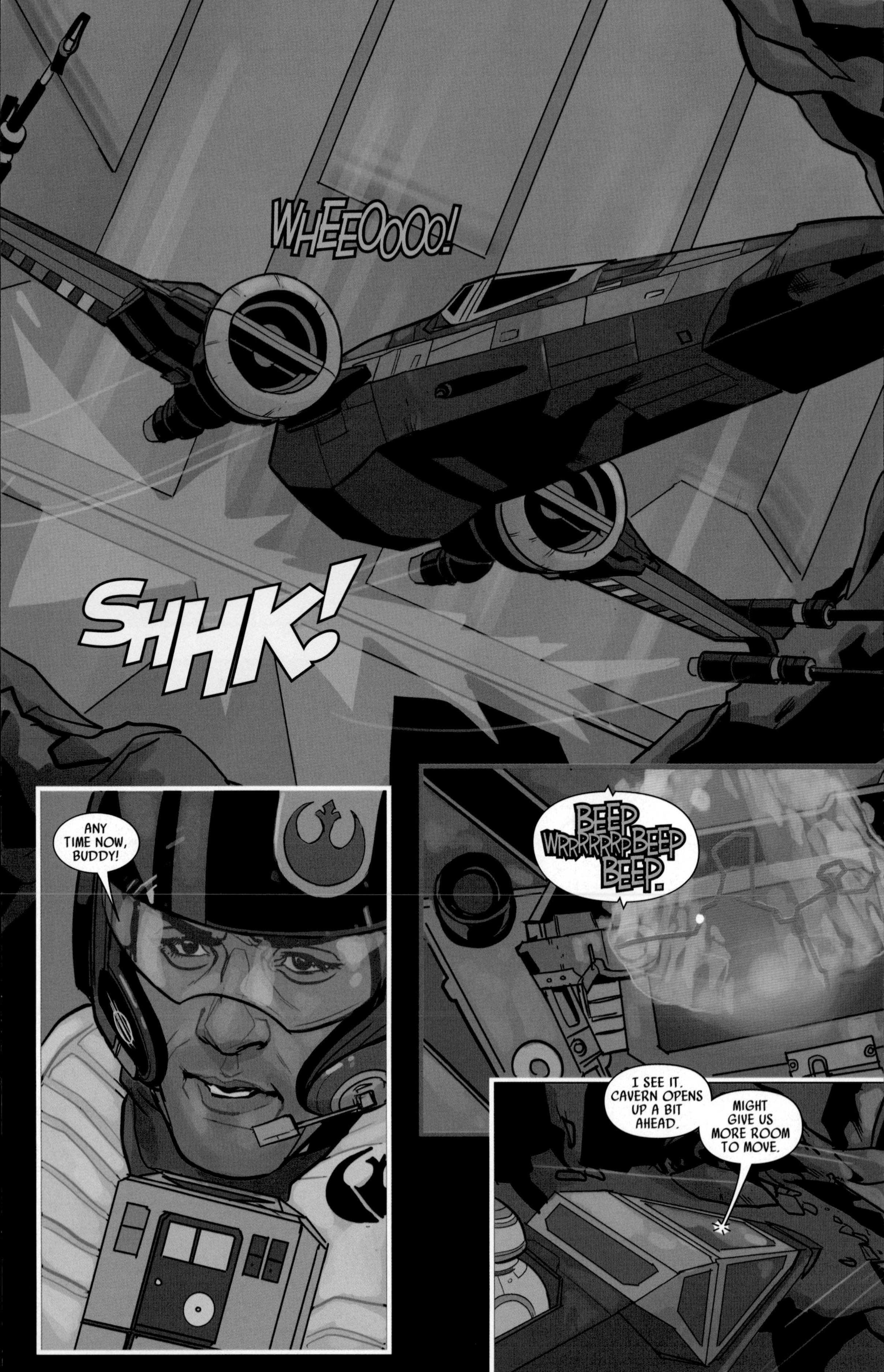
WHEEOOOO!
SHHK!
ANY TIME NOW, BUDDY!
BEEP WRRRRRRP BEEP BEEP.
I SEE IT. CAVERN OPENS UP A BIT AHEAD.
MIGHT GIVE US MORE ROOM TO MOVE.

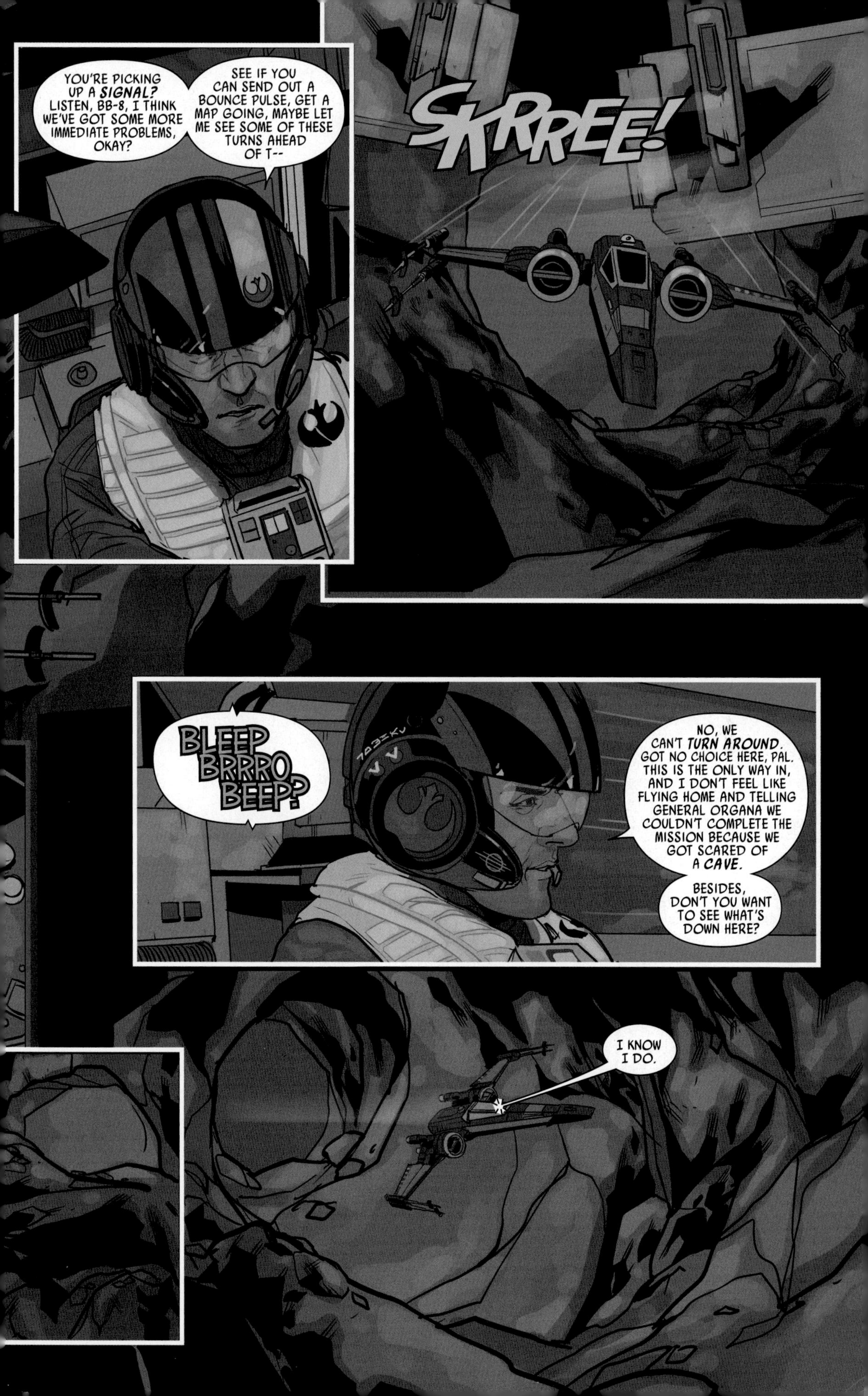
YOU'RE PICKING UP A SIGNAL? LISTEN, BB-8, I THINK WE'VE GOT SOME MORE IMMEDIATE PROBLEMS, OKAY?
SEE IF YOU CAN SEND OUT A BOUNCE PULSE, GET A MAP GOING, MAYBE LET ME SEE SOME OF THESE TURNS AHEAD OF T--
SKRREE!
BLEEP BRRRO BEEP?
NO, WE CAN'T TURN AROUND. GOT NO CHOICE HERE, PAL. THIS IS THE ONLY WAY IN, AND I DON'T FEEL LIKE FLYING HOME AND TELLING GENERAL ORGANA WE COULDN'T COMPLETE THE MISSION BECAUSE WE GOT SCARED OF A CAVE.
BESIDES, DON'T YOU WANT TO SEE WHAT'S DOWN HERE?
I KNOW I DO.

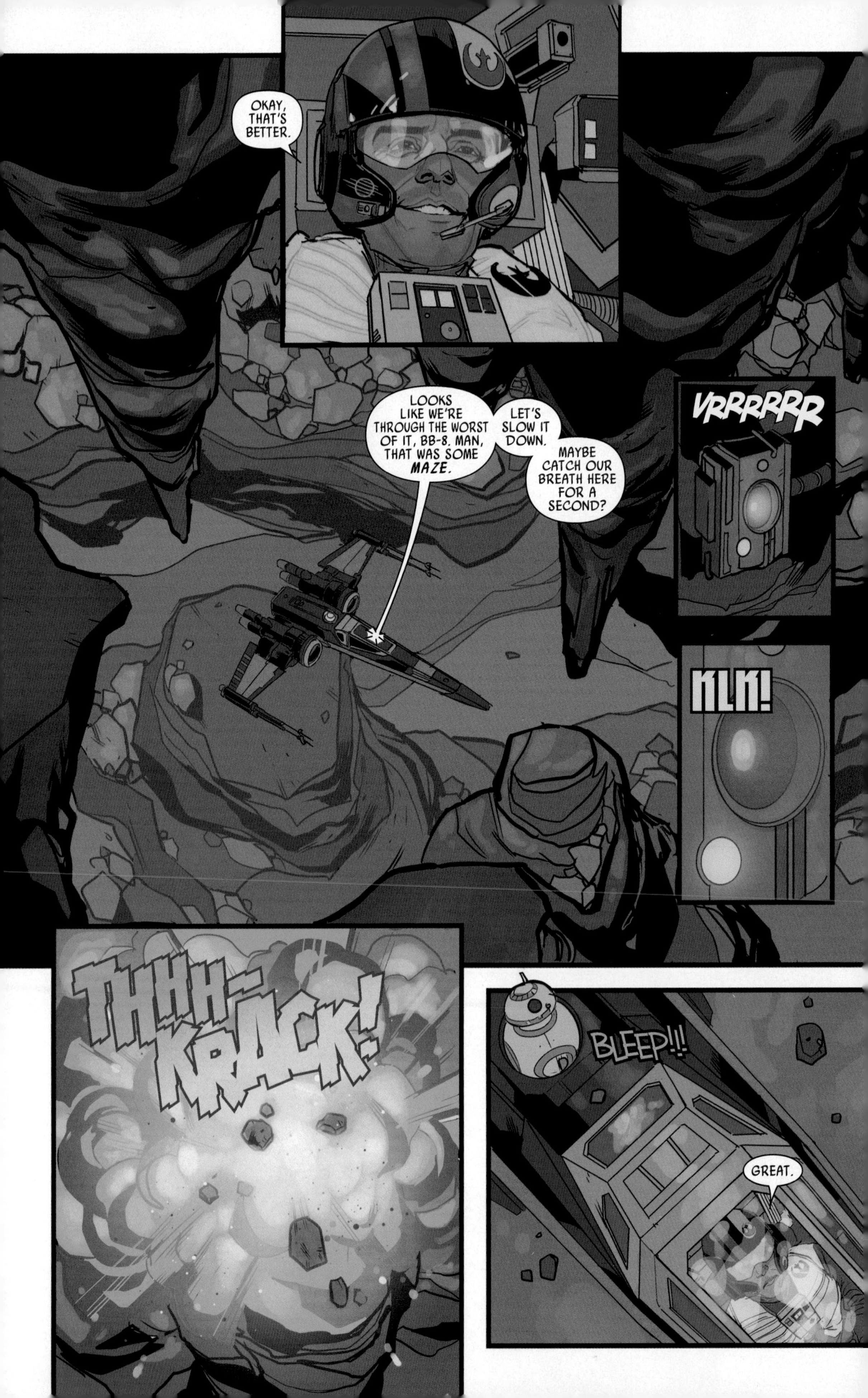
OKAY, THAT'S BETTER.
LOOKS LIKE WE'RE THROUGH THE WORST OF IT, BB-8. MAN, THAT WAS SOME *MAZE*.
LET'S SLOW IT DOWN.
MAYBE CATCH OUR BREATH HERE FOR A SECOND?
VRRRRRR
KLK!
THHH-KRACK!
BLEEP!!!
GREAT.

PROXIMITY MINES IN THE CEILING--THE WHOLE THING'S COMING DOWN ON US!

THIS IS A *KILL BOX*. WE GOTTA GET OUT OF HERE, PAL! FIND ME AN EXIT.

WRRRRP BLEEP BOOP!

GOT IT! HOLD TIGHT!

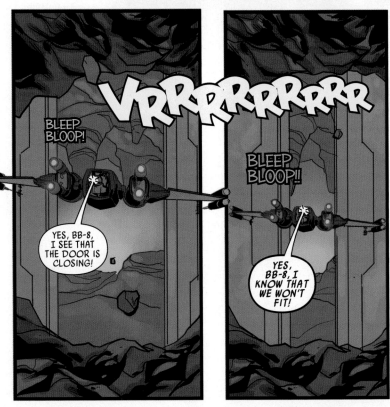

VRRRRRRRR

BLEEP BLOOP!

YES, BB-8, I SEE THAT THE DOOR IS CLOSING!

BLEEP BLOOP!!

YES, BB-8, I KNOW THAT WE WON'T FIT!

COME ON...

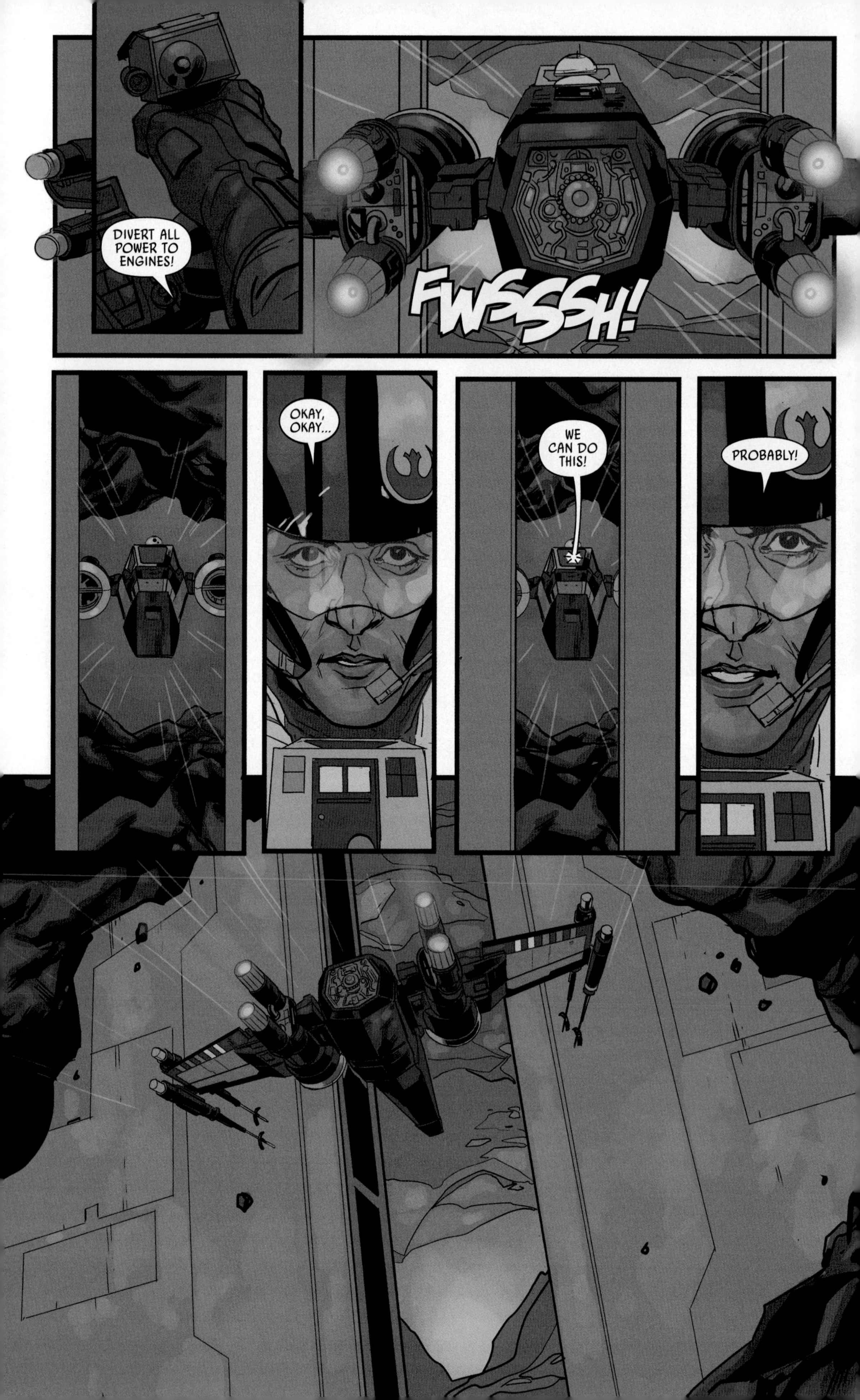
DIVERT ALL POWER TO ENGINES!
FWSSSH!
OKAY, OKAY...
WE CAN DO THIS!
PROBABLY!

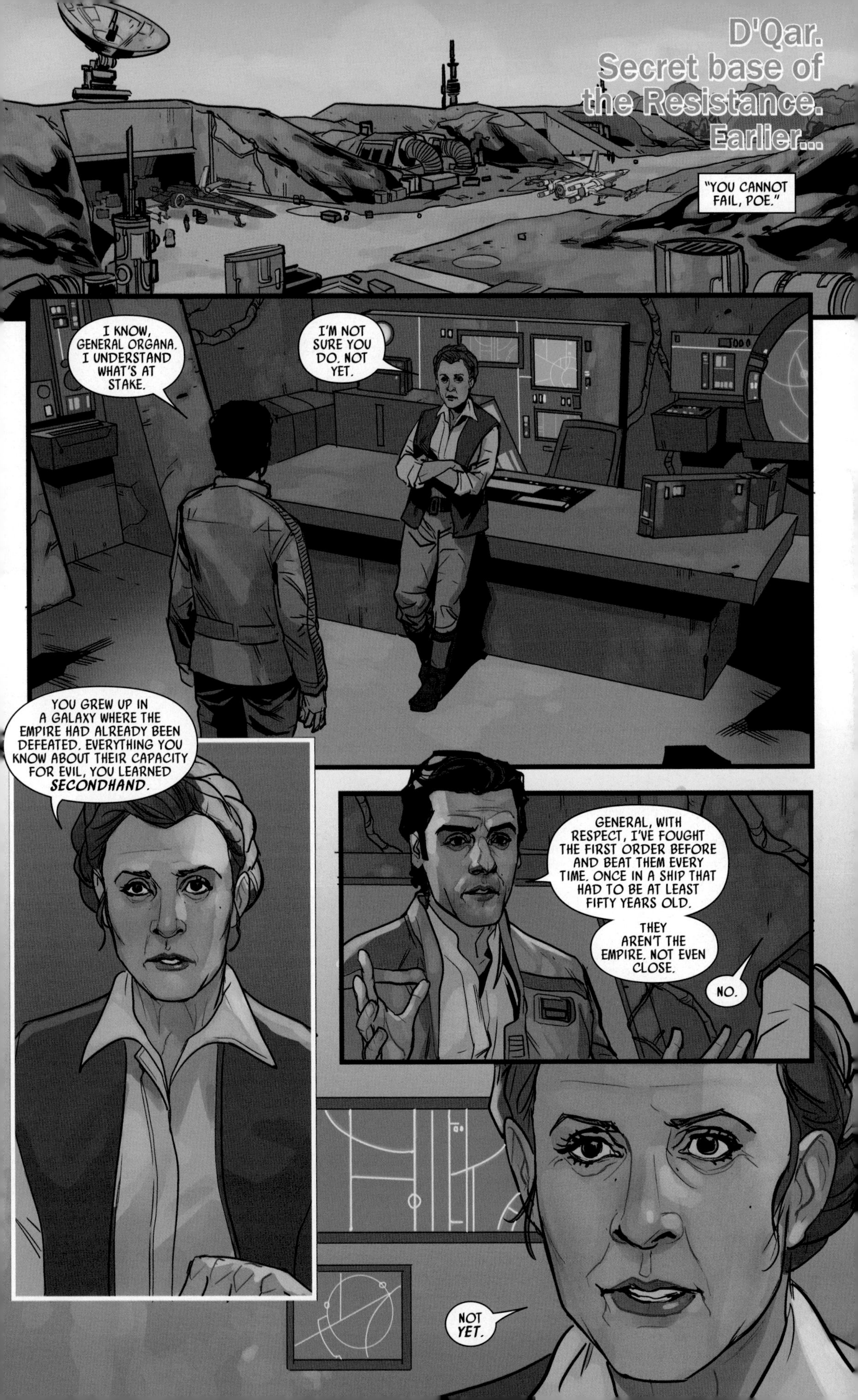
D'Qar.
Secret base of the Resistance.
Earlier...
"YOU CANNOT FAIL, POE."
I KNOW, GENERAL ORGANA. I UNDERSTAND WHAT'S AT STAKE.
I'M NOT SURE YOU DO. NOT YET.
YOU GREW UP IN A GALAXY WHERE THE EMPIRE HAD ALREADY BEEN DEFEATED. EVERYTHING YOU KNOW ABOUT THEIR CAPACITY FOR EVIL, YOU LEARNED SECONDHAND.
GENERAL, WITH RESPECT, I'VE FOUGHT THE FIRST ORDER BEFORE AND BEAT THEM EVERY TIME. ONCE IN A SHIP THAT HAD TO BE AT LEAST FIFTY YEARS OLD.
THEY AREN'T THE EMPIRE. NOT EVEN CLOSE.
NO.
NOT YET.

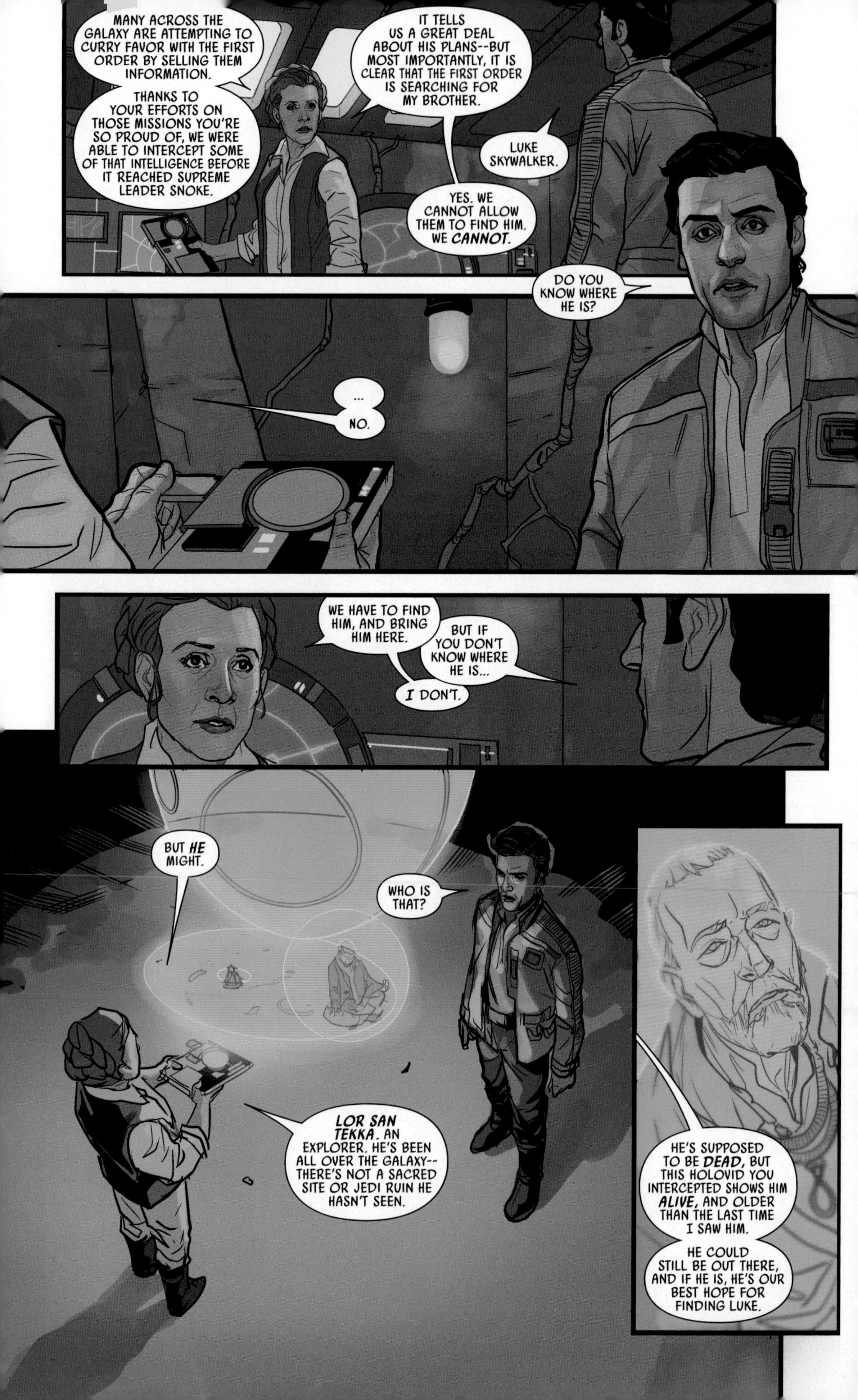
MANY ACROSS THE GALAXY ARE ATTEMPTING TO CURRY FAVOR WITH THE FIRST ORDER BY SELLING THEM INFORMATION.
THANKS TO YOUR EFFORTS ON THOSE MISSIONS YOU'RE SO PROUD OF, WE WERE ABLE TO INTERCEPT SOME OF THAT INTELLIGENCE BEFORE IT REACHED SUPREME LEADER SNOKE.
IT TELLS US A GREAT DEAL ABOUT HIS PLANS--BUT MOST IMPORTANTLY, IT IS CLEAR THAT THE FIRST ORDER IS SEARCHING FOR MY BROTHER.
LUKE SKYWALKER.
YES. WE CANNOT ALLOW THEM TO FIND HIM. WE CANNOT.
DO YOU KNOW WHERE HE IS?
...
NO.
WE HAVE TO FIND HIM, AND BRING HIM HERE.
BUT IF YOU DON'T KNOW WHERE HE IS...
I DON'T.
BUT HE MIGHT.
WHO IS THAT?
LOR SAN TEKKA. AN EXPLORER. HE'S BEEN ALL OVER THE GALAXY--THERE'S NOT A SACRED SITE OR JEDI RUIN HE HASN'T SEEN.
HE'S SUPPOSED TO BE DEAD, BUT THIS HOLOVID YOU INTERCEPTED SHOWS HIM ALIVE, AND OLDER THAN THE LAST TIME I SAW HIM.
HE COULD STILL BE OUT THERE, AND IF HE IS, HE'S OUR BEST HOPE FOR FINDING LUKE.

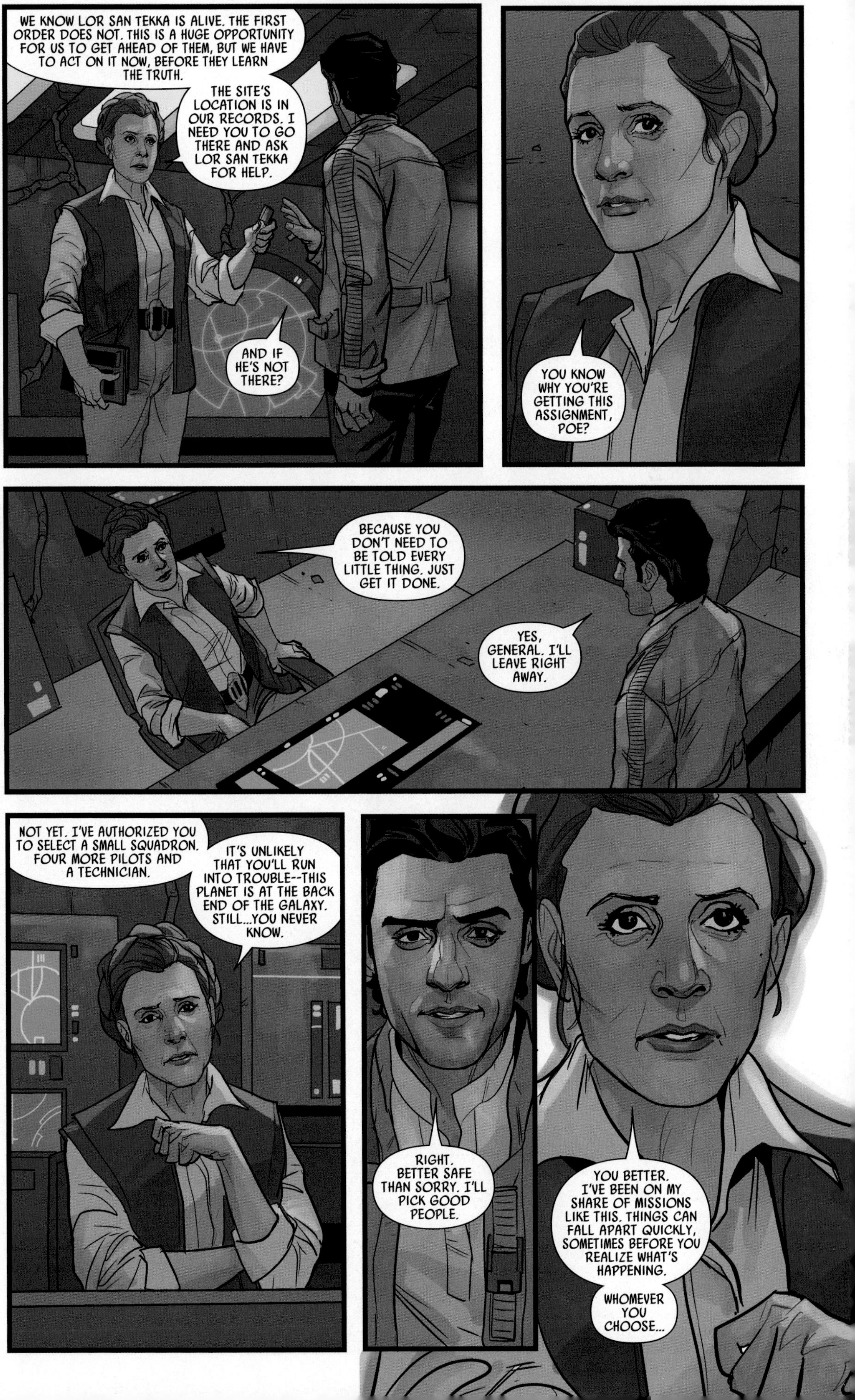
WE KNOW LOR SAN TEKKA IS ALIVE. THE FIRST ORDER DOES NOT. THIS IS A HUGE OPPORTUNITY FOR US TO GET AHEAD OF THEM, BUT WE HAVE TO ACT ON IT NOW, BEFORE THEY LEARN THE TRUTH.
THE SITE'S LOCATION IS IN OUR RECORDS. I NEED YOU TO GO THERE AND ASK LOR SAN TEKKA FOR HELP.
AND IF HE'S NOT THERE?
YOU KNOW WHY YOU'RE GETTING THIS ASSIGNMENT, POE?
BECAUSE YOU DON'T NEED TO BE TOLD EVERY LITTLE THING. JUST GET IT DONE.
YES, GENERAL. I'LL LEAVE RIGHT AWAY.
NOT YET. I'VE AUTHORIZED YOU TO SELECT A SMALL SQUADRON. FOUR MORE PILOTS AND A TECHNICIAN.
IT'S UNLIKELY THAT YOU'LL RUN INTO TROUBLE--THIS PLANET IS AT THE BACK END OF THE GALAXY. STILL...YOU NEVER KNOW.
RIGHT. BETTER SAFE THAN SORRY. I'LL PICK GOOD PEOPLE.
YOU BETTER. I'VE BEEN ON MY SHARE OF MISSIONS LIKE THIS. THINGS CAN FALL APART QUICKLY, SOMETIMES BEFORE YOU REALIZE WHAT'S HAPPENING.
WHOMEVER YOU CHOOSE...

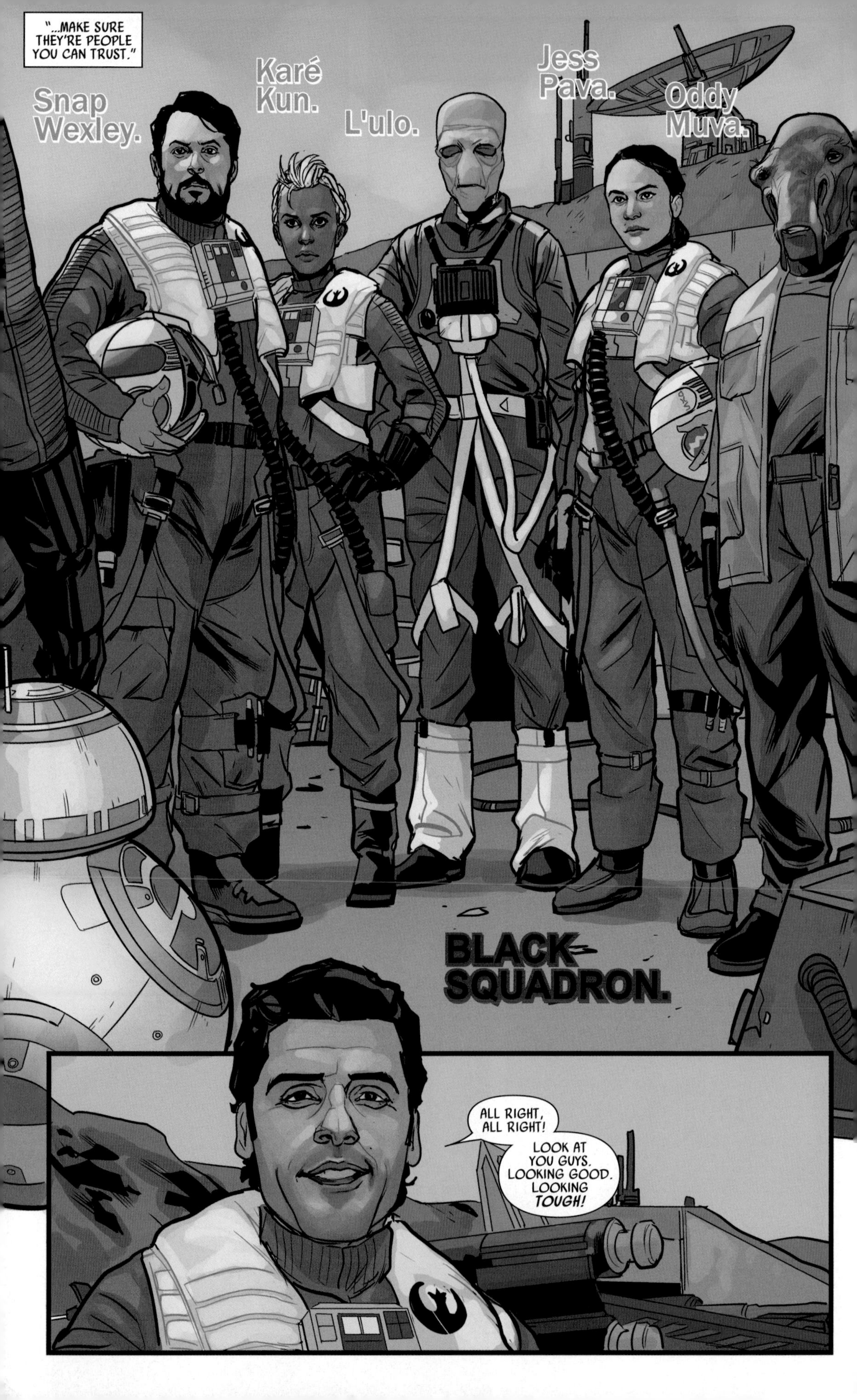
"...MAKE SURE THEY'RE PEOPLE YOU CAN TRUST."
Snap Wexley.
Karé Kun.
L'ulo.
Jess Pava.
Oddy Muva.
BLACK SQUADRON.
ALL RIGHT, ALL RIGHT!
LOOK AT YOU GUYS. LOOKING GOOD. LOOKING *TOUGH!*

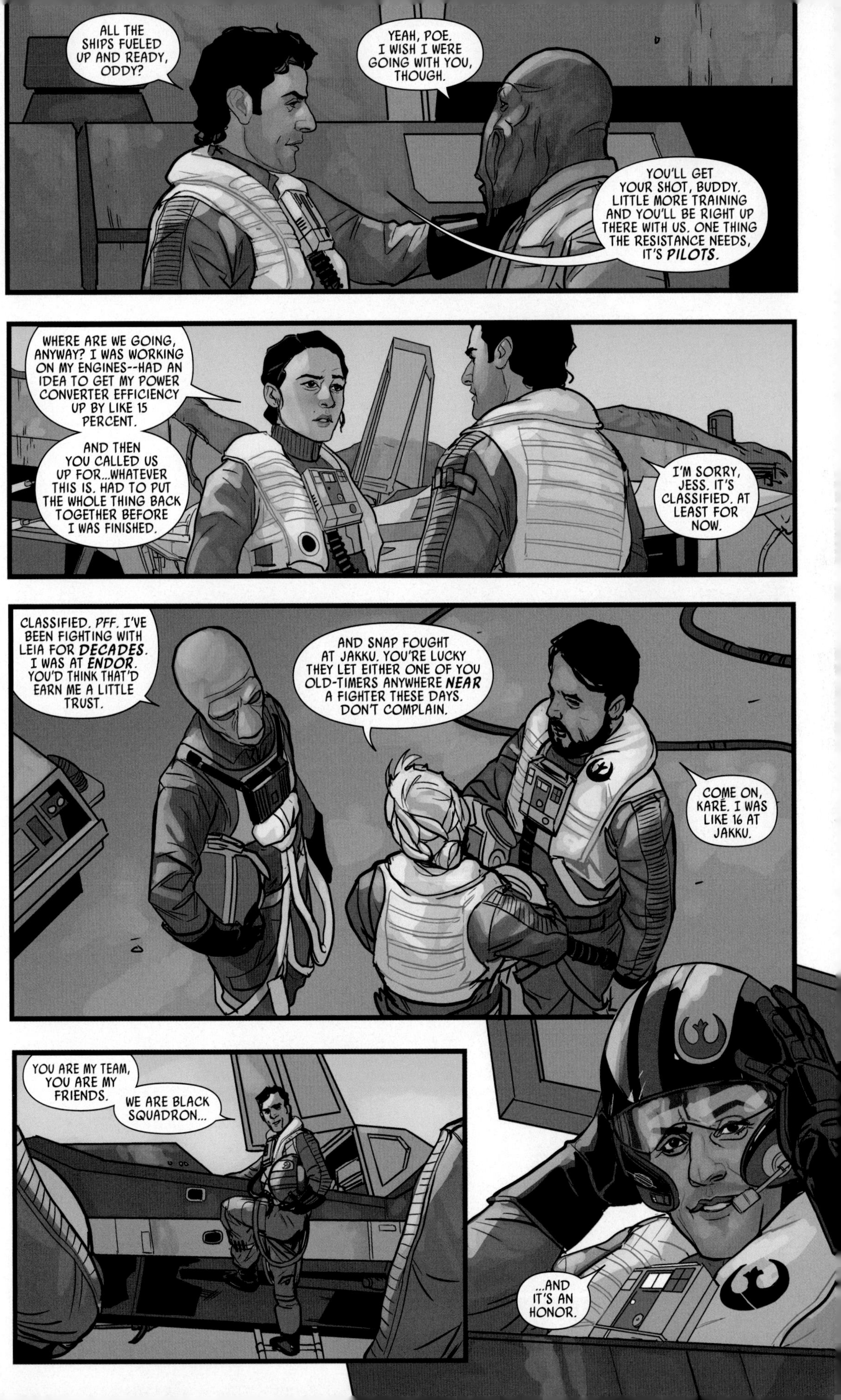
ALL THE SHIPS FUELED UP AND READY, ODDY?
YEAH, POE. I WISH I WERE GOING WITH YOU, THOUGH.
YOU'LL GET YOUR SHOT, BUDDY. LITTLE MORE TRAINING AND YOU'LL BE RIGHT UP THERE WITH US. ONE THING THE RESISTANCE NEEDS, IT'S PILOTS.
WHERE ARE WE GOING, ANYWAY? I WAS WORKING ON MY ENGINES--HAD AN IDEA TO GET MY POWER CONVERTER EFFICIENCY UP BY LIKE 15 PERCENT.
AND THEN YOU CALLED US UP FOR...WHATEVER THIS IS. HAD TO PUT THE WHOLE THING BACK TOGETHER BEFORE I WAS FINISHED.
I'M SORRY, JESS. IT'S CLASSIFIED. AT LEAST FOR NOW.
CLASSIFIED. PFF. I'VE BEEN FIGHTING WITH LEIA FOR DECADES. I WAS AT ENDOR. YOU'D THINK THAT'D EARN ME A LITTLE TRUST.
AND SNAP FOUGHT AT JAKKU. YOU'RE LUCKY THEY LET EITHER ONE OF YOU OLD-TIMERS ANYWHERE NEAR A FIGHTER THESE DAYS. DON'T COMPLAIN.
COME ON, KARÉ. I WAS LIKE 16 AT JAKKU.
YOU ARE MY TEAM, YOU ARE MY FRIENDS.
WE ARE BLACK SQUADRON...
...AND IT'S AN HONOR.

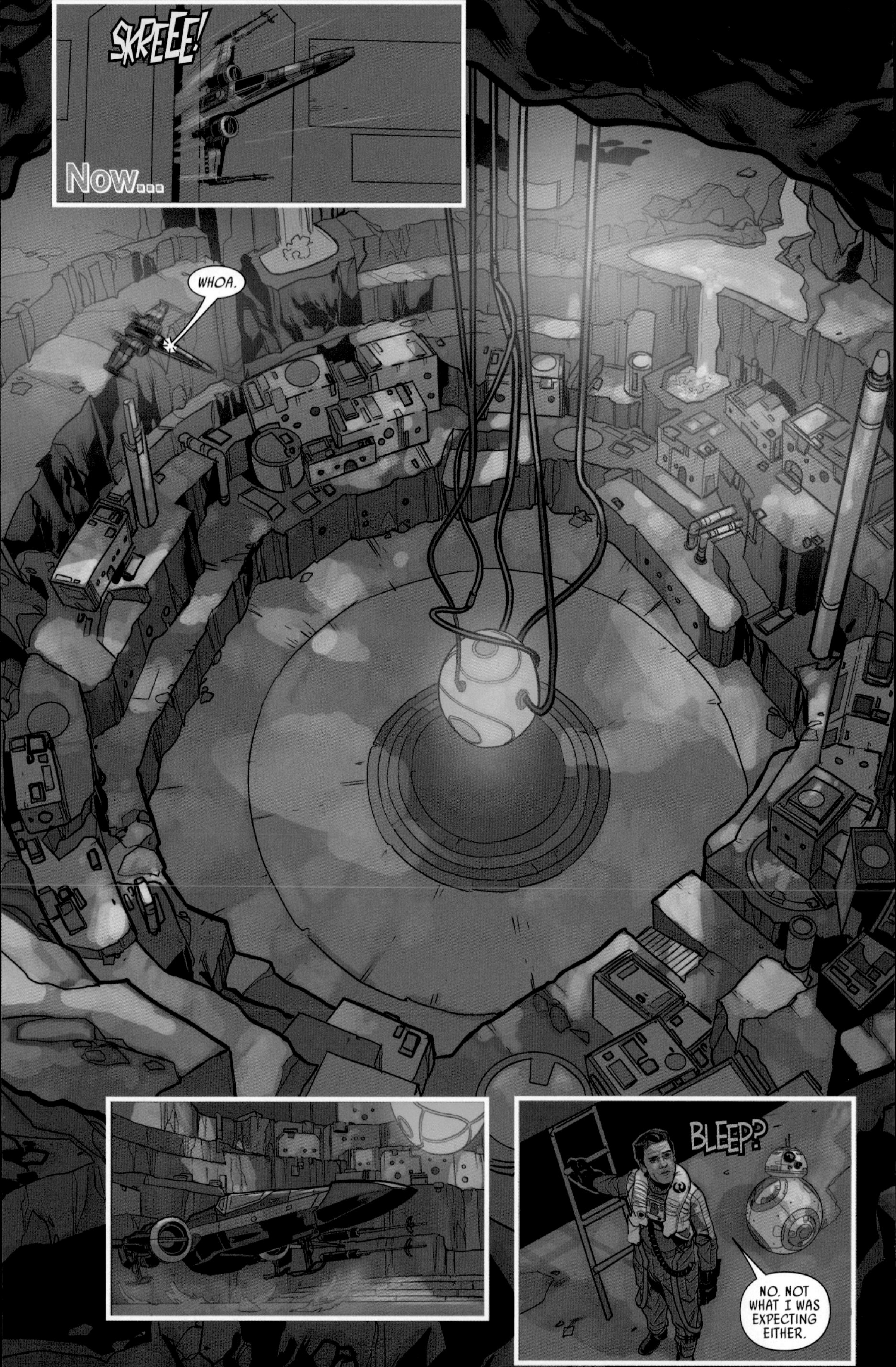
SKREEE!
Now...
WHOA.
BLEEP?
NO. NOT WHAT I WAS EXPECTING EITHER.

I'M GONNA CHECK IN WITH THE OTHERS. LET 'EM KNOW WE MADE IT.

WRRRRP BEEP BEEP?

SURE. GO FOR IT. TRACK DOWN THAT SIGNAL YOU WERE SO WORRIED ABOUT.

BLACK TWO, COME IN.

I READ YOU, BLACK LEADER. YOU MAKE IT THROUGH ALL RIGHT?

YEAH. GOT A LITTLE DICEY, BUT I'M IN.

WHAT'S DOWN THERE?

HARD TO SAY--LOOKS LIKE A SETTLEMENT, MAYBE. DESERTED, FAR AS I CAN TELL. THERE IS A PRETTY BIG EGG, THOUGH.

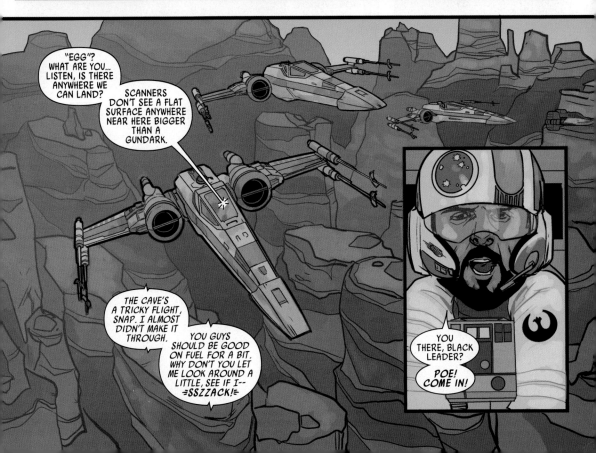

"EGG"? WHAT ARE YOU... LISTEN, IS THERE ANYWHERE WE CAN LAND?

SCANNERS DON'T SEE A FLAT SURFACE ANYWHERE NEAR HERE BIGGER THAN A GUNDARK.

THE CAVE'S A TRICKY FLIGHT, SNAP. I ALMOST DIDN'T MAKE IT THROUGH.

YOU GUYS SHOULD BE GOOD ON FUEL FOR A BIT. WHY DON'T YOU LET ME LOOK AROUND A LITTLE, SEE IF I-- =SSZZACK!=

YOU THERE, BLACK LEADER?

POE! COME IN!

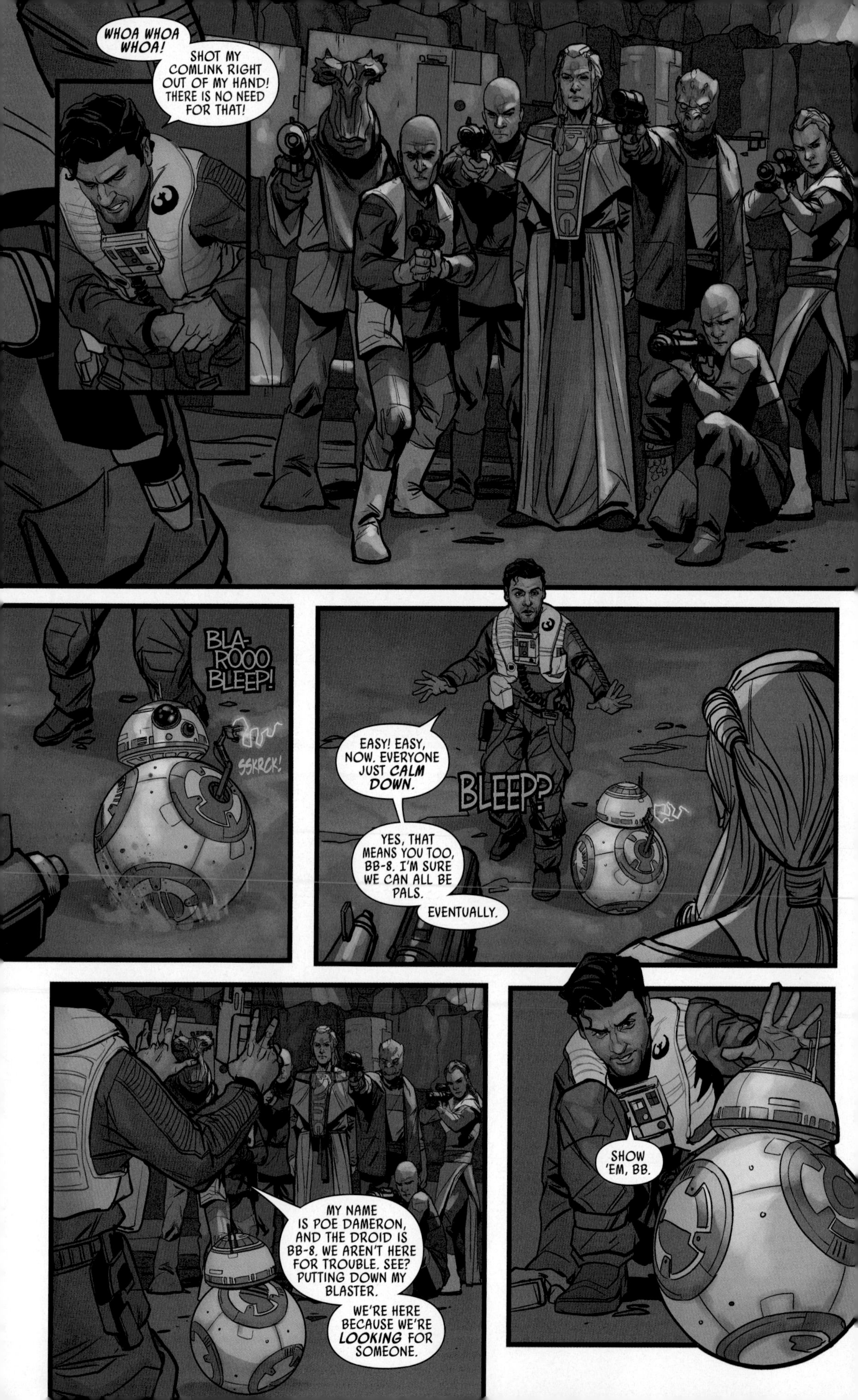
WHOA WHOA WHOA!
SHOT MY COMLINK RIGHT OUT OF MY HAND! THERE IS NO NEED FOR THAT!
BLA-ROOO BLEEP!
SSKRCK!
EASY! EASY, NOW. EVERYONE JUST CALM DOWN.
BLEEP?
YES, THAT MEANS YOU TOO, BB-8. I'M SURE WE CAN ALL BE PALS.
EVENTUALLY.
MY NAME IS POE DAMERON, AND THE DROID IS BB-8. WE AREN'T HERE FOR TROUBLE. SEE? PUTTING DOWN MY BLASTER.
WE'RE HERE BECAUSE WE'RE LOOKING FOR SOMEONE.
SHOW 'EM, BB.

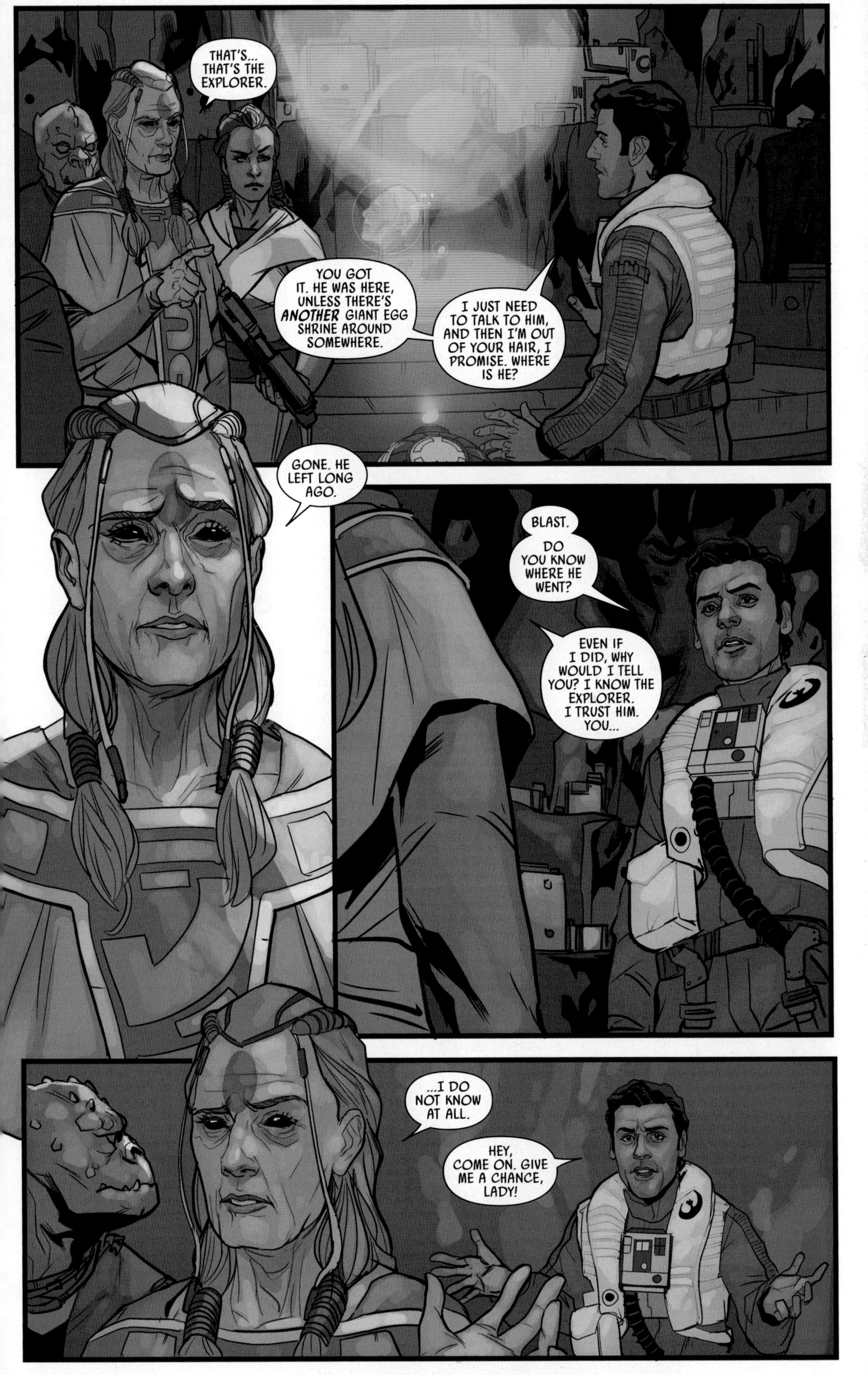
THAT'S... THAT'S THE EXPLORER.
YOU GOT IT. HE WAS HERE, UNLESS THERE'S ANOTHER GIANT EGG SHRINE AROUND SOMEWHERE.
I JUST NEED TO TALK TO HIM, AND THEN I'M OUT OF YOUR HAIR, I PROMISE. WHERE IS HE?
GONE. HE LEFT LONG AGO.
BLAST.
DO YOU KNOW WHERE HE WENT?
EVEN IF I DID, WHY WOULD I TELL YOU? I KNOW THE EXPLORER. I TRUST HIM. YOU...
...I DO NOT KNOW AT ALL.
HEY, COME ON. GIVE ME A CHANCE, LADY!

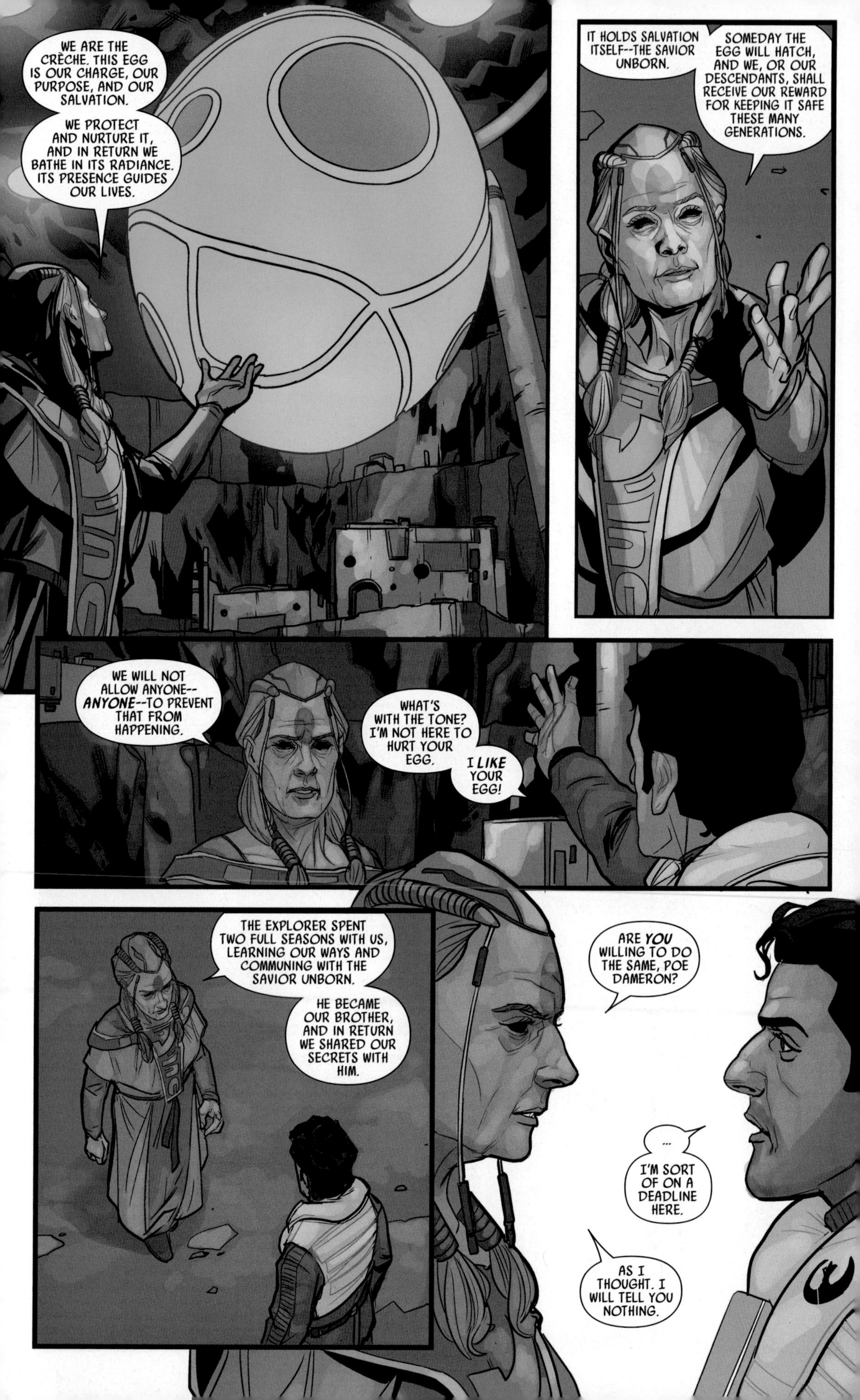
WE ARE THE CRÈCHE. THIS EGG IS OUR CHARGE, OUR PURPOSE, AND OUR SALVATION.
WE PROTECT AND NURTURE IT, AND IN RETURN WE BATHE IN ITS RADIANCE. ITS PRESENCE GUIDES OUR LIVES.
IT HOLDS SALVATION ITSELF--THE SAVIOR UNBORN.
SOMEDAY THE EGG WILL HATCH, AND WE, OR OUR DESCENDANTS, SHALL RECEIVE OUR REWARD FOR KEEPING IT SAFE THESE MANY GENERATIONS.
WE WILL NOT ALLOW ANYONE-- ANYONE--TO PREVENT THAT FROM HAPPENING.
WHAT'S WITH THE TONE? I'M NOT HERE TO HURT YOUR EGG.
I LIKE YOUR EGG!
THE EXPLORER SPENT TWO FULL SEASONS WITH US, LEARNING OUR WAYS AND COMMUNING WITH THE SAVIOR UNBORN.
HE BECAME OUR BROTHER, AND IN RETURN WE SHARED OUR SECRETS WITH HIM.
ARE YOU WILLING TO DO THE SAME, POE DAMERON?
...
I'M SORT OF ON A DEADLINE HERE.
AS I THOUGHT. I WILL TELL YOU NOTHING.

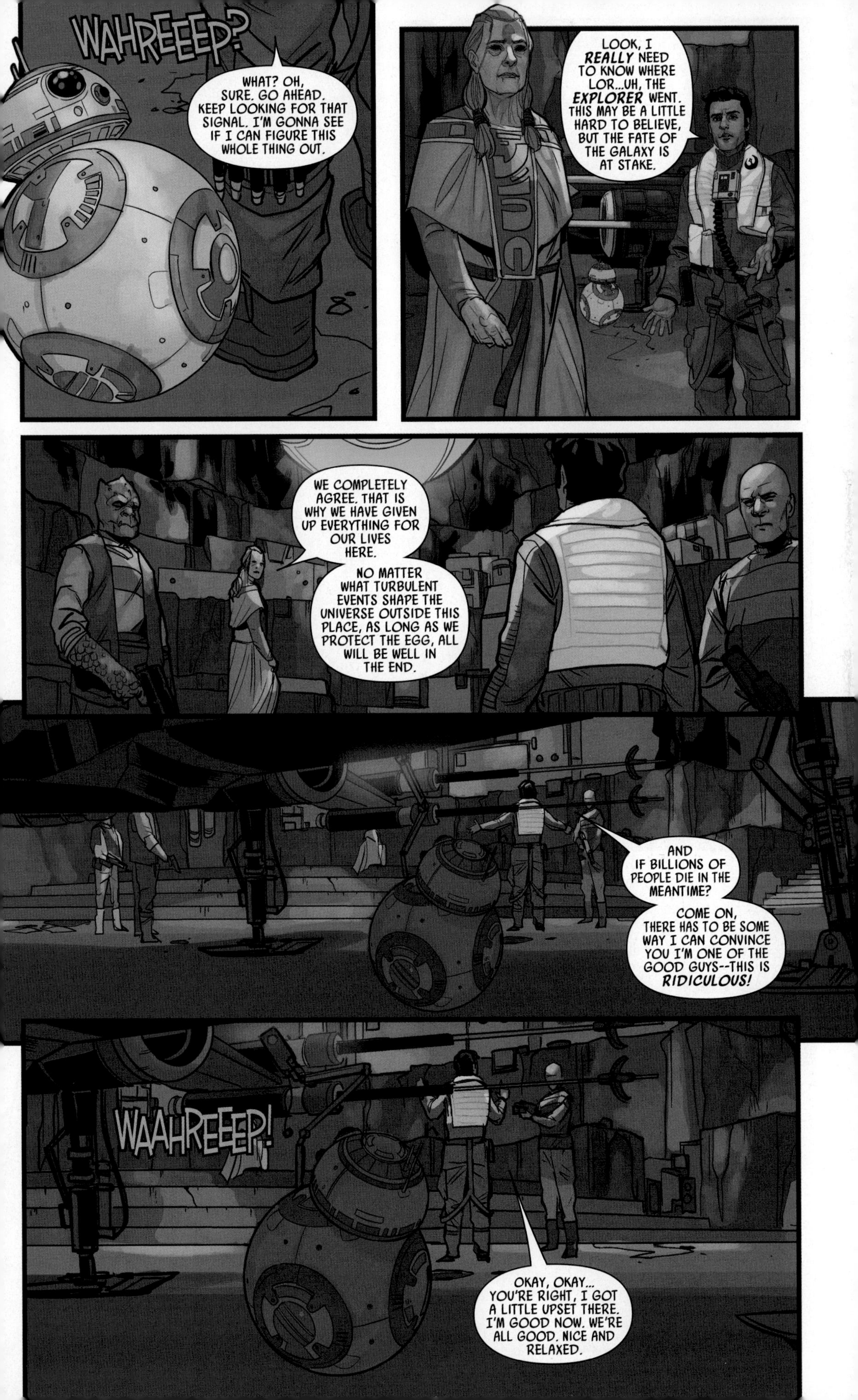
WAHREEEP?
WHAT? OH, SURE. GO AHEAD. KEEP LOOKING FOR THAT SIGNAL. I'M GONNA SEE IF I CAN FIGURE THIS WHOLE THING OUT.
LOOK, I *REALLY* NEED TO KNOW WHERE LOR...UH, THE *EXPLORER* WENT. THIS MAY BE A LITTLE HARD TO BELIEVE, BUT THE FATE OF THE GALAXY IS AT STAKE.
WE COMPLETELY AGREE. THAT IS WHY WE HAVE GIVEN UP EVERYTHING FOR OUR LIVES HERE.
NO MATTER WHAT TURBULENT EVENTS SHAPE THE UNIVERSE OUTSIDE THIS PLACE, AS LONG AS WE PROTECT THE EGG, ALL WILL BE WELL IN THE END.
AND IF BILLIONS OF PEOPLE DIE IN THE MEANTIME?
COME ON, THERE HAS TO BE SOME WAY I CAN CONVINCE YOU I'M ONE OF THE GOOD GUYS--THIS IS *RIDICULOUS!*
WAAHREEEP!
OKAY, OKAY... YOU'RE RIGHT, I GOT A LITTLE UPSET THERE. I'M GOOD NOW. WE'RE ALL GOOD. NICE AND RELAXED.

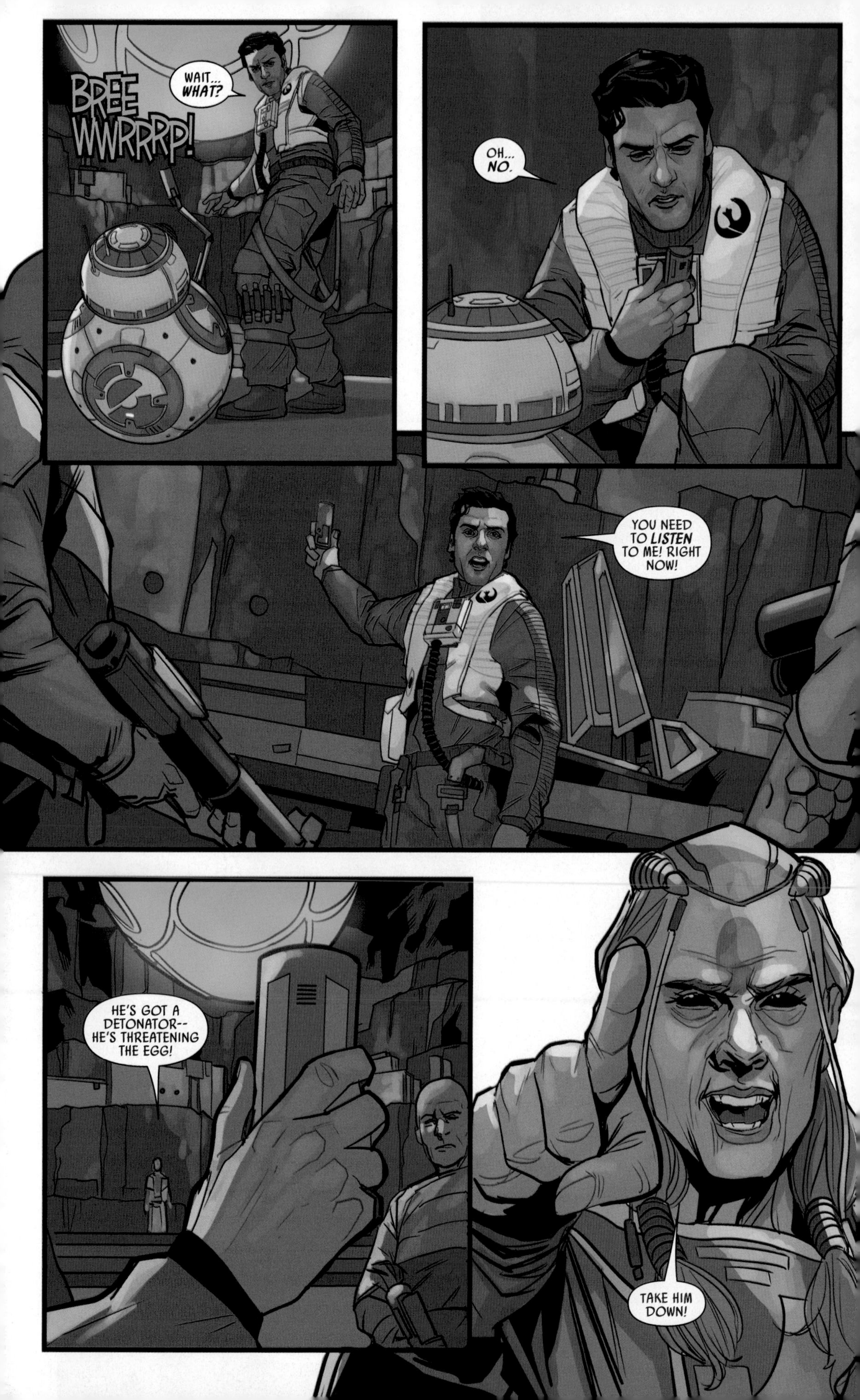
BREE WWRRRP!
WAIT... WHAT?
OH... NO.
YOU NEED TO LISTEN TO ME! RIGHT NOW!
HE'S GOT A DETONATOR-- HE'S THREATENING THE EGG!
TAKE HIM DOWN!

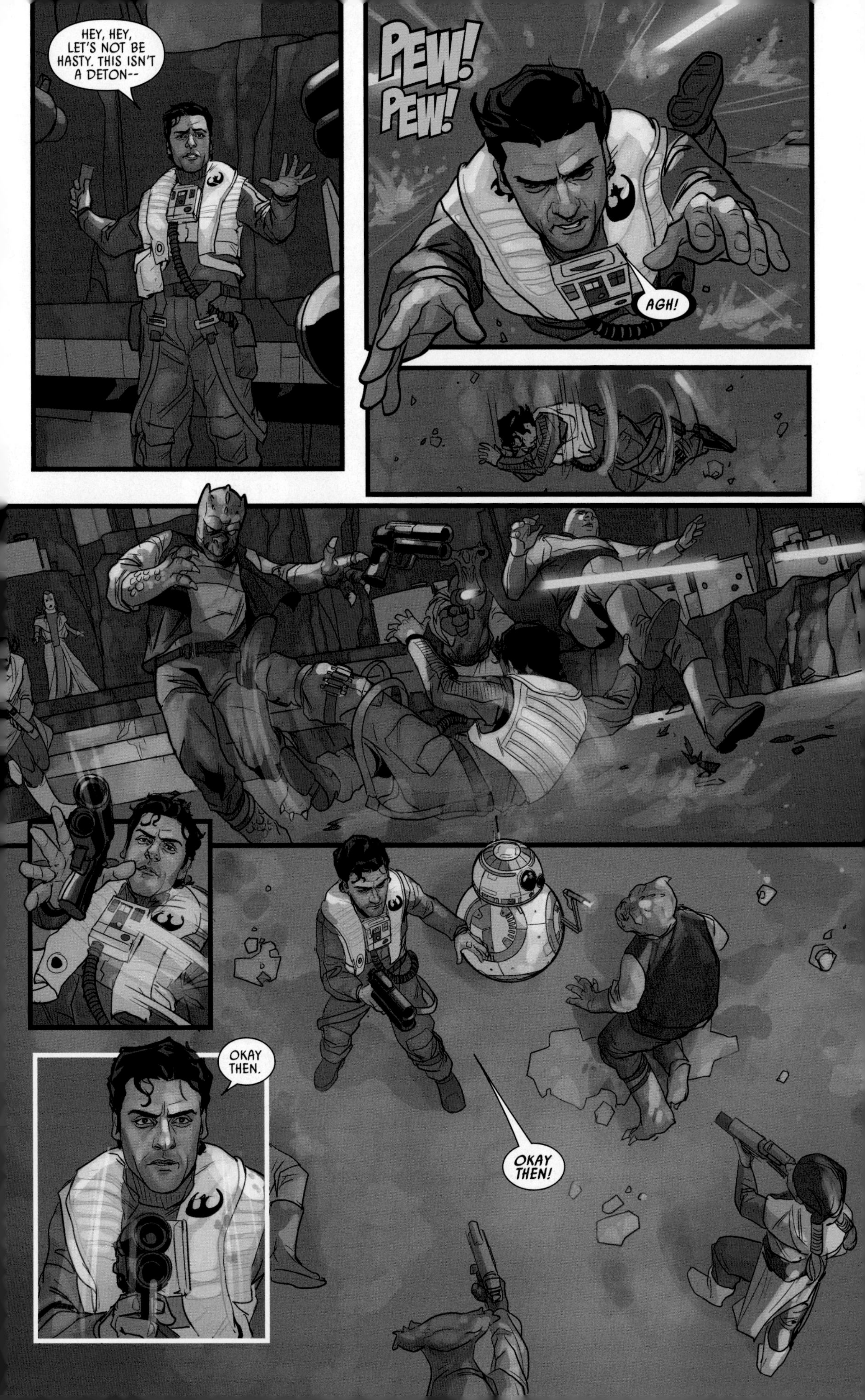
HEY, HEY, LET'S NOT BE HASTY. THIS ISN'T A DETON--
PEW! PEW!
AGH!
OKAY THEN.
OKAY THEN!

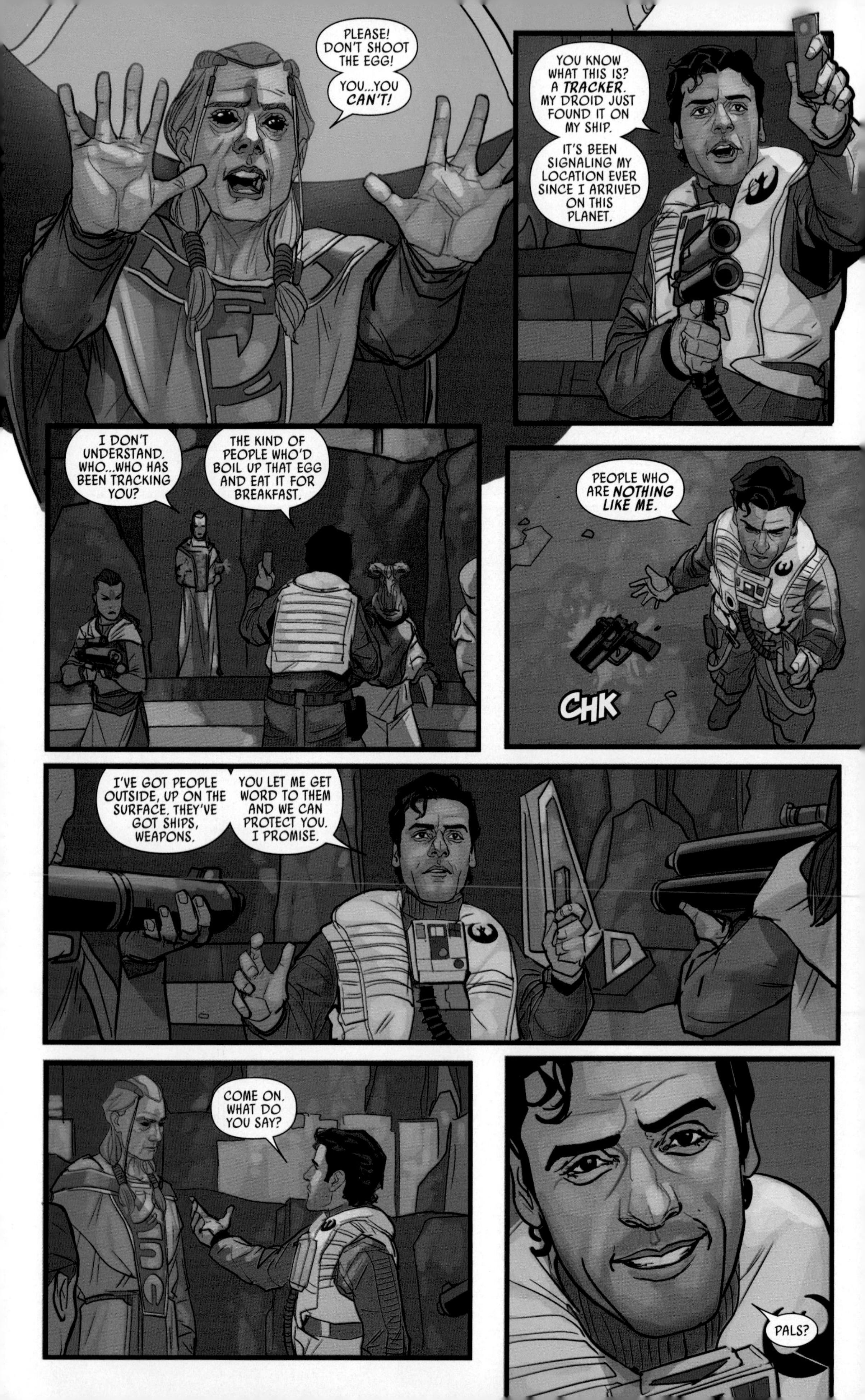
PLEASE! DON'T SHOOT THE EGG!
YOU...YOU CAN'T!
YOU KNOW WHAT THIS IS? A TRACKER. MY DROID JUST FOUND IT ON MY SHIP.
IT'S BEEN SIGNALING MY LOCATION EVER SINCE I ARRIVED ON THIS PLANET.
I DON'T UNDERSTAND. WHO...WHO HAS BEEN TRACKING YOU?
THE KIND OF PEOPLE WHO'D BOIL UP THAT EGG AND EAT IT FOR BREAKFAST.
PEOPLE WHO ARE NOTHING LIKE ME.
CHK
I'VE GOT PEOPLE OUTSIDE, UP ON THE SURFACE. THEY'VE GOT SHIPS, WEAPONS.
YOU LET ME GET WORD TO THEM AND WE CAN PROTECT YOU. I PROMISE.
COME ON. WHAT DO YOU SAY?
PALS?

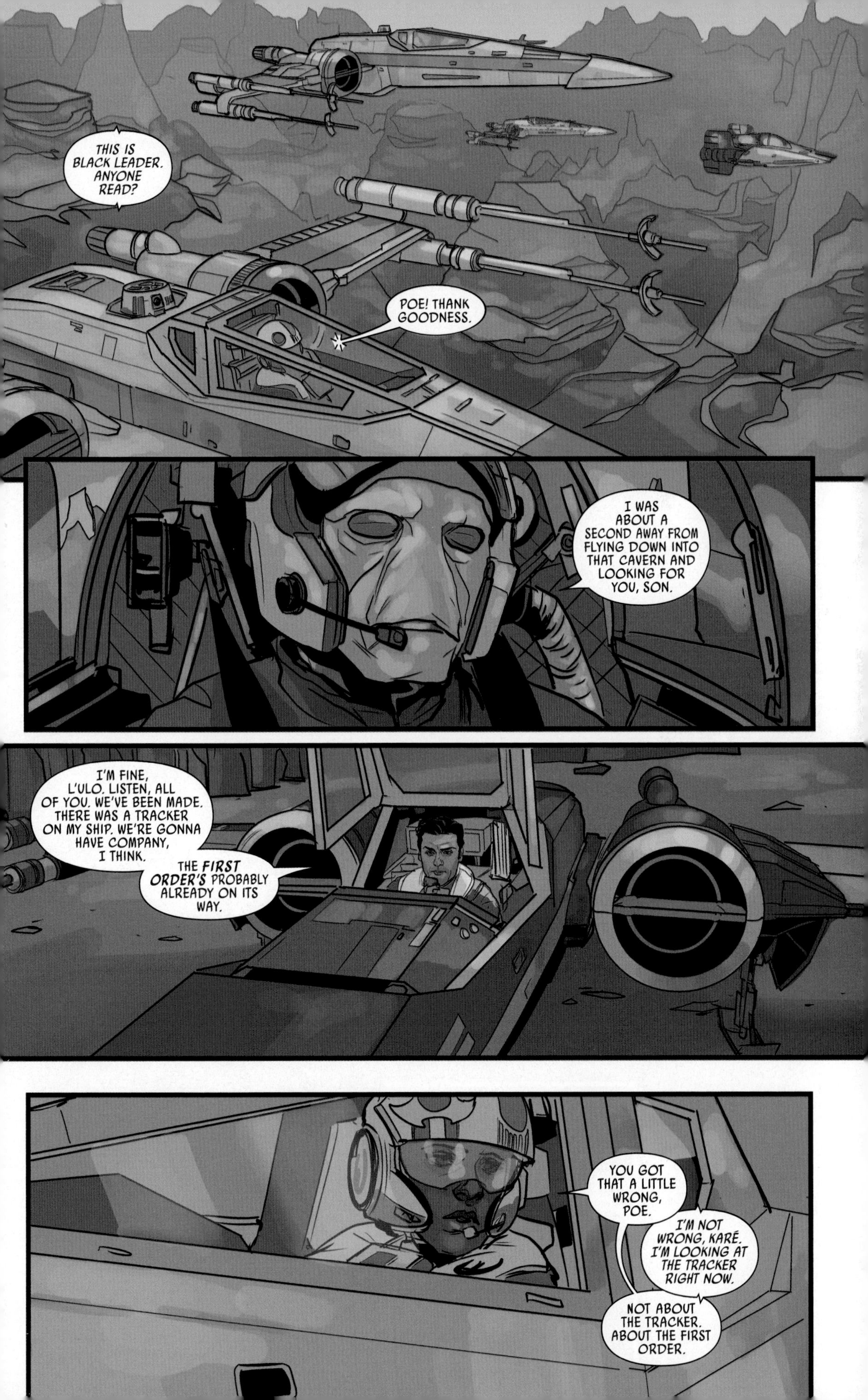
THIS IS BLACK LEADER. ANYONE READ?
POE! THANK GOODNESS.
I WAS ABOUT A SECOND AWAY FROM FLYING DOWN INTO THAT CAVERN AND LOOKING FOR YOU, SON.
I'M FINE, L'ULO. LISTEN, ALL OF YOU. WE'VE BEEN MADE. THERE WAS A TRACKER ON MY SHIP. WE'RE GONNA HAVE COMPANY, I THINK.
THE FIRST ORDER'S PROBABLY ALREADY ON ITS WAY.
YOU GOT THAT A LITTLE WRONG, POE.
I'M NOT WRONG, KARÉ. I'M LOOKING AT THE TRACKER RIGHT NOW.
NOT ABOUT THE TRACKER. ABOUT THE FIRST ORDER.

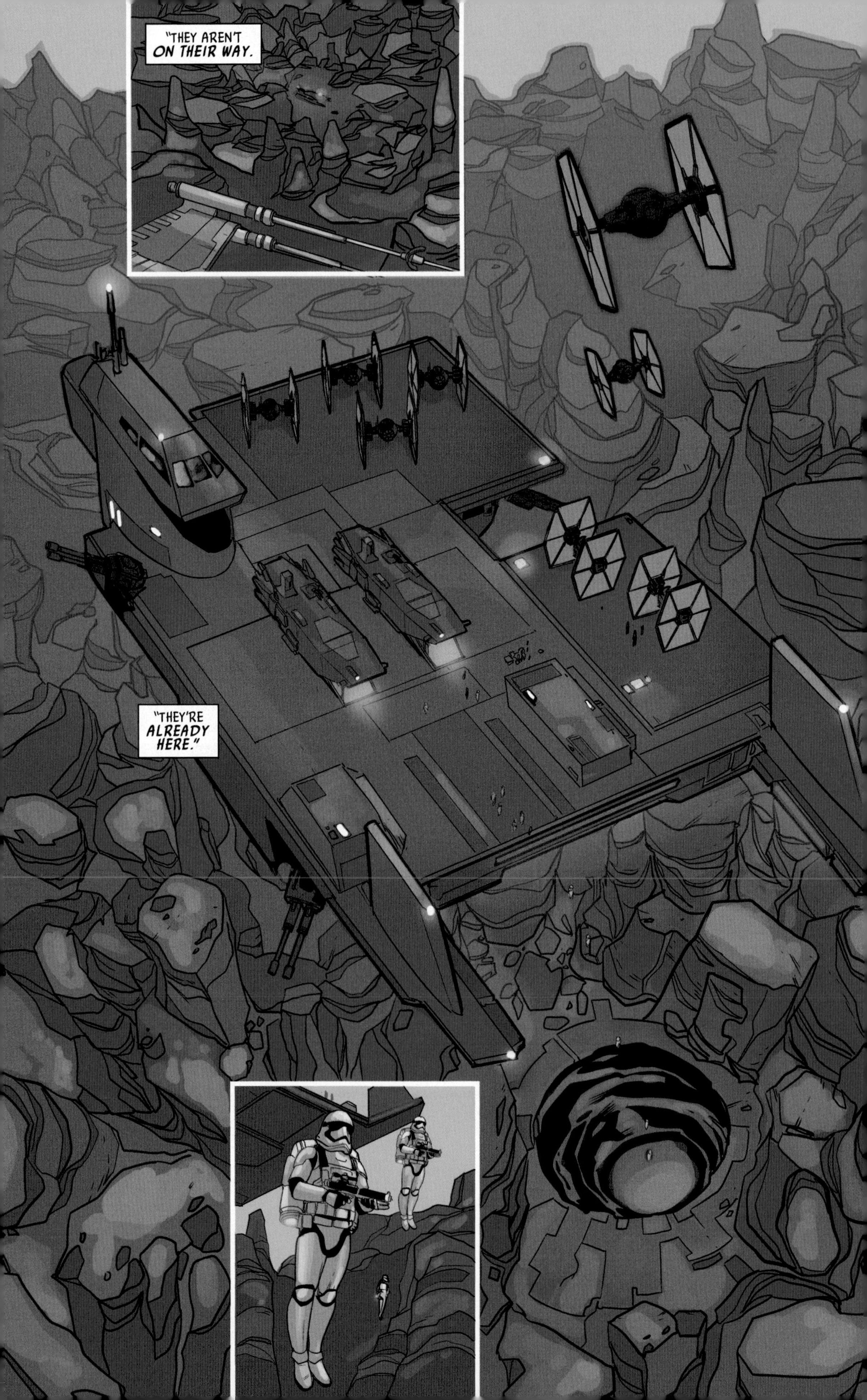
"THEY AREN'T ON THEIR WAY.
"THEY'RE ALREADY HERE."

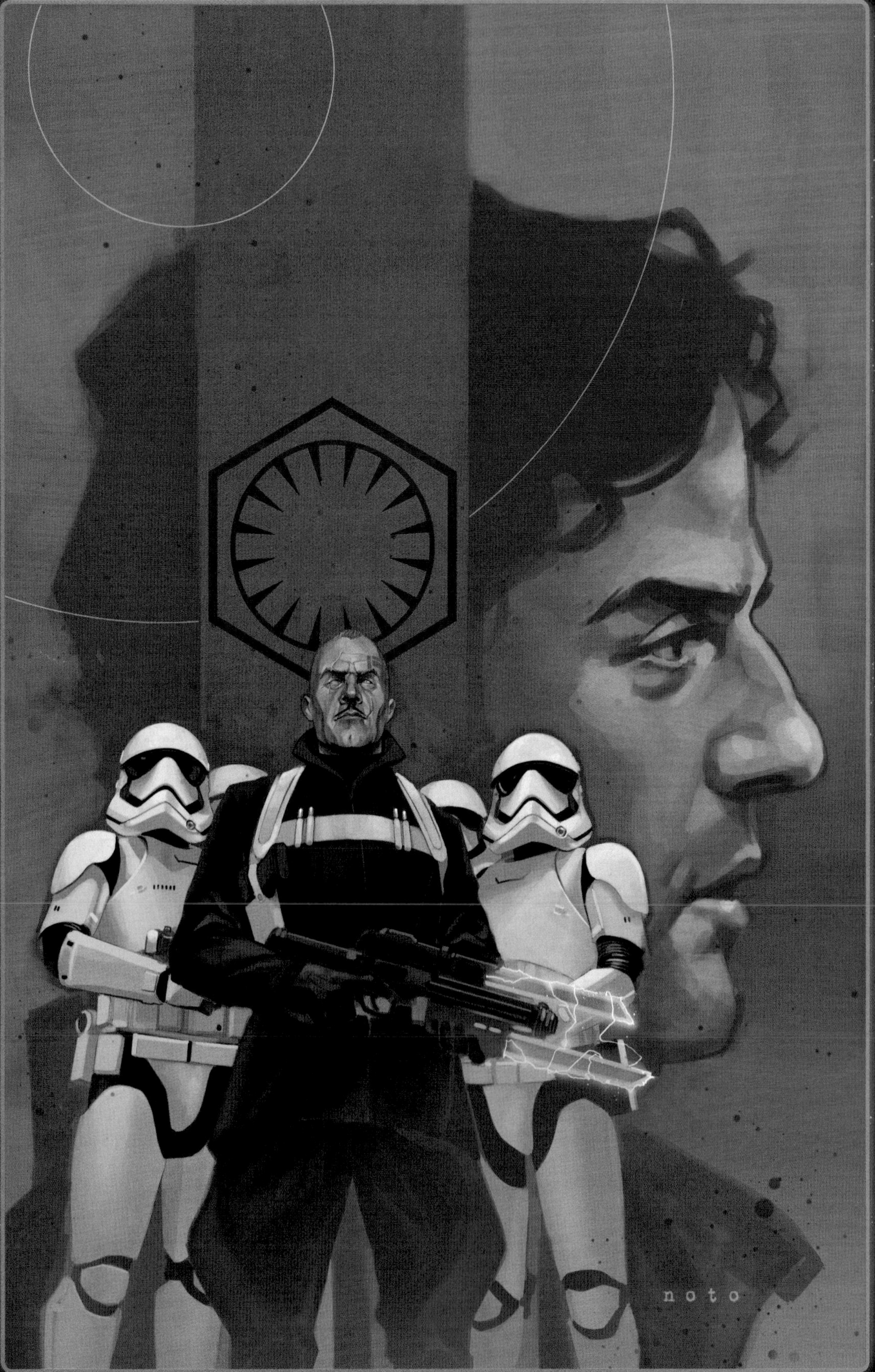
noto

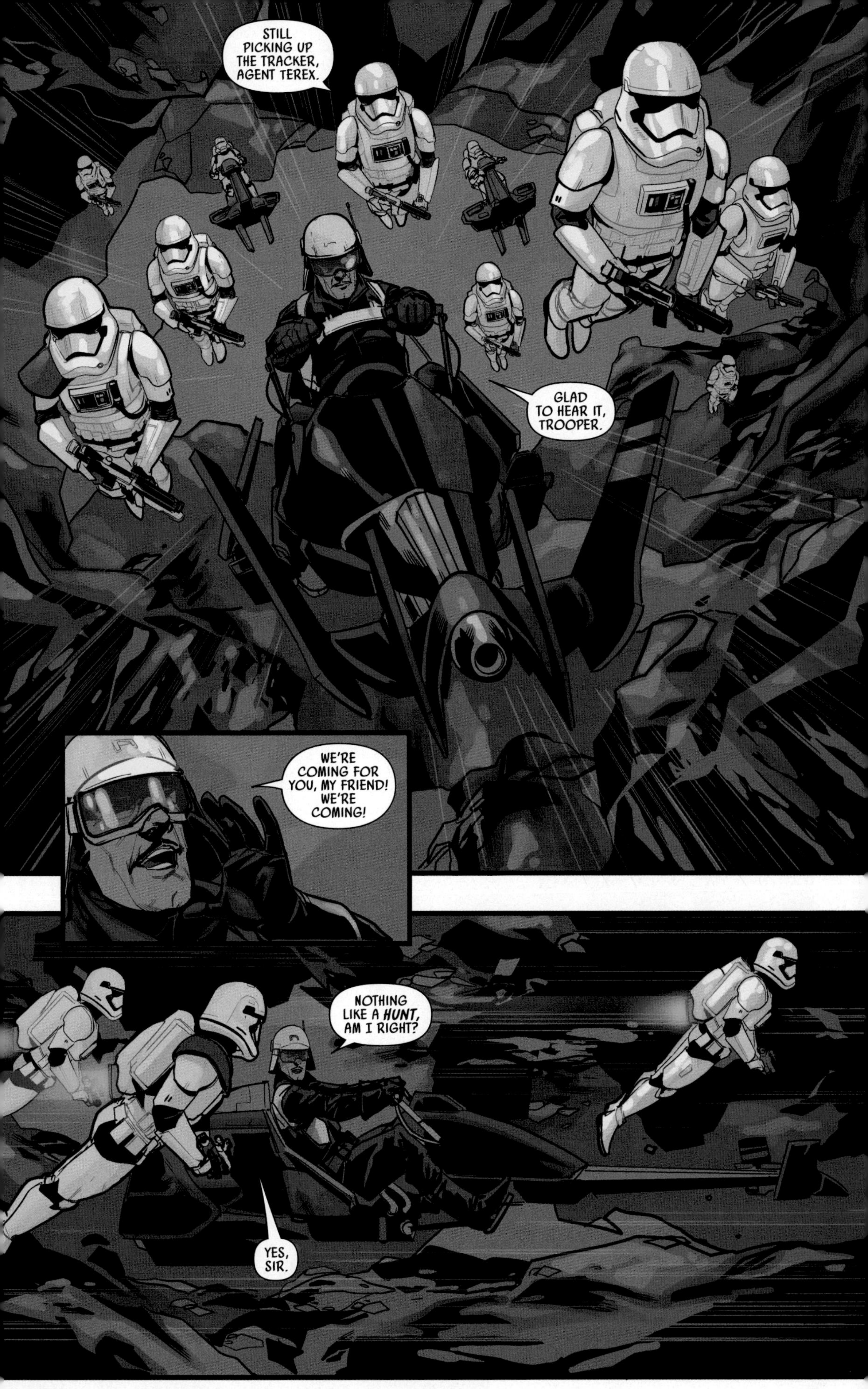
STILL PICKING UP THE TRACKER, AGENT TEREX.
GLAD TO HEAR IT, TROOPER.
WE'RE COMING FOR YOU, MY FRIEND! WE'RE COMING!
NOTHING LIKE A *HUNT*, AM I RIGHT?
YES, SIR.

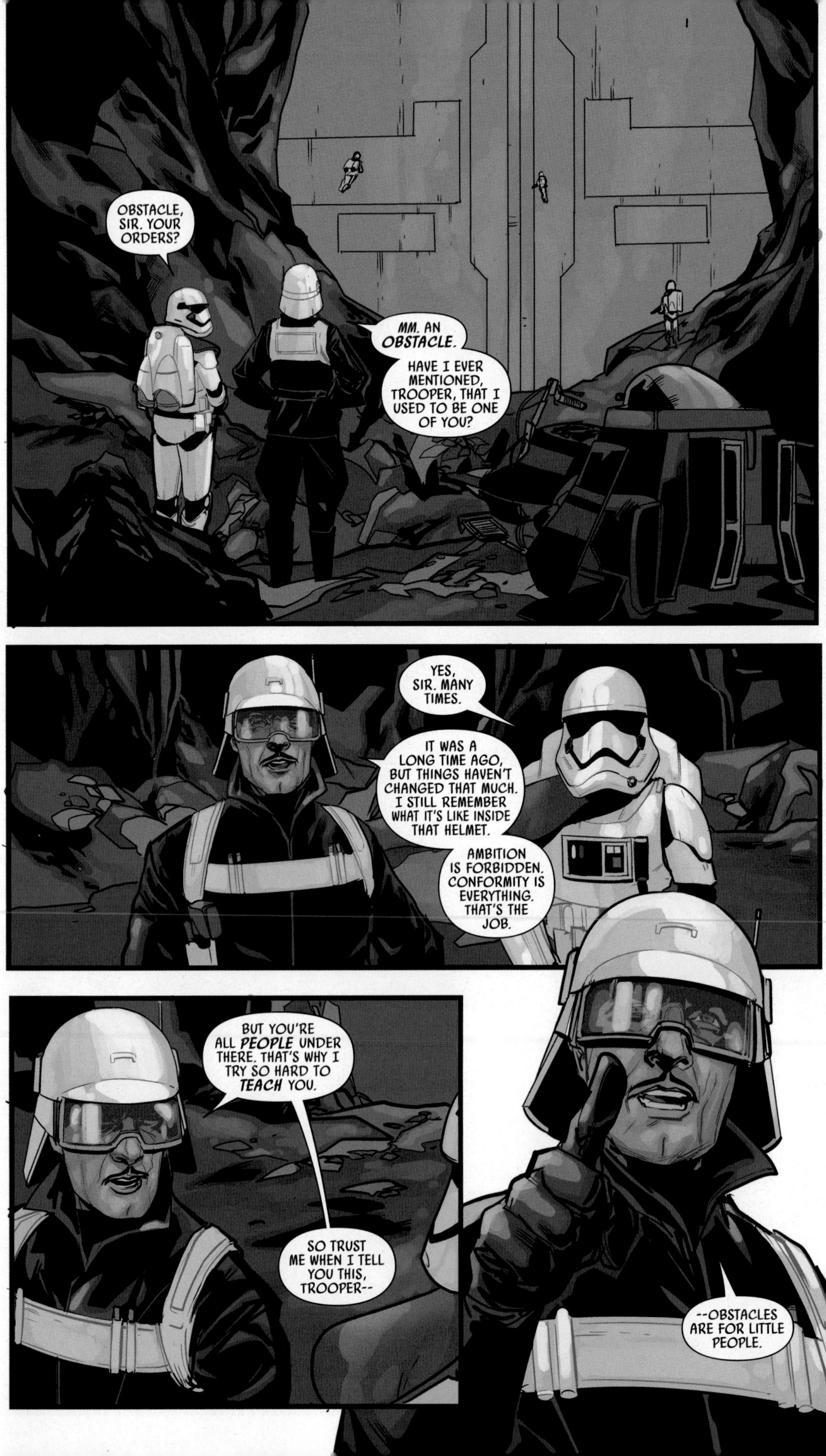
OBSTACLE, SIR. YOUR ORDERS?
MM. AN *OBSTACLE.*
HAVE I EVER MENTIONED, TROOPER, THAT I USED TO BE ONE OF YOU?
YES, SIR. MANY TIMES.
IT WAS A LONG TIME AGO, BUT THINGS HAVEN'T CHANGED THAT MUCH. I STILL REMEMBER WHAT IT'S LIKE INSIDE THAT HELMET.
AMBITION IS FORBIDDEN. CONFORMITY IS EVERYTHING. THAT'S THE JOB.
BUT YOU'RE ALL *PEOPLE* UNDER THERE. THAT'S WHY I TRY SO HARD TO *TEACH* YOU.
SO TRUST ME WHEN I TELL YOU THIS, TROOPER--
--OBSTACLES ARE FOR LITTLE PEOPLE.

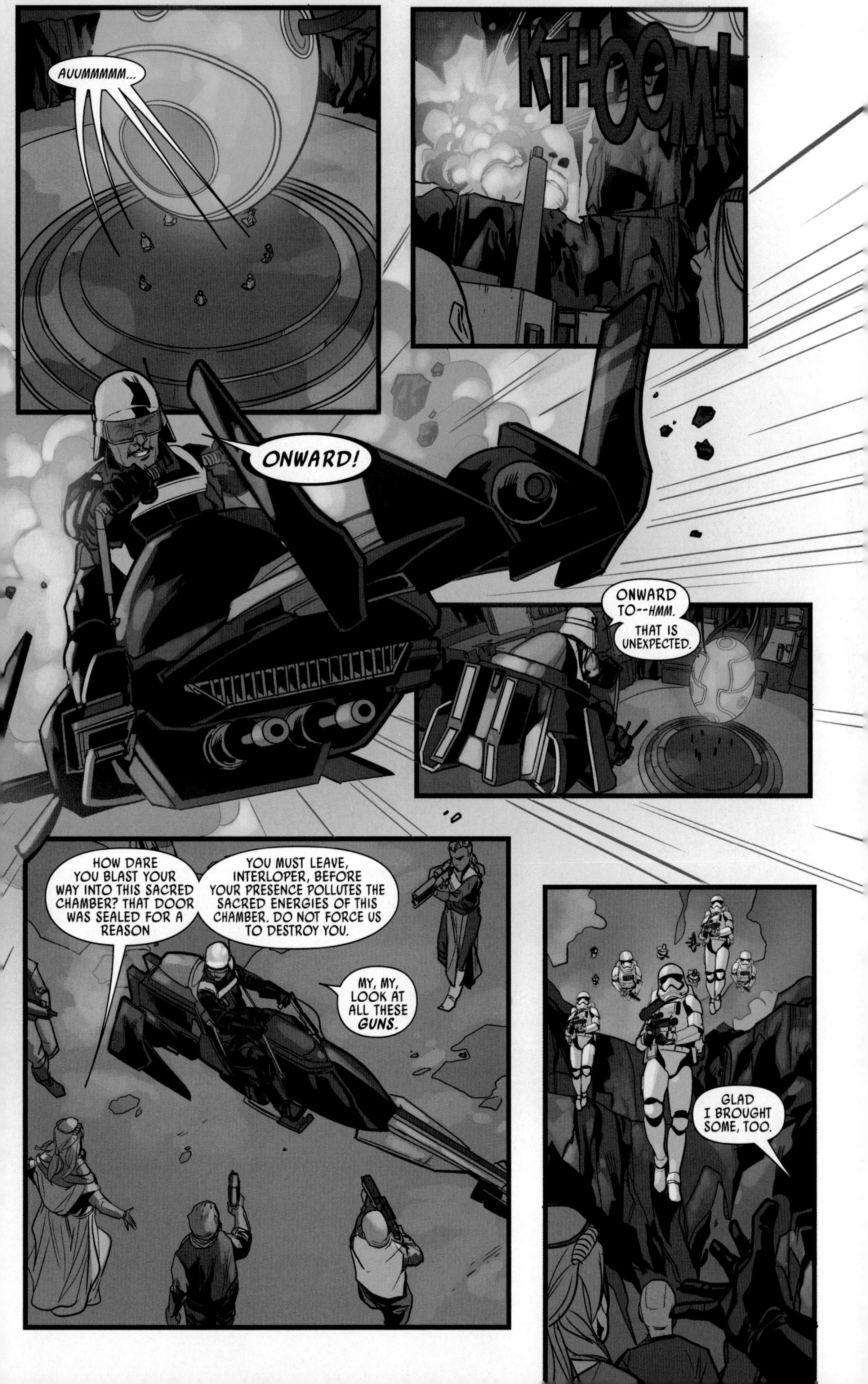
AUUMMMMM...
KTHOOM!
ONWARD!
ONWARD TO--HMM.
THAT IS UNEXPECTED.
HOW DARE YOU BLAST YOUR WAY INTO THIS SACRED CHAMBER? THAT DOOR WAS SEALED FOR A REASON
YOU MUST LEAVE, INTERLOPER, BEFORE YOUR PRESENCE POLLUTES THE SACRED ENERGIES OF THIS CHAMBER. DO NOT FORCE US TO DESTROY YOU.
MY, MY, LOOK AT ALL THESE GUNS.
GLAD I BROUGHT SOME, TOO.

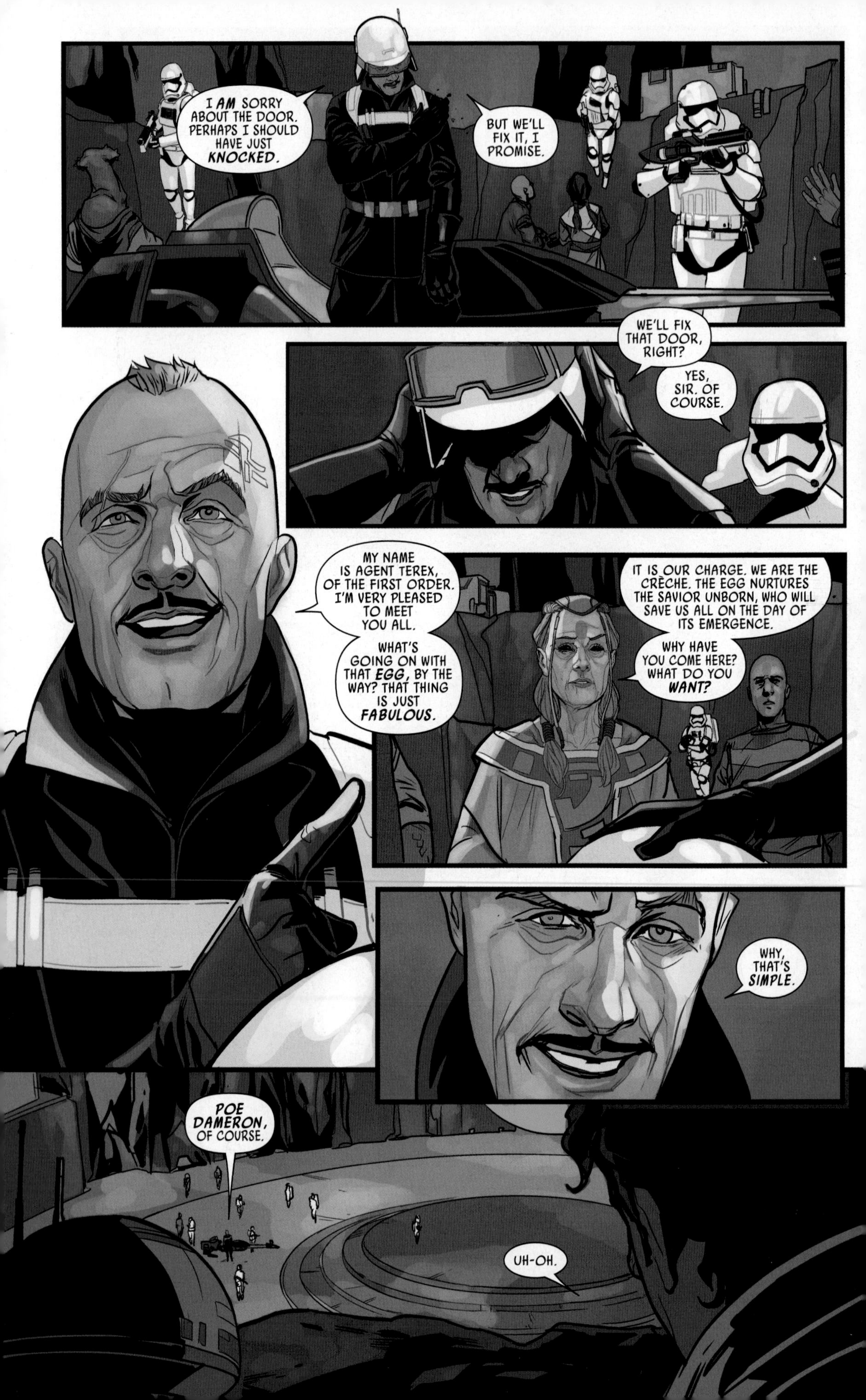
I AM SORRY ABOUT THE DOOR. PERHAPS I SHOULD HAVE JUST KNOCKED.
BUT WE'LL FIX IT, I PROMISE.
WE'LL FIX THAT DOOR, RIGHT?
YES, SIR. OF COURSE.
MY NAME IS AGENT TEREX, OF THE FIRST ORDER. I'M VERY PLEASED TO MEET YOU ALL.
WHAT'S GOING ON WITH THAT EGG, BY THE WAY? THAT THING IS JUST FABULOUS.
IT IS OUR CHARGE. WE ARE THE CRÈCHE. THE EGG NURTURES THE SAVIOR UNBORN, WHO WILL SAVE US ALL ON THE DAY OF ITS EMERGENCE.
WHY HAVE YOU COME HERE? WHAT DO YOU WANT?
WHY, THAT'S SIMPLE.
POE DAMERON, OF COURSE.
UH-OH.

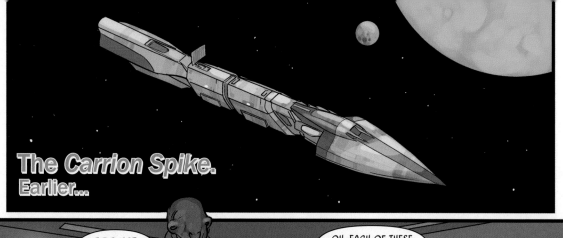

The *Carrion Spike.*
Earlier...

I DO NOT UNDERSTAND WHY YOU KEEP THESE... PEOPLE, AGENT TEREX.

OH, EACH OF THESE FOLKS IS PARTICULARLY, *SPECIFICALLY* USEFUL TO ME, PHASMA.

BESIDES, THE EMPIRE HAD PLENTY OF SLAVES. EVERY LAST WOOKIEE ON KASHYYYK, FOR EXAMPLE. AND THANK GOODNESS FOR THAT.

THIS BRANDY WAS AGED FOR FIFTY YEARS, BUT IT WOULDN'T TASTE *NEARLY* AS FINE WITHOUT THAT KESSEL SPICE.

THE FIRST ORDER IS *NOT* THE EMPIRE. WE ARE PURER. WE HAVE BEEN THROUGH THE *CRUCIBLE* AND EMERGED *STRONGER.*

I AGREE, PHASMA. THE FIRST ORDER IS NOT THE EMPIRE. BUT PERHAPS, ONE DAY, IF WE ALL WORK VERY HARD AND DO OUR VERY, VERY BEST...

...IT *COULD* BE.

AWAY NOW, MY FRIENDS. CAPTAIN PHASMA AND I NEED TO SPEAK IN PRIVATE.

THIS IS ABOUT A MAN NAMED POE DAMERON. HE IS--

A YOUNG PILOT IN THE REPUBLIC NAVY. EXTREMELY SKILLED, BY ALL ACCOUNTS.

RECENTLY RECRUITED INTO ORGANA'S RESISTANCE, WHICH IS WORKING TO THWART THE FIRST ORDER'S NOBLE EFFORTS TO TIDY UP THE GALAXY.

HISTORY DOES LIKE A CIRCLE, EH?

YOUR SOURCES ARE GOOD.

OF COURSE THEY ARE. THAT IS WHY I HAVE A PLACE IN THE FIRST ORDER. HUX AND THE REST CAN BARELY HIDE THEIR DISTASTE FOR ME--BUT THEY'RE MORE THAN HAPPY TO USE THE INFORMATION I PROVIDE.

CAN WE GET ON WITH THIS, PHASMA? I HAVE BRANDY TO DRINK.

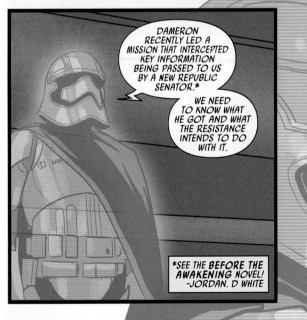

DAMERON RECENTLY LED A MISSION THAT INTERCEPTED KEY INFORMATION BEING PASSED TO US BY A NEW REPUBLIC SENATOR.*

WE NEED TO KNOW WHAT HE GOT AND WHAT THE RESISTANCE INTENDS TO DO WITH IT.

*SEE THE BEFORE THE AWAKENING NOVEL! -JORDAN. D WHITE

YOU'VE BEEN ASSIGNED SIGNIFICANT RESOURCES TO COMPLETE THIS MISSION.

THE TRUE OFFENSIVE WILL BEGIN SOON...BUT ONLY IF THERE ARE NO LOOSE ENDS.

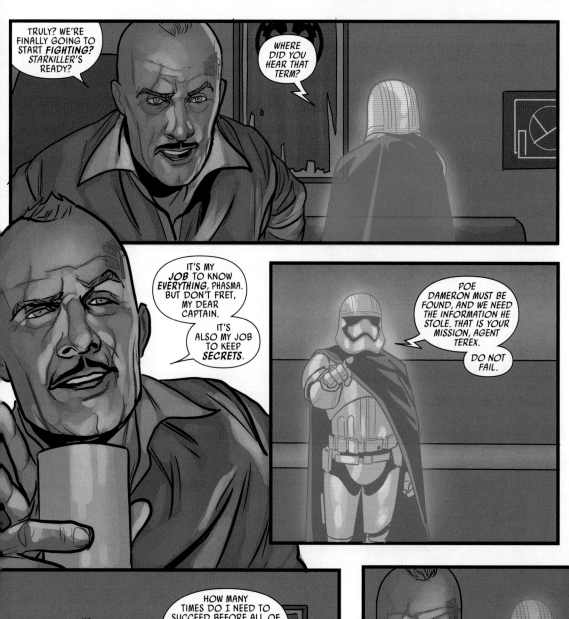

TRULY? WE'RE FINALLY GOING TO START *FIGHTING?* *STARKILLER'S* READY?

WHERE DID YOU HEAR THAT TERM?

IT'S MY *JOB* TO KNOW *EVERYTHING,* PHASMA. BUT DON'T FRET, MY DEAR CAPTAIN.

IT'S ALSO MY JOB TO KEEP *SECRETS.*

POE DAMERON MUST BE FOUND, AND WE NEED THE INFORMATION HE STOLE. THAT IS YOUR MISSION, AGENT TEREX.

DO NOT FAIL.

HOW MANY TIMES DO I NEED TO SUCCEED BEFORE ALL OF YOU STOP TELLING ME NOT TO *FAIL?* I'VE BEEN DOING THIS WORK SINCE BEFORE YOU WERE *BORN,* PHASMA.

YES, TEREX. EVERY OFFICER IN THE FIRST ORDER KNOWS *EXACTLY* WHERE YOU CAME FROM. THAT IS WHY WE SAY IT.

DO NOT FAIL, TEREX.

FIND POE DAMERON.

POE DAMERON? WHO IS THAT?

BB-8, GET IN TOUCH WITH SNAP AND THE REST OF BLACK SQUADRON.

THIS COULD GET *BAD*. I CAN FEEL IT. WE HAVE TO TRY TO HELP THESE PEOPLE.

WRRRP BLEEP.

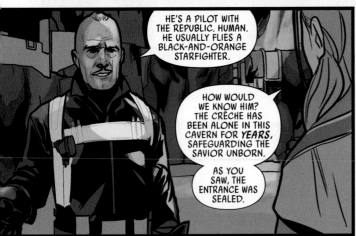

HE'S A PILOT WITH THE REPUBLIC, HUMAN. HE USUALLY FLIES A BLACK-AND-ORANGE STARFIGHTER.

HOW WOULD WE KNOW HIM? THE CRÈCHE HAS BEEN ALONE IN THIS CAVERN FOR *YEARS,* SAFEGUARDING THE SAVIOR UNBORN.

AS YOU SAW, THE ENTRANCE WAS SEALED.

AWWW. LOOK AT YOU. THAT'S ADORABLE.

YES, SIR.

BRRRO BLEEP?

THAT'S POE'S ORDER? THAT'S IT? ALL RIGHT, BB-8, WE'LL DO OUR BEST. YOU GUYS STAYING SAFE DOWN THERE?

WRRRRP BLEEP BOOP.

OKAY. GOOD LUCK. WEXLEY OUT.

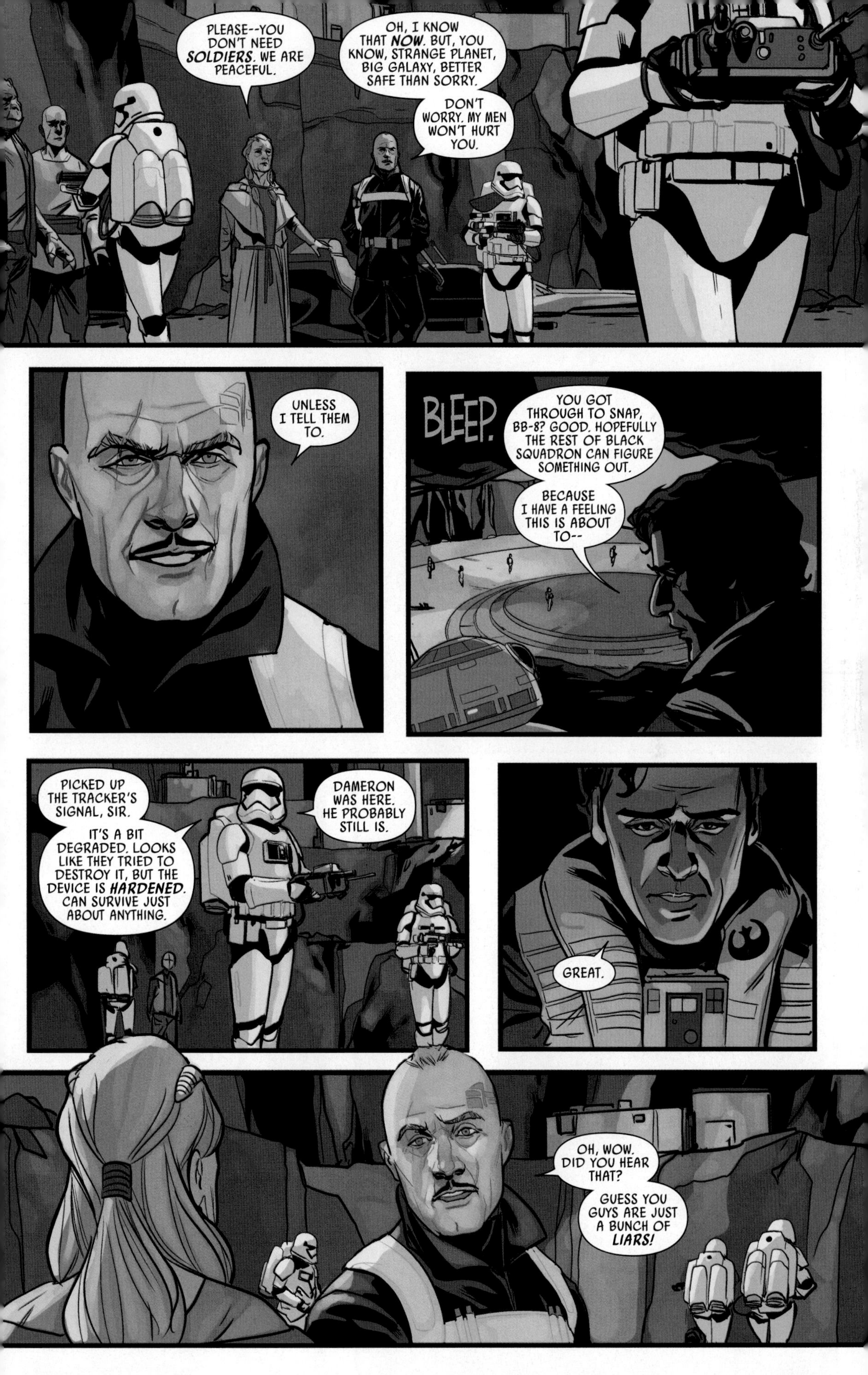
PLEASE--YOU DON'T NEED **SOLDIERS**. WE ARE PEACEFUL.
OH, I KNOW THAT **NOW**. BUT, YOU KNOW, STRANGE PLANET, BIG GALAXY, BETTER SAFE THAN SORRY.
DON'T WORRY. MY MEN WON'T HURT YOU.
UNLESS I TELL THEM TO.
BLEEP.
YOU GOT THROUGH TO SNAP, BB-8? GOOD. HOPEFULLY THE REST OF BLACK SQUADRON CAN FIGURE SOMETHING OUT.
BECAUSE I HAVE A FEELING THIS IS ABOUT TO--
PICKED UP THE TRACKER'S SIGNAL, SIR.
IT'S A BIT DEGRADED. LOOKS LIKE THEY TRIED TO DESTROY IT, BUT THE DEVICE IS **HARDENED**. CAN SURVIVE JUST ABOUT ANYTHING.
DAMERON WAS HERE. HE PROBABLY STILL IS.
GREAT.
OH, WOW. DID YOU HEAR THAT?
GUESS YOU GUYS ARE JUST A BUNCH OF ***LIARS!***

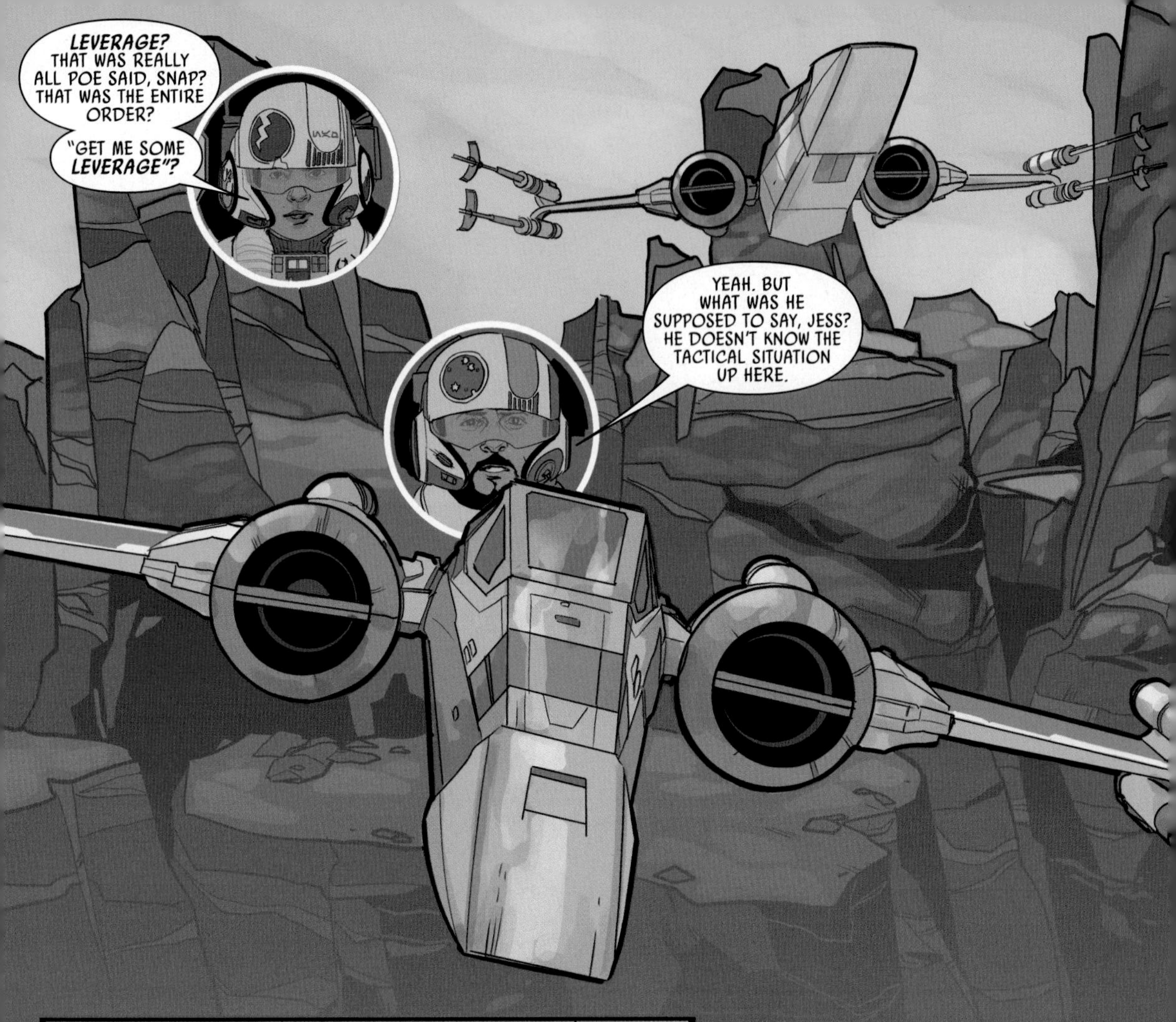
LEVERAGE? THAT WAS REALLY ALL POE SAID, SNAP? THAT WAS THE ENTIRE ORDER?
"GET ME SOME *LEVERAGE*"?
YEAH. BUT WHAT WAS HE SUPPOSED TO SAY, JESS? HE DOESN'T KNOW THE TACTICAL SITUATION UP HERE.

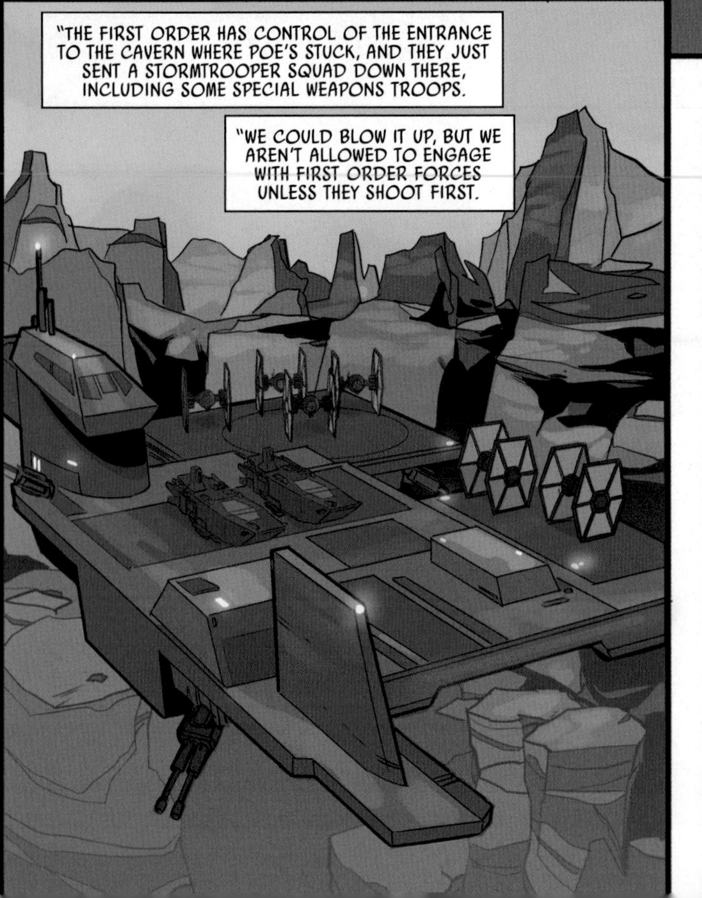
"THE FIRST ORDER HAS CONTROL OF THE ENTRANCE TO THE CAVERN WHERE POE'S STUCK, AND THEY JUST SENT A STORMTROOPER SQUAD DOWN THERE, INCLUDING SOME SPECIAL WEAPONS TROOPS.
"WE COULD BLOW IT UP, BUT WE AREN'T ALLOWED TO ENGAGE WITH FIRST ORDER FORCES UNLESS THEY SHOOT FIRST.

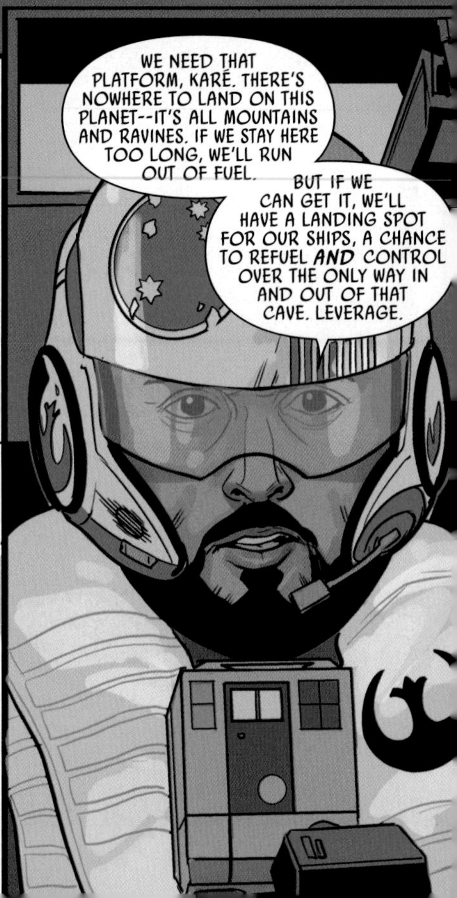
WE NEED THAT PLATFORM, KARÉ. THERE'S NOWHERE TO LAND ON THIS PLANET--IT'S ALL MOUNTAINS AND RAVINES. IF WE STAY HERE TOO LONG, WE'LL RUN OUT OF FUEL.
BUT IF WE CAN GET IT, WE'LL HAVE A LANDING SPOT FOR OUR SHIPS, A CHANCE TO REFUEL *AND* CONTROL OVER THE ONLY WAY IN AND OUT OF THAT CAVE. LEVERAGE.

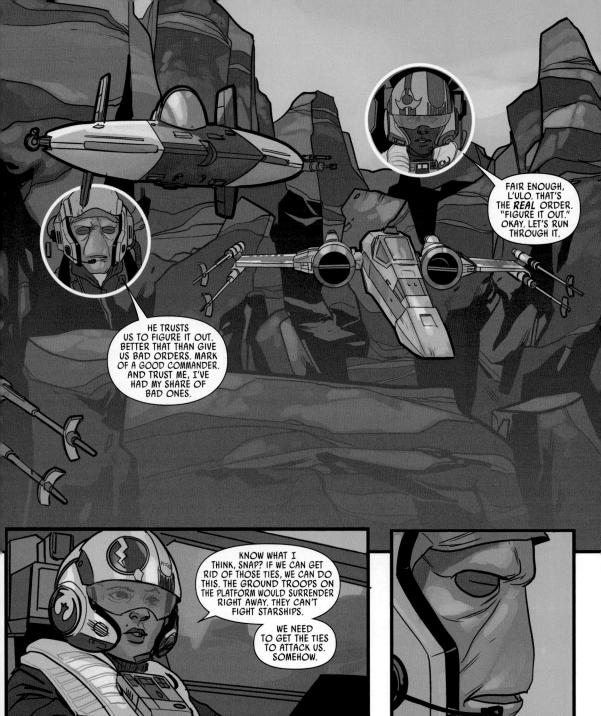

FAIR ENOUGH, L'ULO. THAT'S THE *REAL* ORDER. "FIGURE IT OUT." OKAY. LET'S RUN THROUGH IT.

HE TRUSTS US TO FIGURE IT OUT. BETTER THAT THAN GIVE US BAD ORDERS. MARK OF A GOOD COMMANDER. AND TRUST ME, I'VE HAD MY SHARE OF BAD ONES.

KNOW WHAT I THINK, SNAP? IF WE CAN GET RID OF THOSE TIES, WE CAN DO THIS. THE GROUND TROOPS ON THE PLATFORM WOULD SURRENDER RIGHT AWAY. THEY CAN'T FIGHT STARSHIPS.

WE NEED TO GET THE TIES TO ATTACK US. SOMEHOW.

IT'S A GOOD IDEA, JESS, BUT TIES ARE FASTER AND MORE MANEUVERABLE THAN X-WINGS.

ESPECIALLY THOSE NEW SPECIAL FORCES MODELS. ON A PLANET LIKE THIS, WITH THESE *CANYONS*... COULD BE TRICKY.

GOOD THING WE'RE NOT ALL FLYING X-WINGS, THEN, ISN'T IT?

LEAVE IT TO ME.

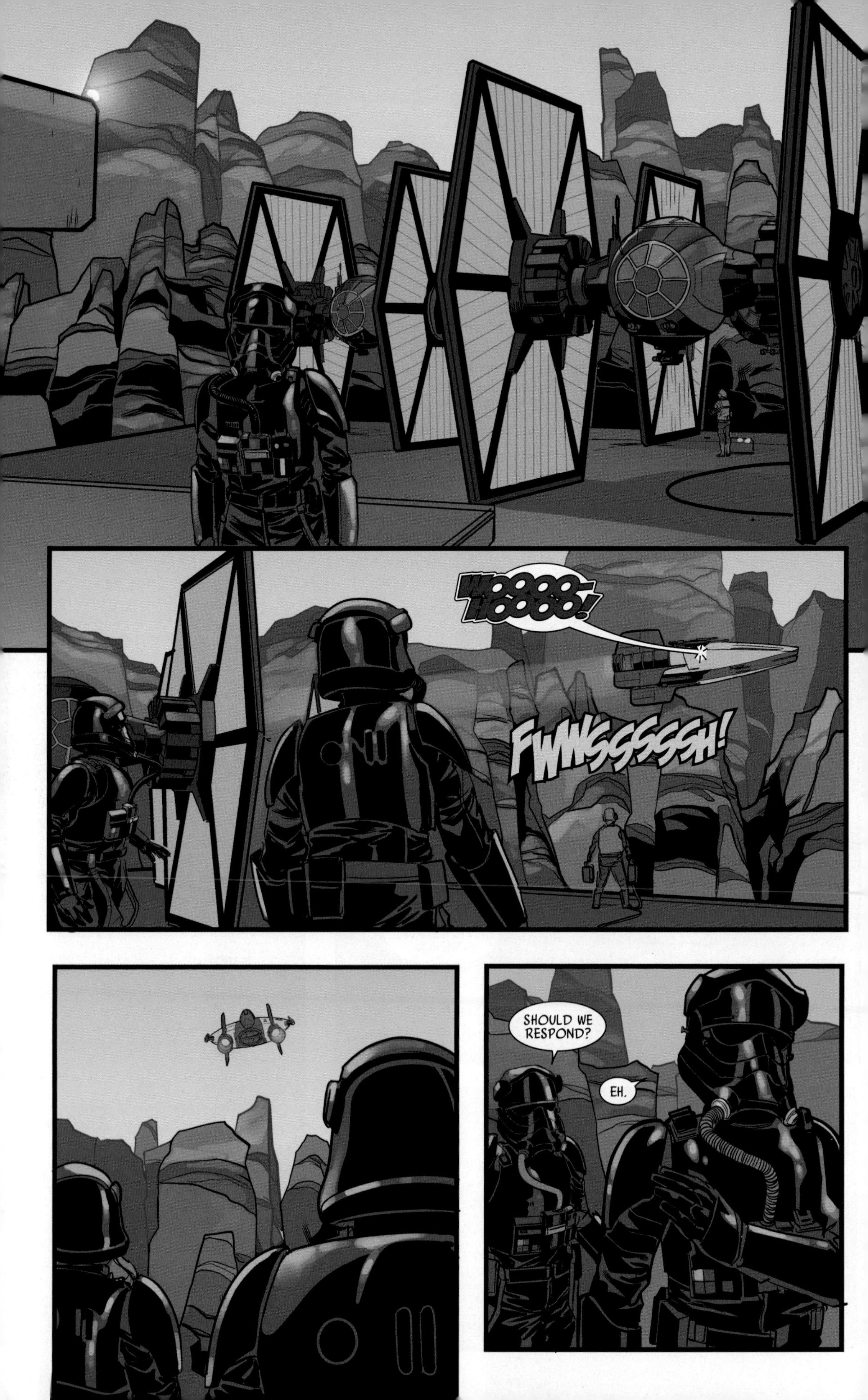
WOOOO-HOOOO!
FWWSSSSSH!
SHOULD WE RESPOND?
EH.

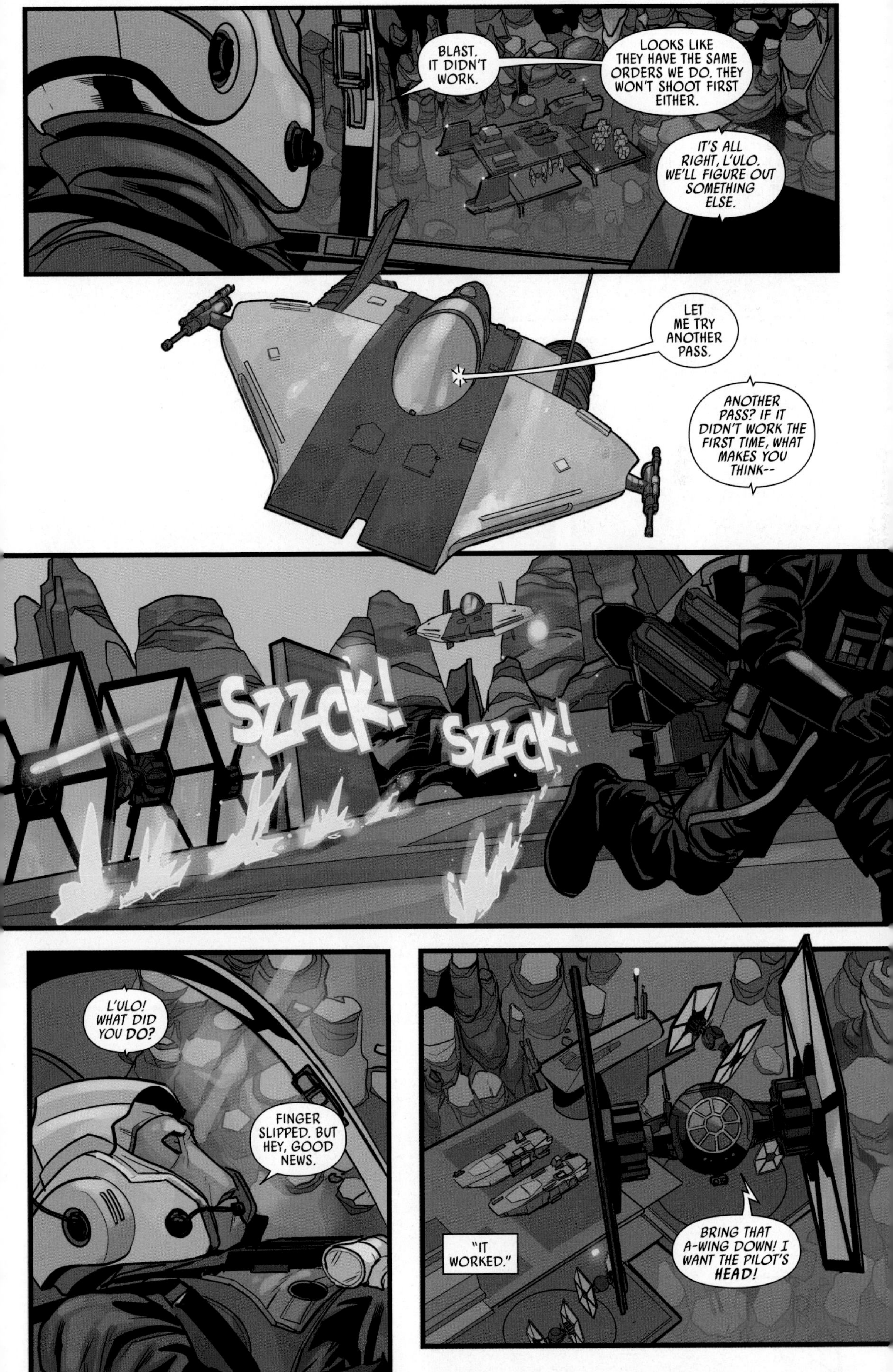
BLAST. IT DIDN'T WORK.
LOOKS LIKE THEY HAVE THE SAME ORDERS WE DO. THEY WON'T SHOOT FIRST EITHER.
IT'S ALL RIGHT, L'ULO. WE'LL FIGURE OUT SOMETHING ELSE.
LET ME TRY ANOTHER PASS.
ANOTHER PASS? IF IT DIDN'T WORK THE FIRST TIME, WHAT MAKES YOU THINK--
SZZCK!
SZZCK!
L'ULO! WHAT DID YOU DO?
FINGER SLIPPED. BUT HEY, GOOD NEWS.
"IT WORKED."
BRING THAT A-WING DOWN! I WANT THE PILOT'S HEAD!

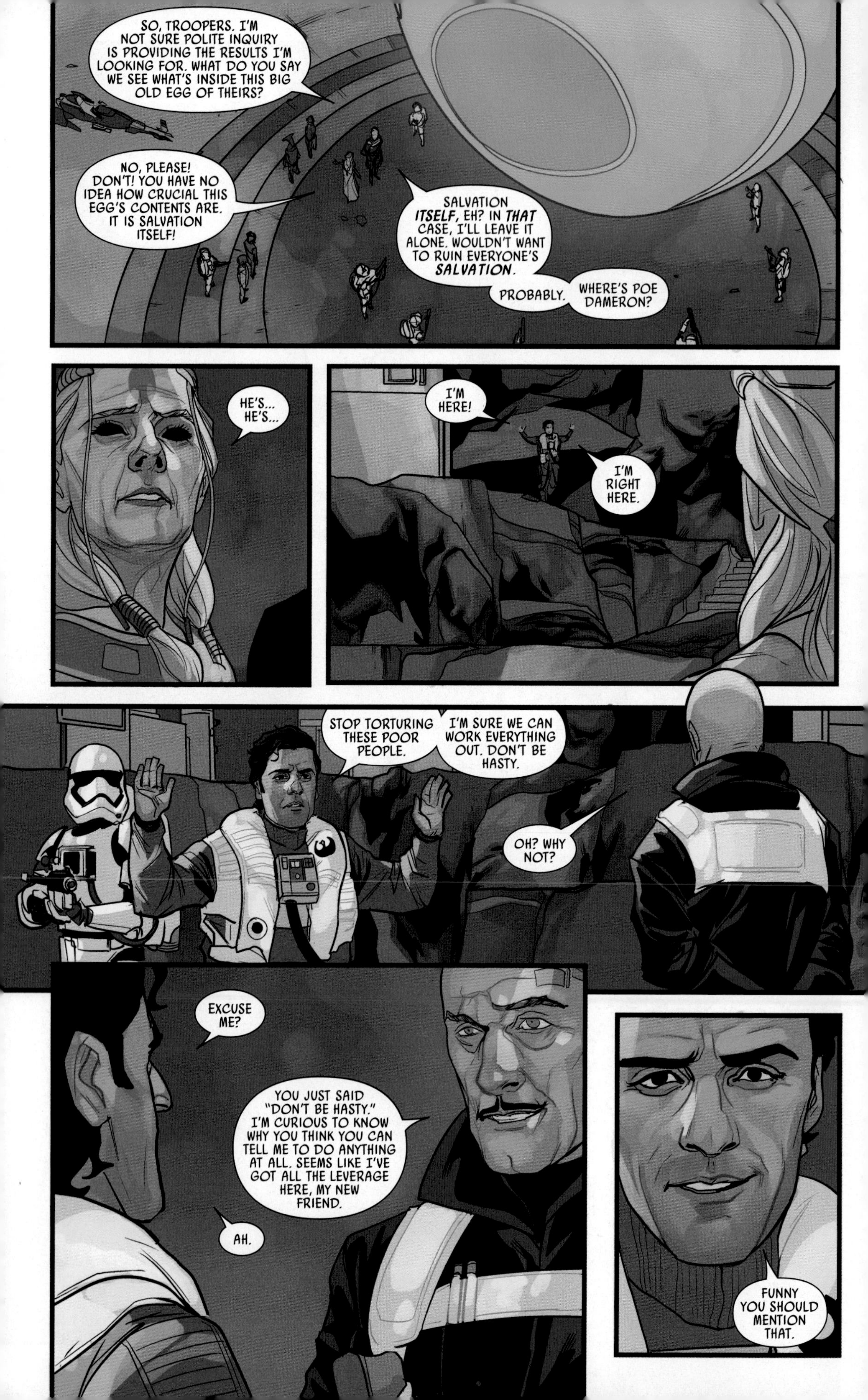
SO, TROOPERS. I'M NOT SURE POLITE INQUIRY IS PROVIDING THE RESULTS I'M LOOKING FOR. WHAT DO YOU SAY WE SEE WHAT'S INSIDE THIS BIG OLD EGG OF THEIRS?
NO, PLEASE! DON'T! YOU HAVE NO IDEA HOW CRUCIAL THIS EGG'S CONTENTS ARE. IT IS SALVATION ITSELF!
SALVATION ITSELF, EH? IN THAT CASE, I'LL LEAVE IT ALONE. WOULDN'T WANT TO RUIN EVERYONE'S SALVATION.
PROBABLY.
WHERE'S POE DAMERON?
HE'S... HE'S...
I'M HERE!
I'M RIGHT HERE.
STOP TORTURING THESE POOR PEOPLE.
I'M SURE WE CAN WORK EVERYTHING OUT. DON'T BE HASTY.
OH? WHY NOT?
EXCUSE ME?
YOU JUST SAID "DON'T BE HASTY." I'M CURIOUS TO KNOW WHY YOU THINK YOU CAN TELL ME TO DO ANYTHING AT ALL. SEEMS LIKE I'VE GOT ALL THE LEVERAGE HERE, MY NEW FRIEND.
AH.
FUNNY YOU SHOULD MENTION THAT.

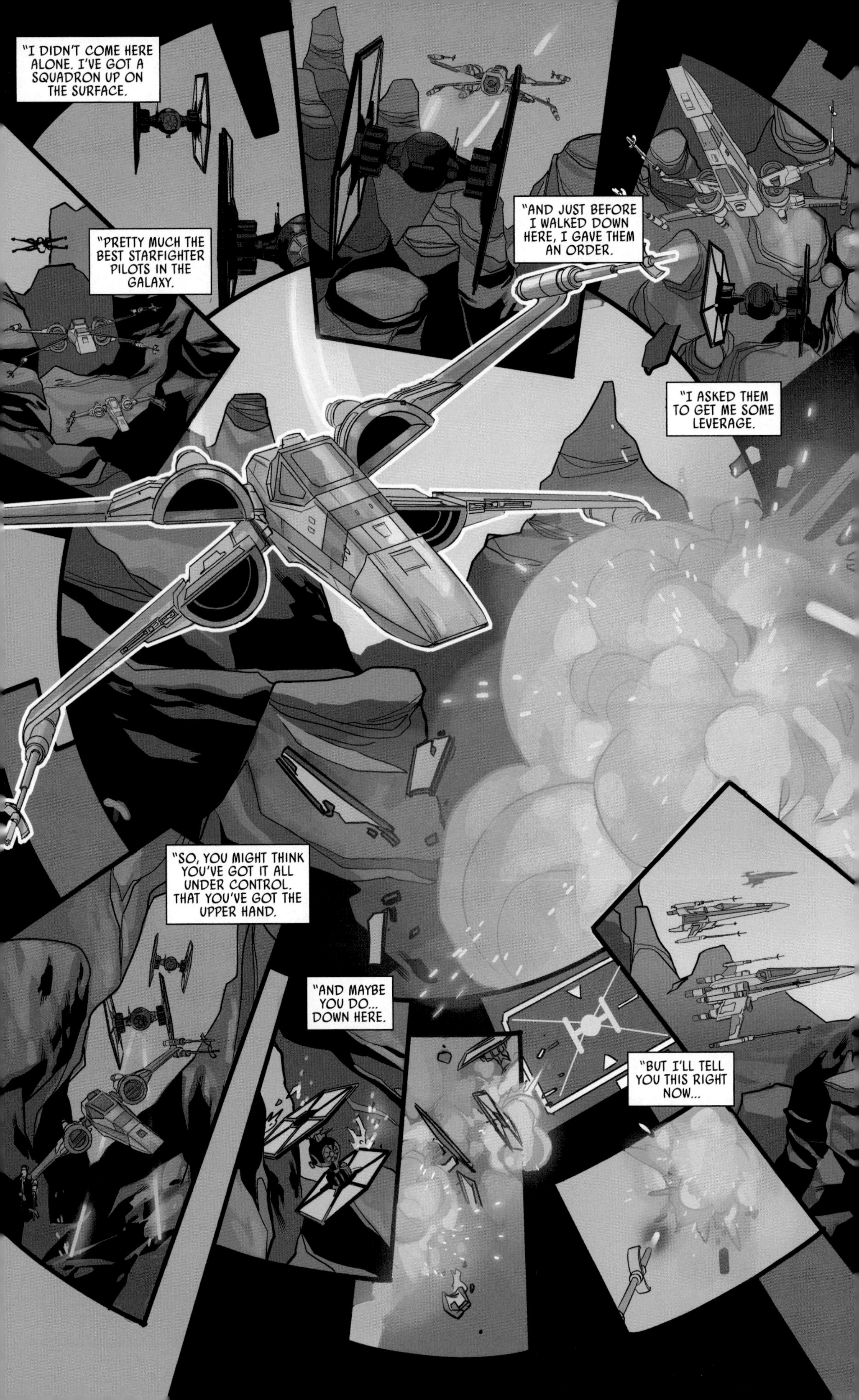
"I DIDN'T COME HERE ALONE. I'VE GOT A SQUADRON UP ON THE SURFACE.
"PRETTY MUCH THE BEST STARFIGHTER PILOTS IN THE GALAXY.
"AND JUST BEFORE I WALKED DOWN HERE, I GAVE THEM AN ORDER.
"I ASKED THEM TO GET ME SOME LEVERAGE.
"SO, YOU MIGHT THINK YOU'VE GOT IT ALL UNDER CONTROL. THAT YOU'VE GOT THE UPPER HAND.
"AND MAYBE YOU DO... DOWN HERE.
"BUT I'LL TELL YOU THIS RIGHT NOW...

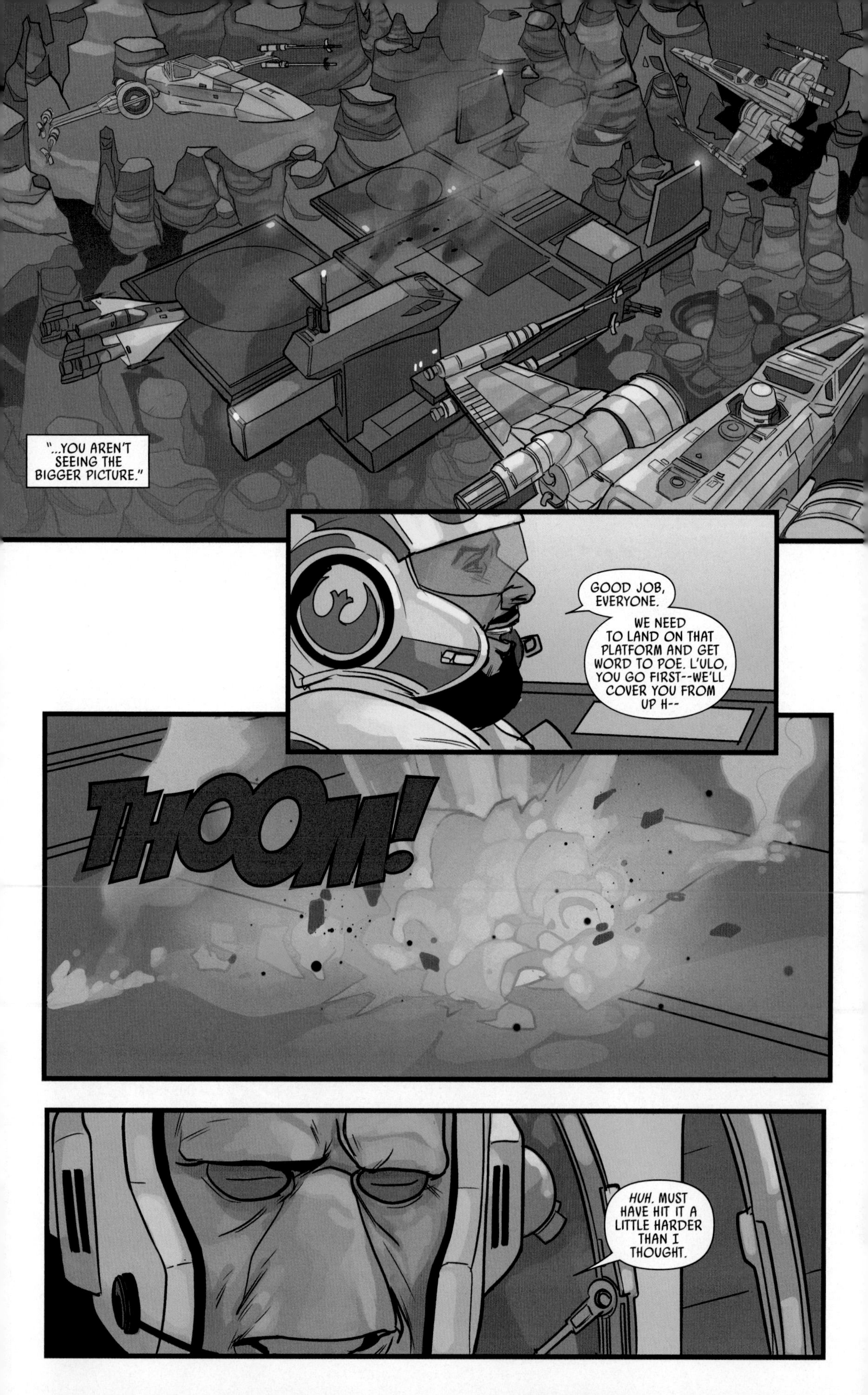
"...YOU AREN'T SEEING THE BIGGER PICTURE."
GOOD JOB, EVERYONE.
WE NEED TO LAND ON THAT PLATFORM AND GET WORD TO POE. L'ULO, YOU GO FIRST--WE'LL COVER YOU FROM UP H--
THOOM!
HUH. MUST HAVE HIT IT A LITTLE HARDER THAN I THOUGHT.

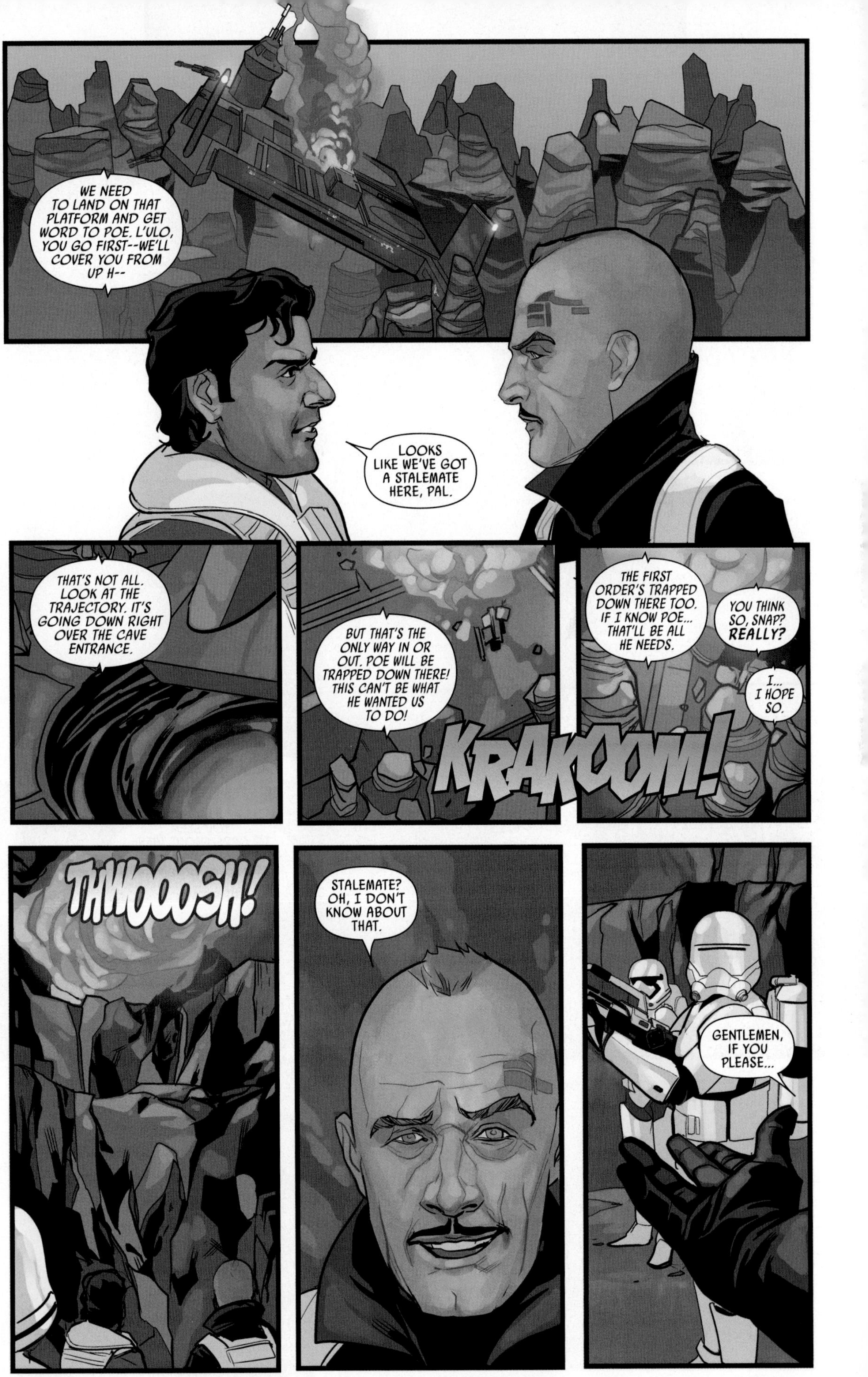

WE NEED TO LAND ON THAT PLATFORM AND GET WORD TO POE. L'ULO, YOU GO FIRST--WE'LL COVER YOU FROM UP H--
LOOKS LIKE WE'VE GOT A STALEMATE HERE, PAL.
THAT'S NOT ALL. LOOK AT THE TRAJECTORY. IT'S GOING DOWN RIGHT OVER THE CAVE ENTRANCE.
BUT THAT'S THE ONLY WAY IN OR OUT. POE WILL BE TRAPPED DOWN THERE! THIS CAN'T BE WHAT HE WANTED US TO DO!
THE FIRST ORDER'S TRAPPED DOWN THERE TOO. IF I KNOW POE... THAT'LL BE ALL HE NEEDS.
YOU THINK SO, SNAP? REALLY?
I... I HOPE SO.
KRAKOOM!
THWOOOSH!
STALEMATE? OH, I DON'T KNOW ABOUT THAT.
GENTLEMEN, IF YOU PLEASE...

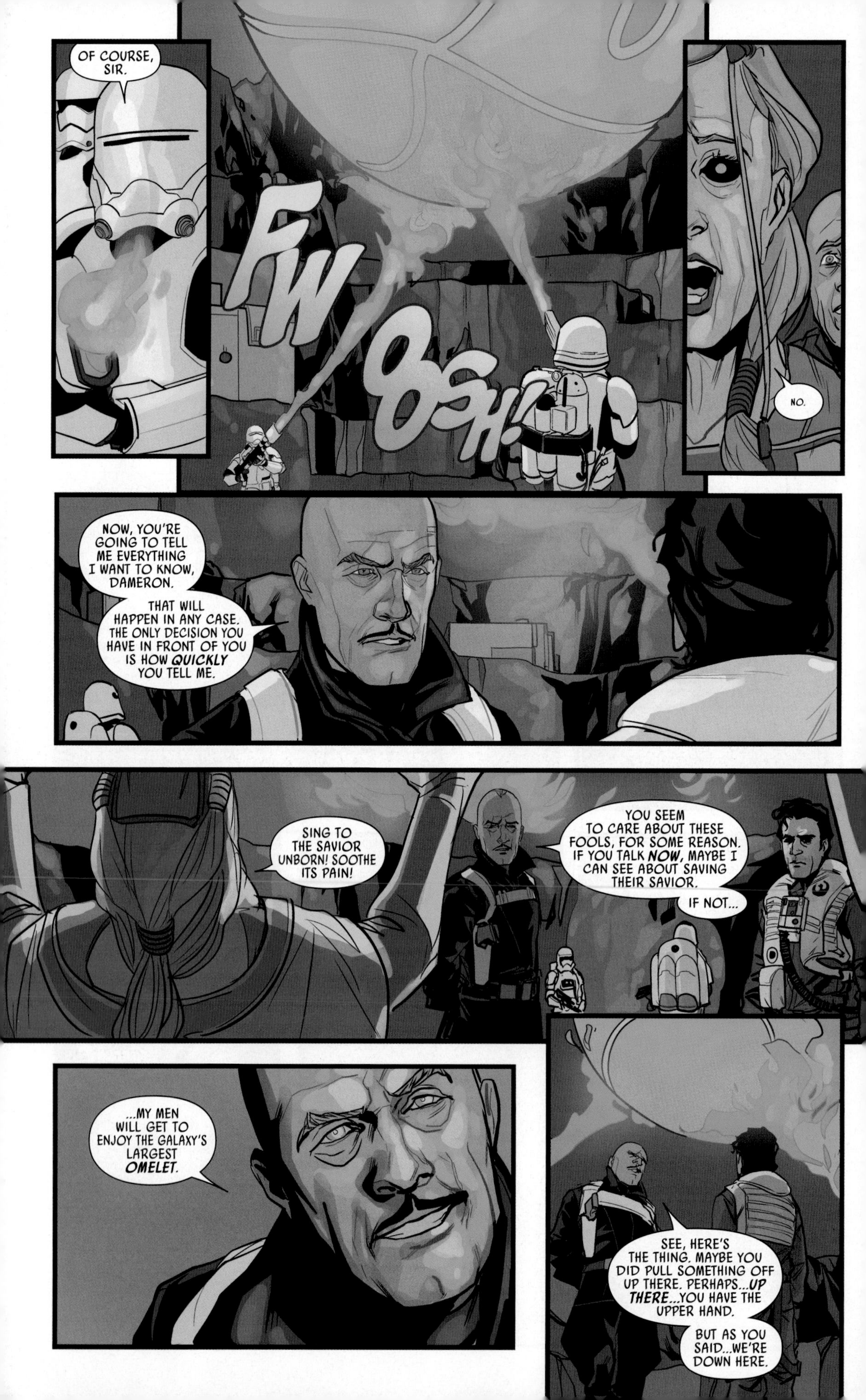
OF COURSE, SIR.
FWOOSH!!
NO.
NOW, YOU'RE GOING TO TELL ME EVERYTHING I WANT TO KNOW, DAMERON.
THAT WILL HAPPEN IN ANY CASE. THE ONLY DECISION YOU HAVE IN FRONT OF YOU IS HOW *QUICKLY* YOU TELL ME.
SING TO THE SAVIOR UNBORN! SOOTHE ITS PAIN!
YOU SEEM TO CARE ABOUT THESE FOOLS, FOR SOME REASON. IF YOU TALK *NOW*, MAYBE I CAN SEE ABOUT SAVING THEIR SAVIOR.
IF NOT...
...MY MEN WILL GET TO ENJOY THE GALAXY'S LARGEST *OMELET*.
SEE, HERE'S THE THING. MAYBE YOU DID PULL SOMETHING OFF UP THERE. PERHAPS...*UP THERE*...YOU HAVE THE UPPER HAND.
BUT AS YOU SAID...WE'RE DOWN HERE.

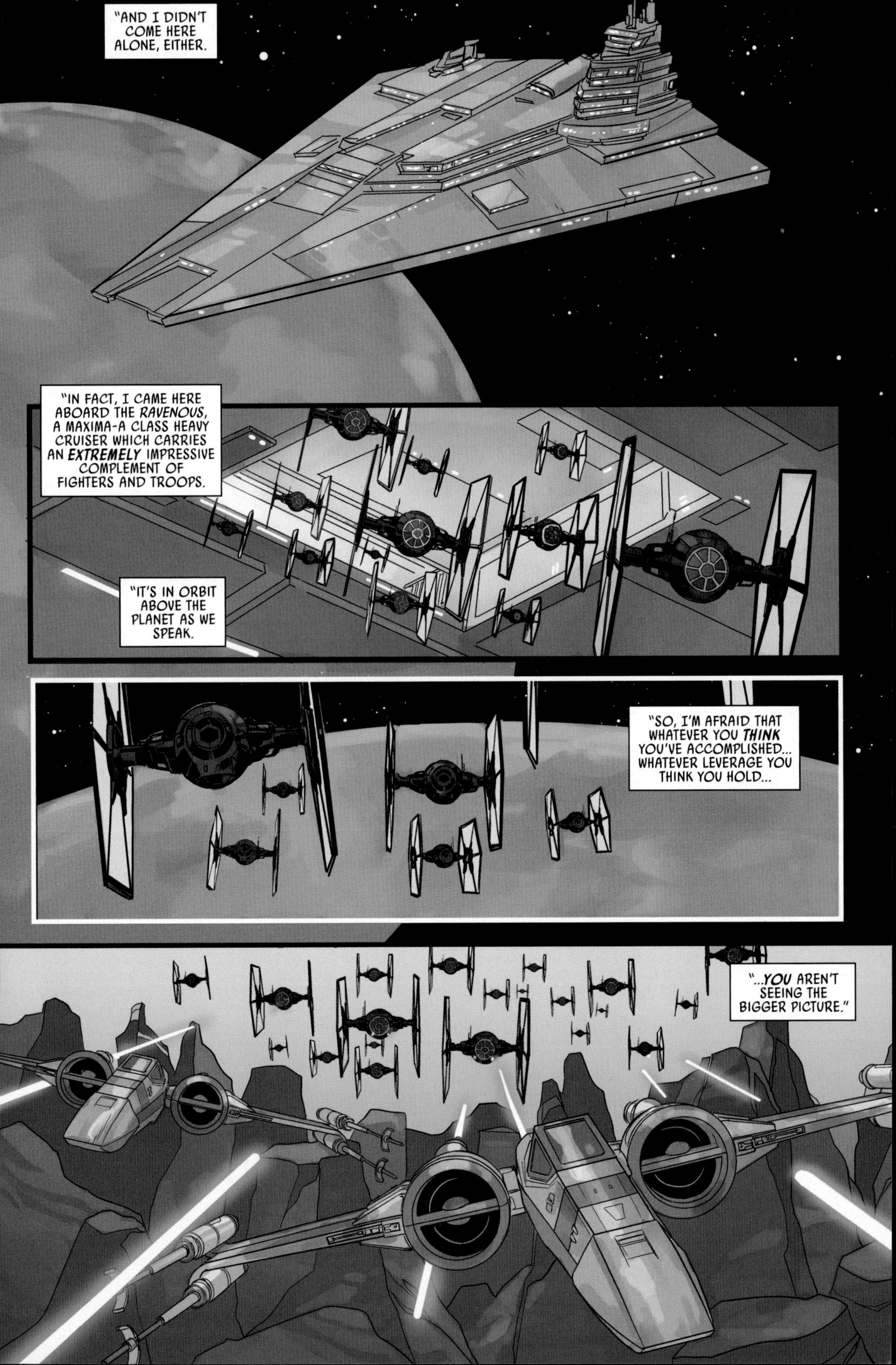
"AND I DIDN'T COME HERE ALONE, EITHER.
"IN FACT, I CAME HERE ABOARD THE *RAVENOUS*, A MAXIMA-A CLASS HEAVY CRUISER WHICH CARRIES AN ***EXTREMELY*** IMPRESSIVE COMPLEMENT OF FIGHTERS AND TROOPS.
"IT'S IN ORBIT ABOVE THE PLANET AS WE SPEAK.
"SO, I'M AFRAID THAT WHATEVER YOU ***THINK*** YOU'VE ACCOMPLISHED... WHATEVER LEVERAGE YOU THINK YOU HOLD...
"...***YOU*** AREN'T SEEING THE BIGGER PICTURE."

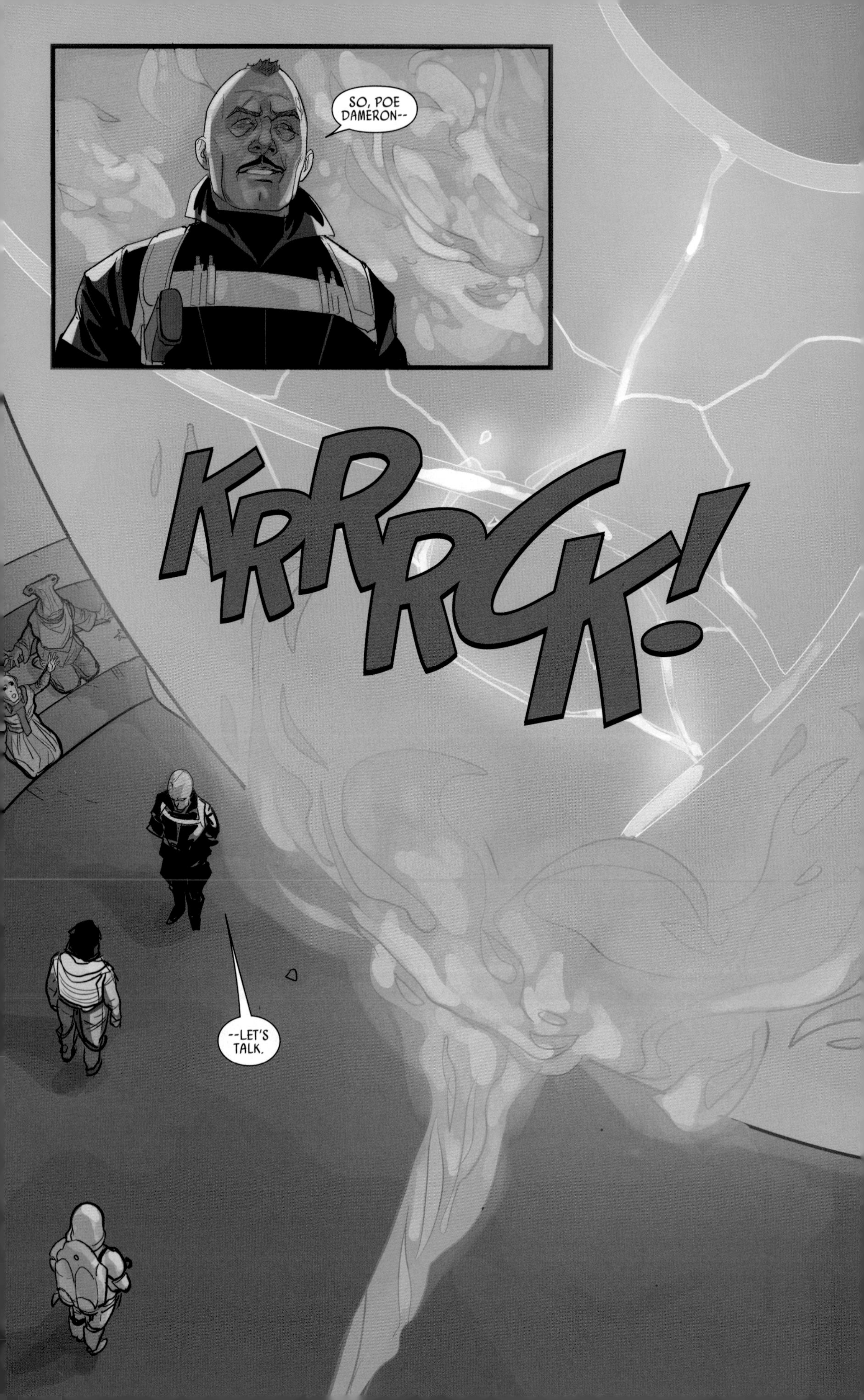
SO, POE DAMERON--
KRRRCK!
--LET'S TALK.

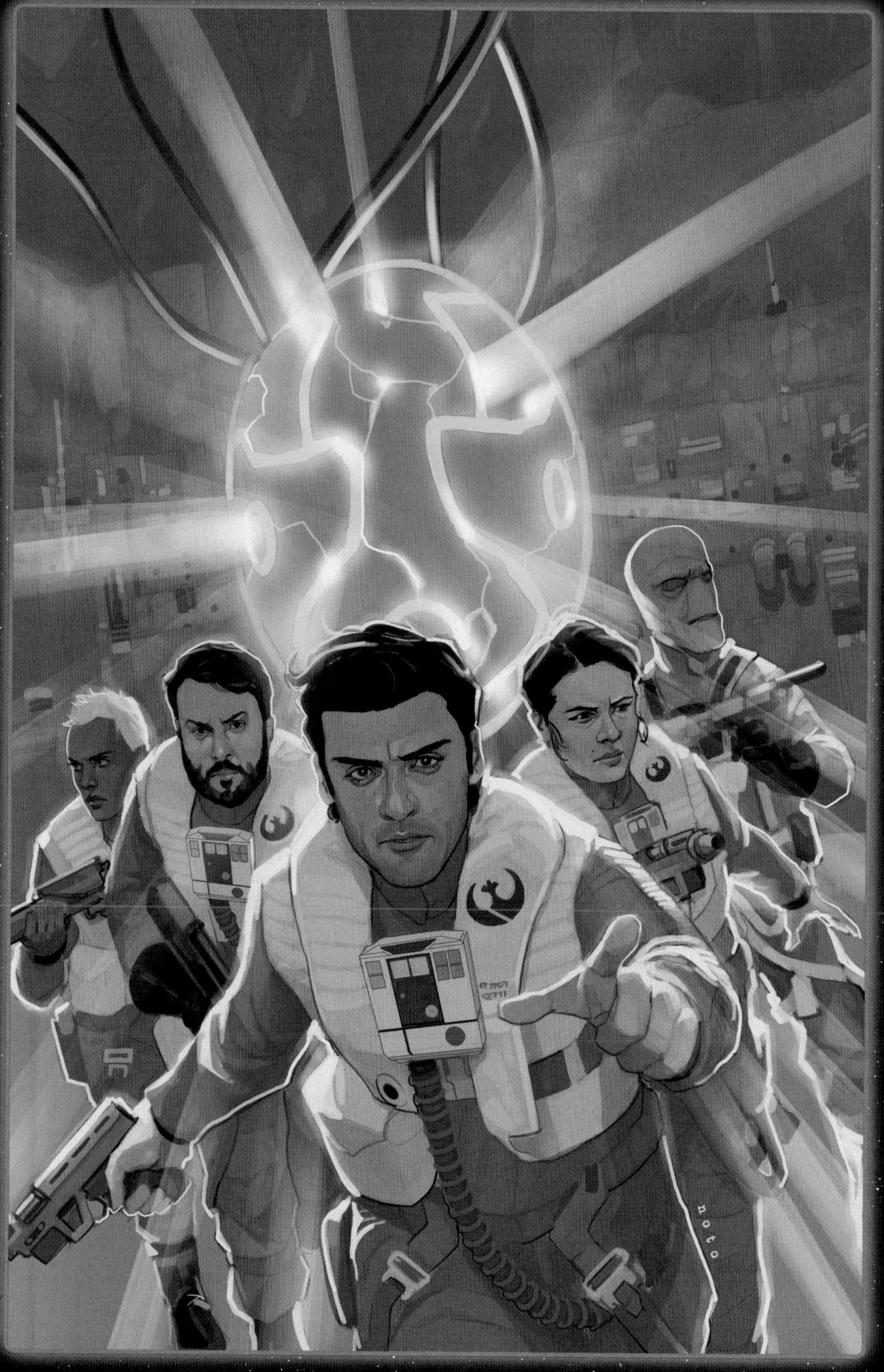
noto

3

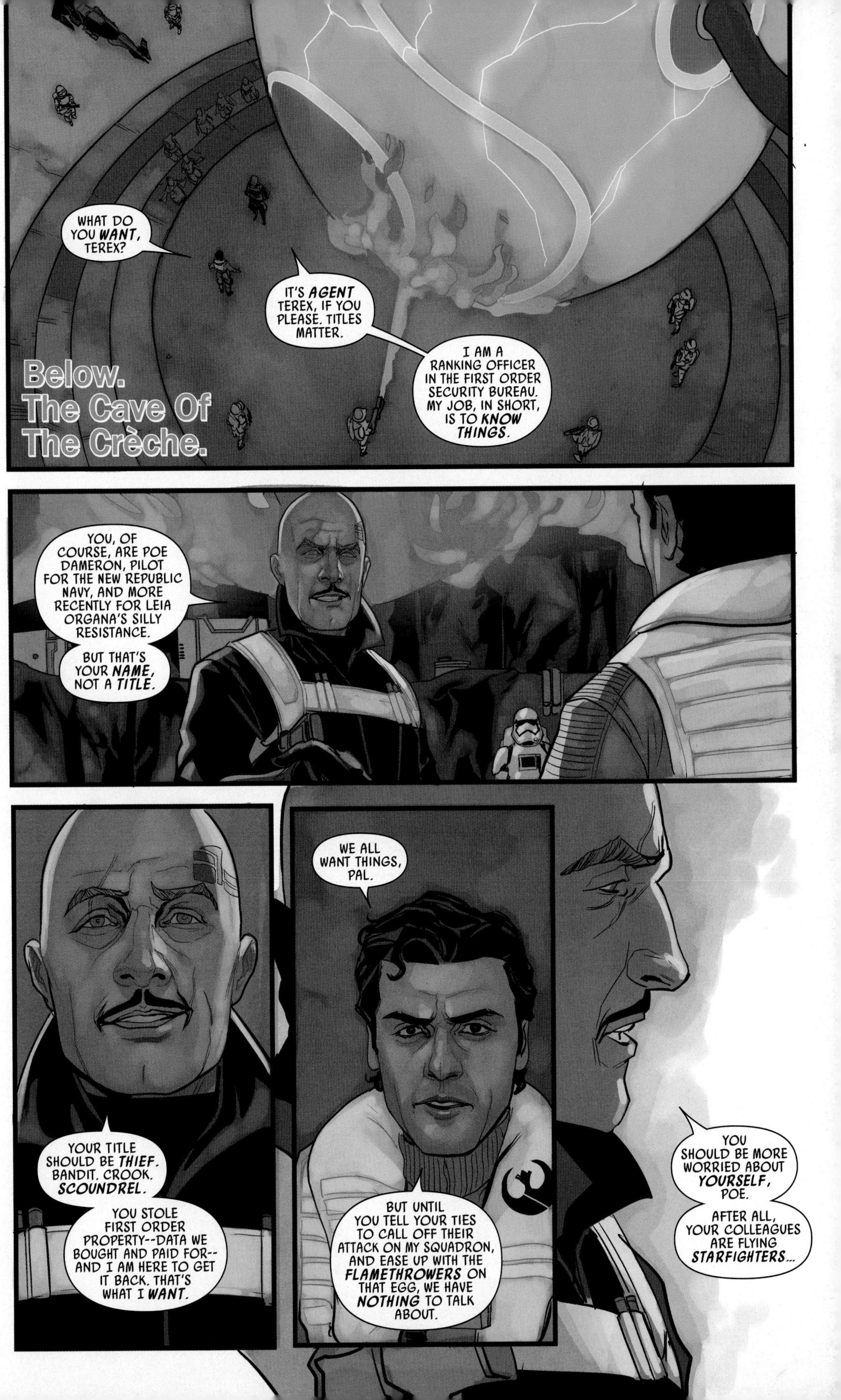
WHAT DO YOU WANT, TEREX?
IT'S AGENT TEREX, IF YOU PLEASE. TITLES MATTER.
I AM A RANKING OFFICER IN THE FIRST ORDER SECURITY BUREAU. MY JOB, IN SHORT, IS TO KNOW THINGS.
Below. The Cave Of The Crèche.
YOU, OF COURSE, ARE POE DAMERON, PILOT FOR THE NEW REPUBLIC NAVY, AND MORE RECENTLY FOR LEIA ORGANA'S SILLY RESISTANCE.
BUT THAT'S YOUR NAME, NOT A TITLE.
YOUR TITLE SHOULD BE THIEF. BANDIT. CROOK. SCOUNDREL.
YOU STOLE FIRST ORDER PROPERTY--DATA WE BOUGHT AND PAID FOR--AND I AM HERE TO GET IT BACK. THAT'S WHAT I WANT.
WE ALL WANT THINGS, PAL.
BUT UNTIL YOU TELL YOUR TIES TO CALL OFF THEIR ATTACK ON MY SQUADRON, AND EASE UP WITH THE FLAMETHROWERS ON THAT EGG, WE HAVE NOTHING TO TALK ABOUT.
YOU SHOULD BE MORE WORRIED ABOUT YOURSELF, POE.
AFTER ALL, YOUR COLLEAGUES ARE FLYING STARFIGHTERS...

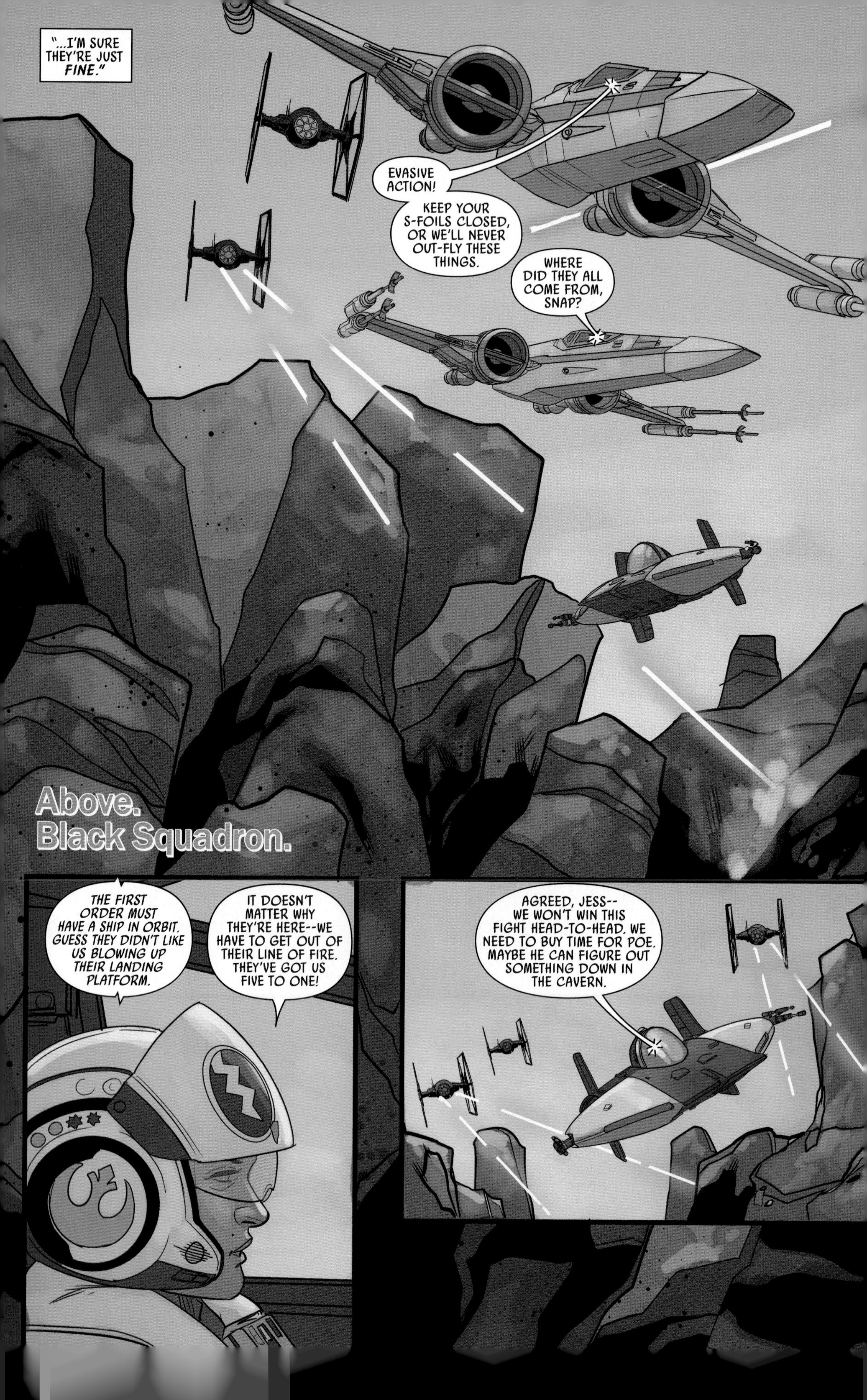
"...I'M SURE THEY'RE JUST FINE."
EVASIVE ACTION!
KEEP YOUR S-FOILS CLOSED, OR WE'LL NEVER OUT-FLY THESE THINGS.
WHERE DID THEY ALL COME FROM, SNAP?
Above. Black Squadron.
THE FIRST ORDER MUST HAVE A SHIP IN ORBIT. GUESS THEY DIDN'T LIKE US BLOWING UP THEIR LANDING PLATFORM.
IT DOESN'T MATTER WHY THEY'RE HERE--WE HAVE TO GET OUT OF THEIR LINE OF FIRE. THEY'VE GOT US FIVE TO ONE!
AGREED, JESS-- WE WON'T WIN THIS FIGHT HEAD-TO-HEAD. WE NEED TO BUY TIME FOR POE. MAYBE HE CAN FIGURE OUT SOMETHING DOWN IN THE CAVERN.

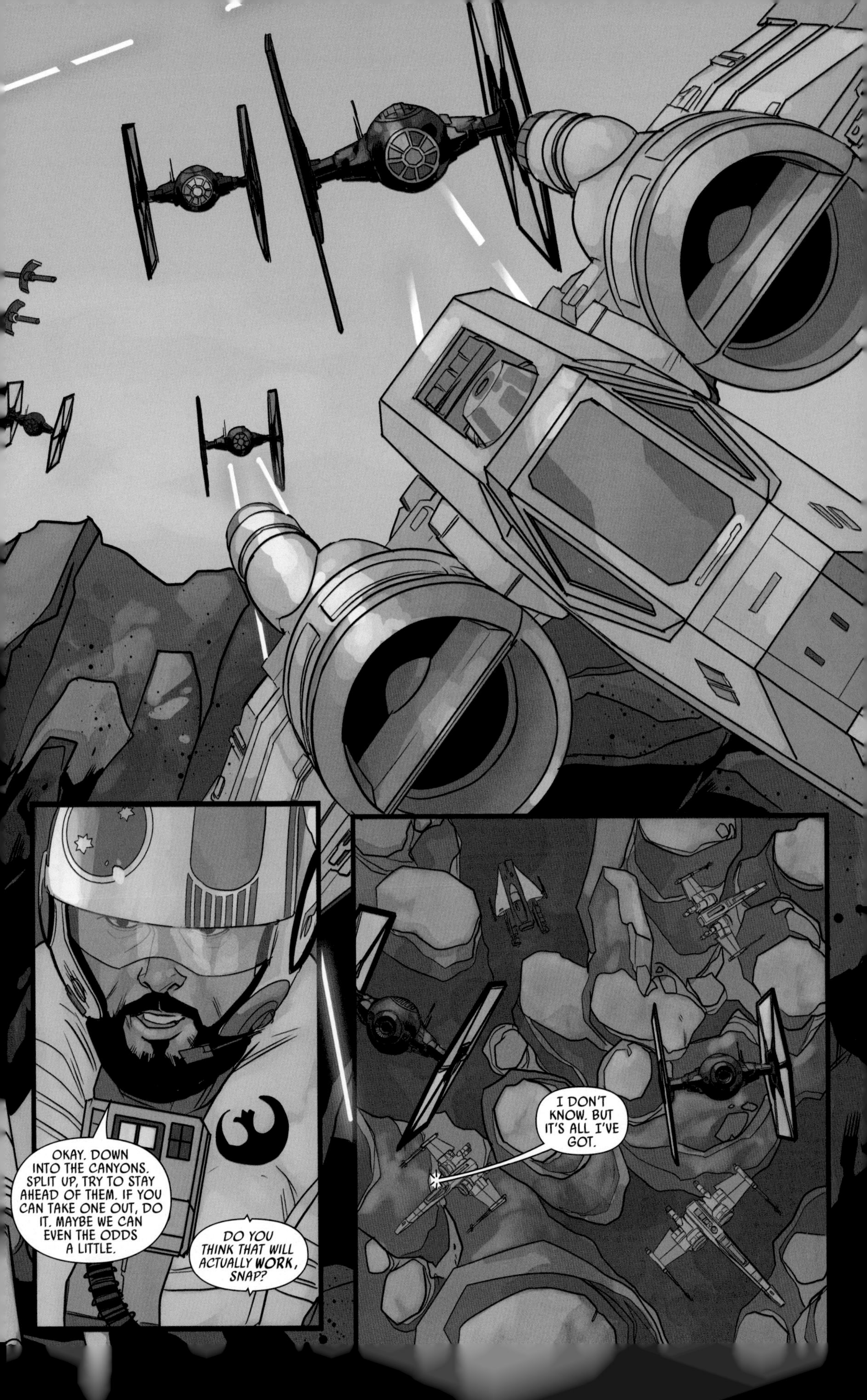
OKAY. DOWN INTO THE CANYONS. SPLIT UP, TRY TO STAY AHEAD OF THEM. IF YOU CAN TAKE ONE OUT, DO IT. MAYBE WE CAN EVEN THE ODDS A LITTLE.
DO YOU THINK THAT WILL ACTUALLY WORK, SNAP?
I DON'T KNOW. BUT IT'S ALL I'VE GOT.

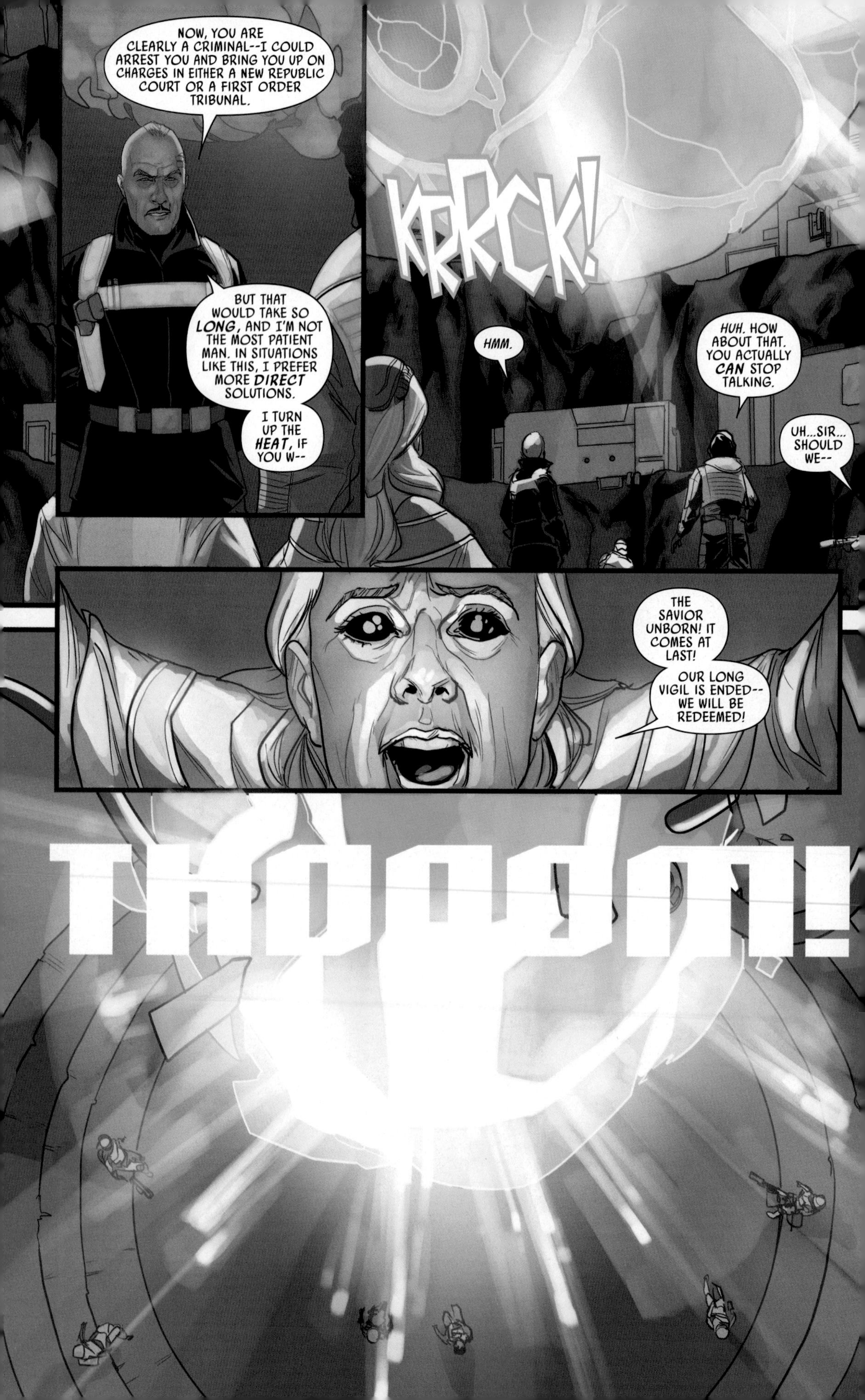
NOW, YOU ARE CLEARLY A CRIMINAL--I COULD ARREST YOU AND BRING YOU UP ON CHARGES IN EITHER A NEW REPUBLIC COURT OR A FIRST ORDER TRIBUNAL.
BUT THAT WOULD TAKE SO LONG, AND I'M NOT THE MOST PATIENT MAN. IN SITUATIONS LIKE THIS, I PREFER MORE DIRECT SOLUTIONS.
I TURN UP THE HEAT, IF YOU W--
KRRCK!
HMM.
HUH. HOW ABOUT THAT. YOU ACTUALLY CAN STOP TALKING.
UH...SIR... SHOULD WE--
THE SAVIOR UNBORN! IT COMES AT LAST!
OUR LONG VIGIL IS ENDED--WE WILL BE REDEEMED!
THOOOM!

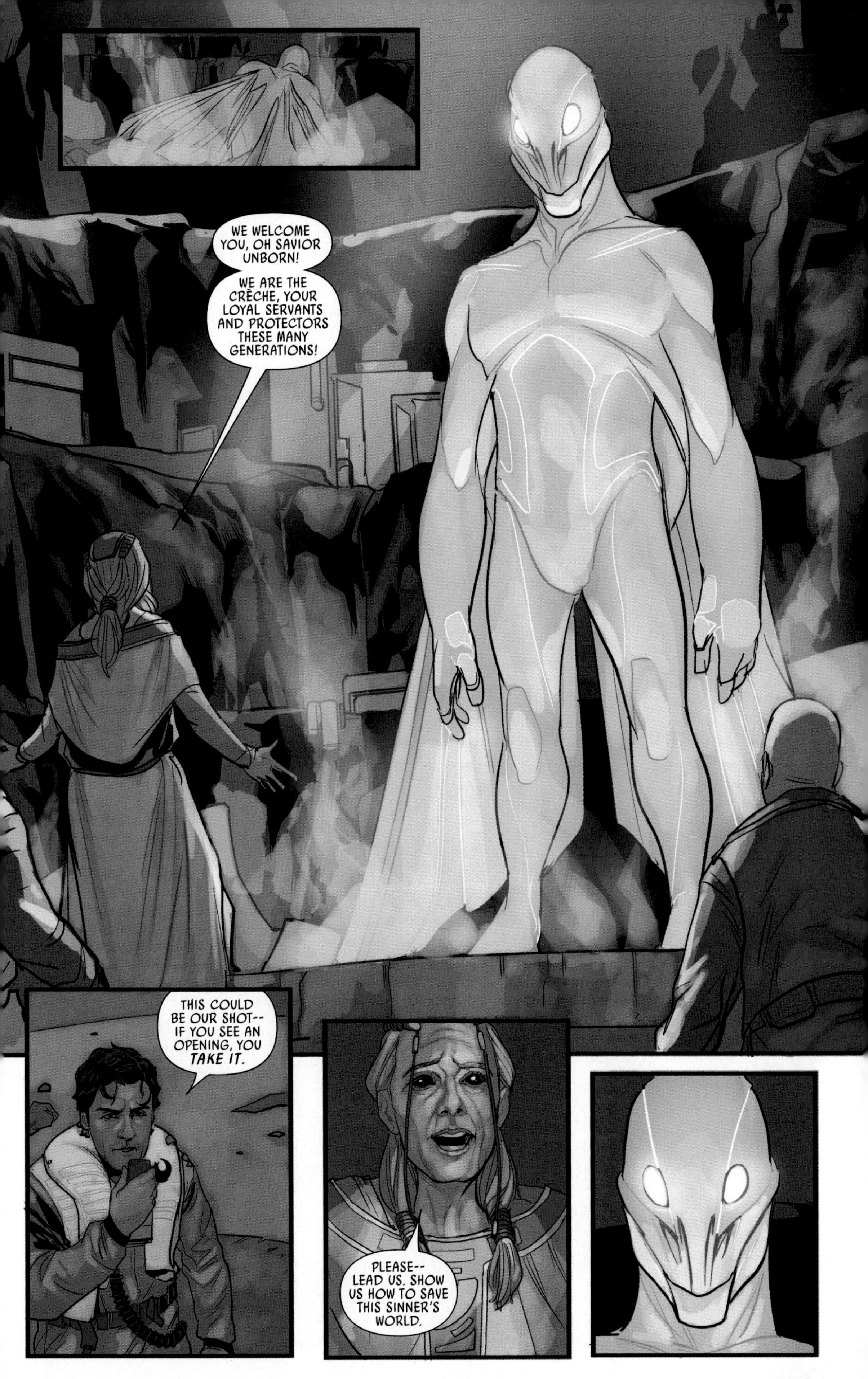
WE WELCOME YOU, OH SAVIOR UNBORN!
WE ARE THE CRÈCHE, YOUR LOYAL SERVANTS AND PROTECTORS THESE MANY GENERATIONS!
THIS COULD BE OUR SHOT--IF YOU SEE AN OPENING, YOU *TAKE IT.*
PLEASE--LEAD US. SHOW US HOW TO SAVE THIS SINNER'S WORLD.

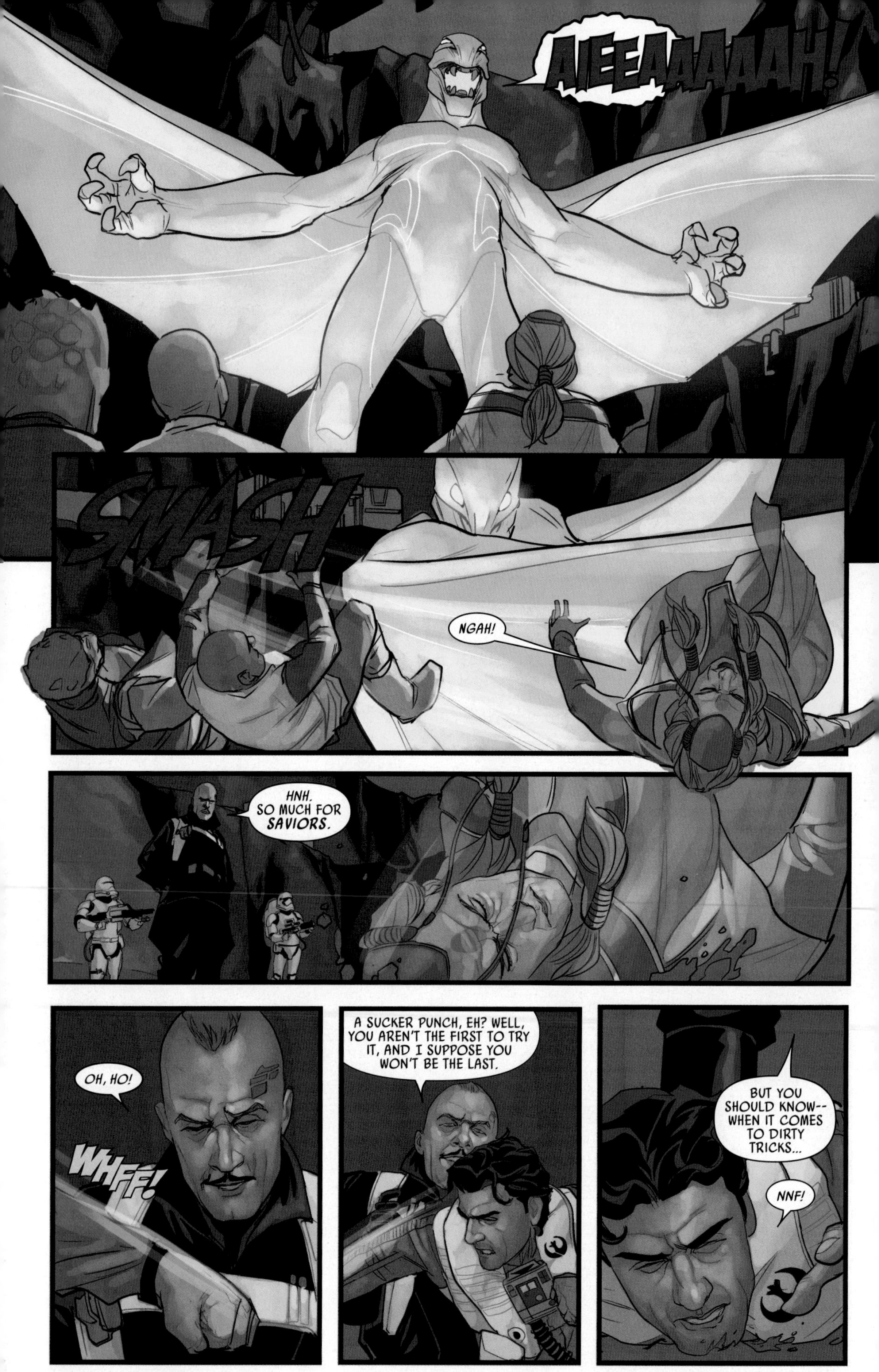
AIEEAAAAAH!
SMASH
NGAH!
HNH. SO MUCH FOR SAVIORS.
OH, HO!
WHFF!
A SUCKER PUNCH, EH? WELL, YOU AREN'T THE FIRST TO TRY IT, AND I SUPPOSE YOU WON'T BE THE LAST.
BUT YOU SHOULD KNOW-- WHEN IT COMES TO DIRTY TRICKS...
NNF!

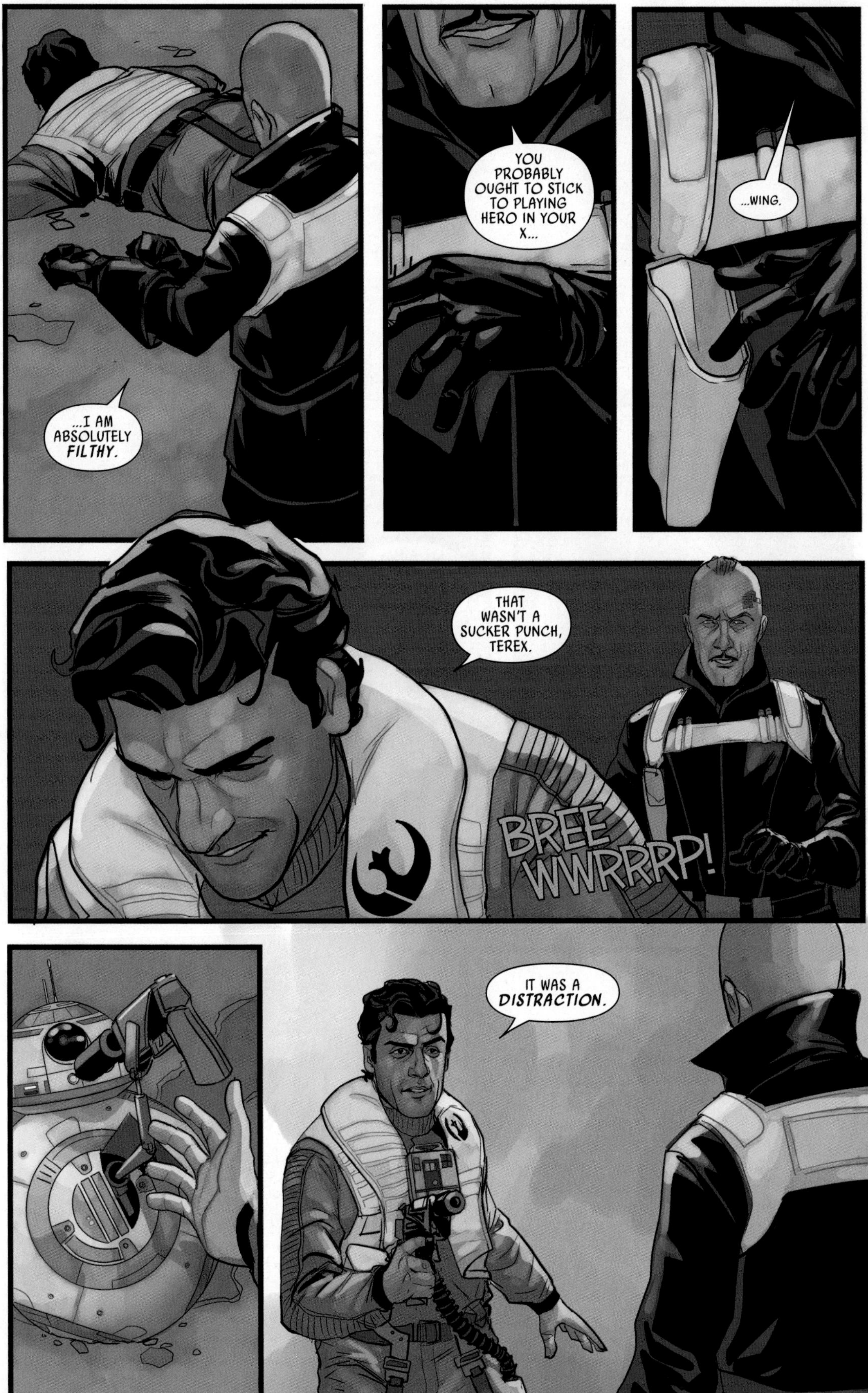
...I AM ABSOLUTELY FILTHY.
YOU PROBABLY OUGHT TO STICK TO PLAYING HERO IN YOUR X...
...WING.
THAT WASN'T A SUCKER PUNCH, TEREX.
BREE WWRRRP!
IT WAS A DISTRACTION.

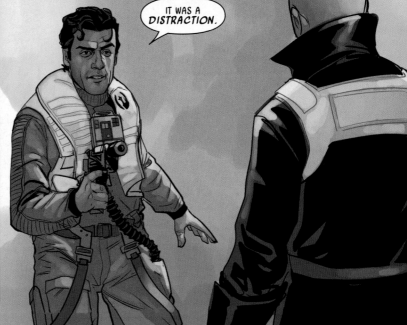

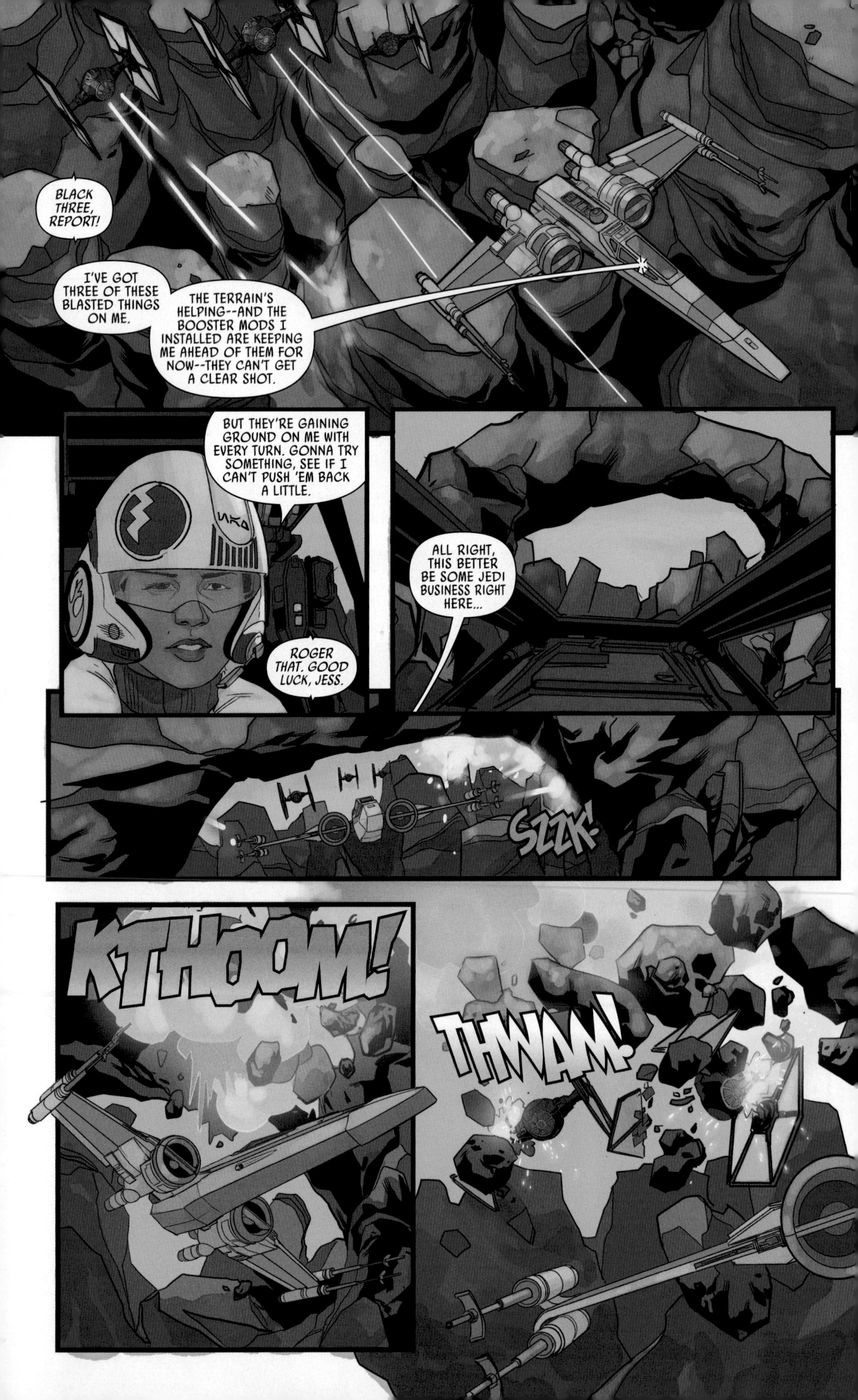
BLACK THREE, REPORT!
I'VE GOT THREE OF THESE BLASTED THINGS ON ME.
THE TERRAIN'S HELPING--AND THE BOOSTER MODS I INSTALLED ARE KEEPING ME AHEAD OF THEM FOR NOW--THEY CAN'T GET A CLEAR SHOT.
BUT THEY'RE GAINING GROUND ON ME WITH EVERY TURN. GONNA TRY SOMETHING, SEE IF I CAN'T PUSH 'EM BACK A LITTLE.
ROGER THAT. GOOD LUCK, JESS.
ALL RIGHT, THIS BETTER BE SOME JEDI BUSINESS RIGHT HERE...
SZZK!
KTHOOM!
THWAM!

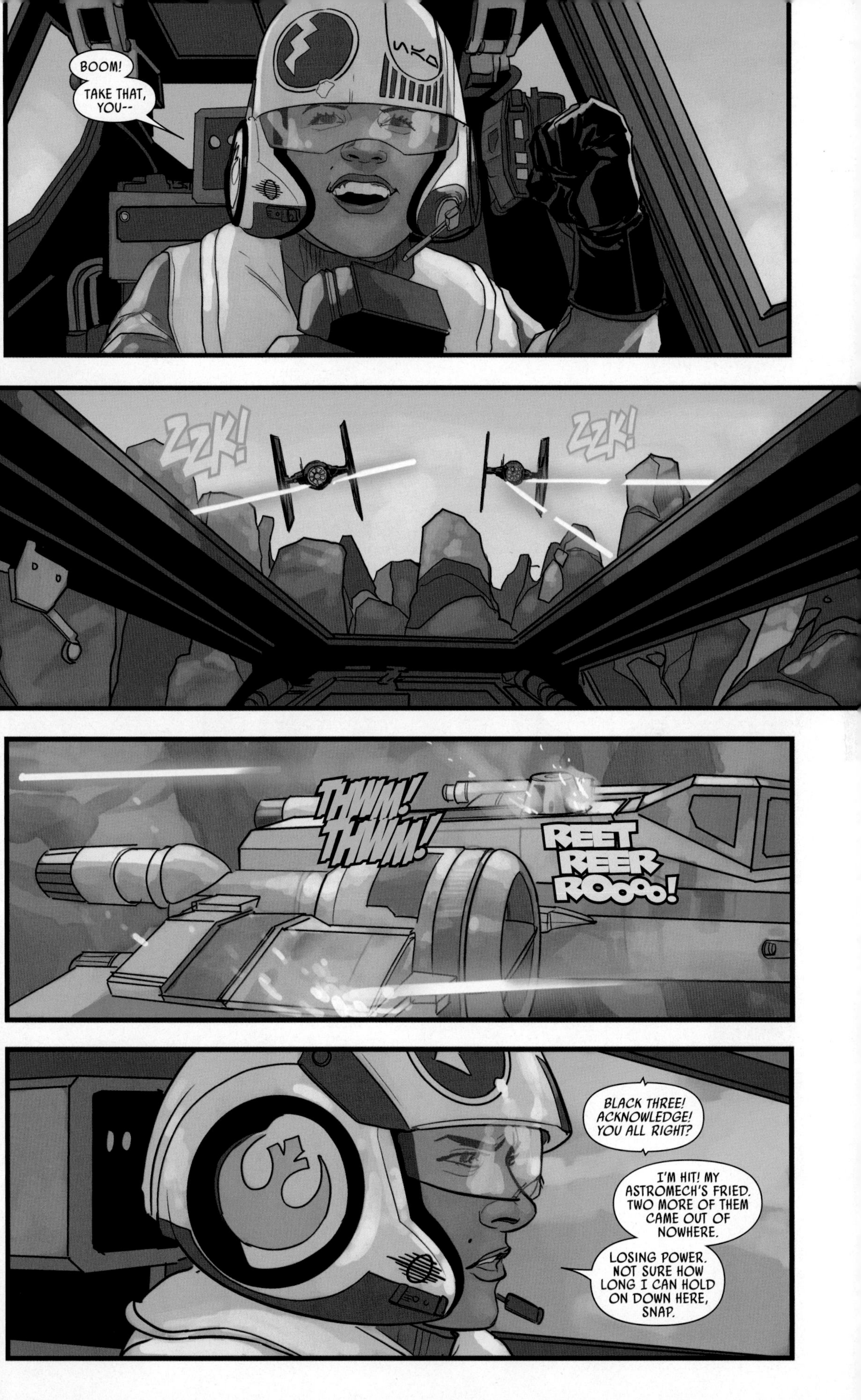
BOOM!
TAKE THAT, YOU--
ZZK!
ZZK!
THWM! THWM!
REET REER ROooo!
BLACK THREE! ACKNOWLEDGE! YOU ALL RIGHT?
I'M HIT! MY ASTROMECH'S FRIED. TWO MORE OF THEM CAME OUT OF NOWHERE.
LOSING POWER. NOT SURE HOW LONG I CAN HOLD ON DOWN HERE, SNAP.

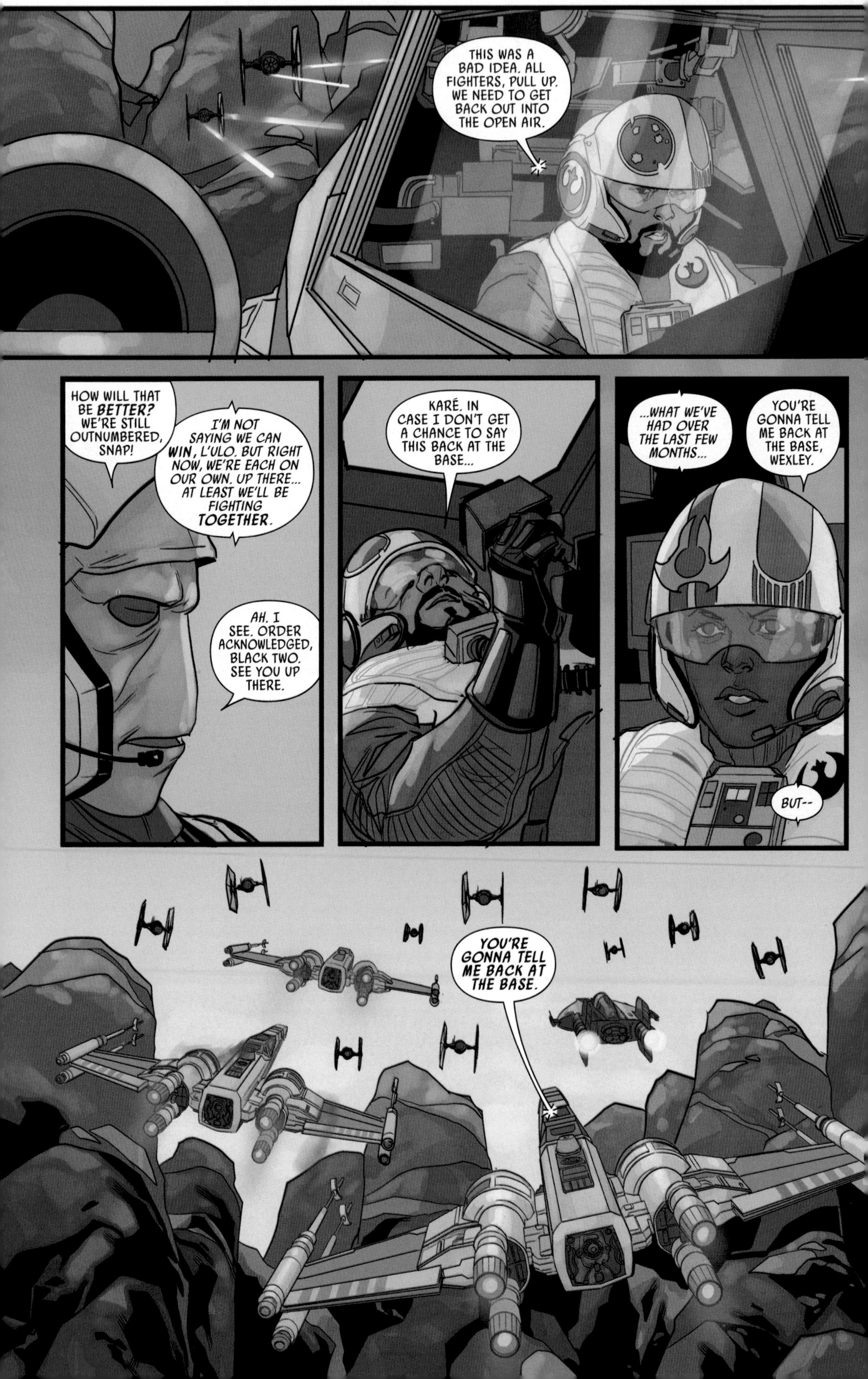

THIS WAS A BAD IDEA. ALL FIGHTERS, PULL UP. WE NEED TO GET BACK OUT INTO THE OPEN AIR.
HOW WILL THAT BE **BETTER?** WE'RE STILL OUTNUMBERED, SNAP!
I'M NOT SAYING WE CAN ***WIN****, L'ULO. BUT RIGHT NOW, WE'RE EACH ON OUR OWN. UP THERE... AT LEAST WE'LL BE FIGHTING* ***TOGETHER****.*
AH. I SEE. ORDER ACKNOWLEDGED, BLACK TWO. SEE YOU UP THERE.
KARÉ. IN CASE I DON'T GET A CHANCE TO SAY THIS BACK AT THE BASE...
...WHAT WE'VE HAD OVER THE LAST FEW MONTHS...
YOU'RE GONNA TELL ME BACK AT THE BASE, WEXLEY.
BUT--
YOU'RE GONNA TELL ME BACK AT THE BASE.

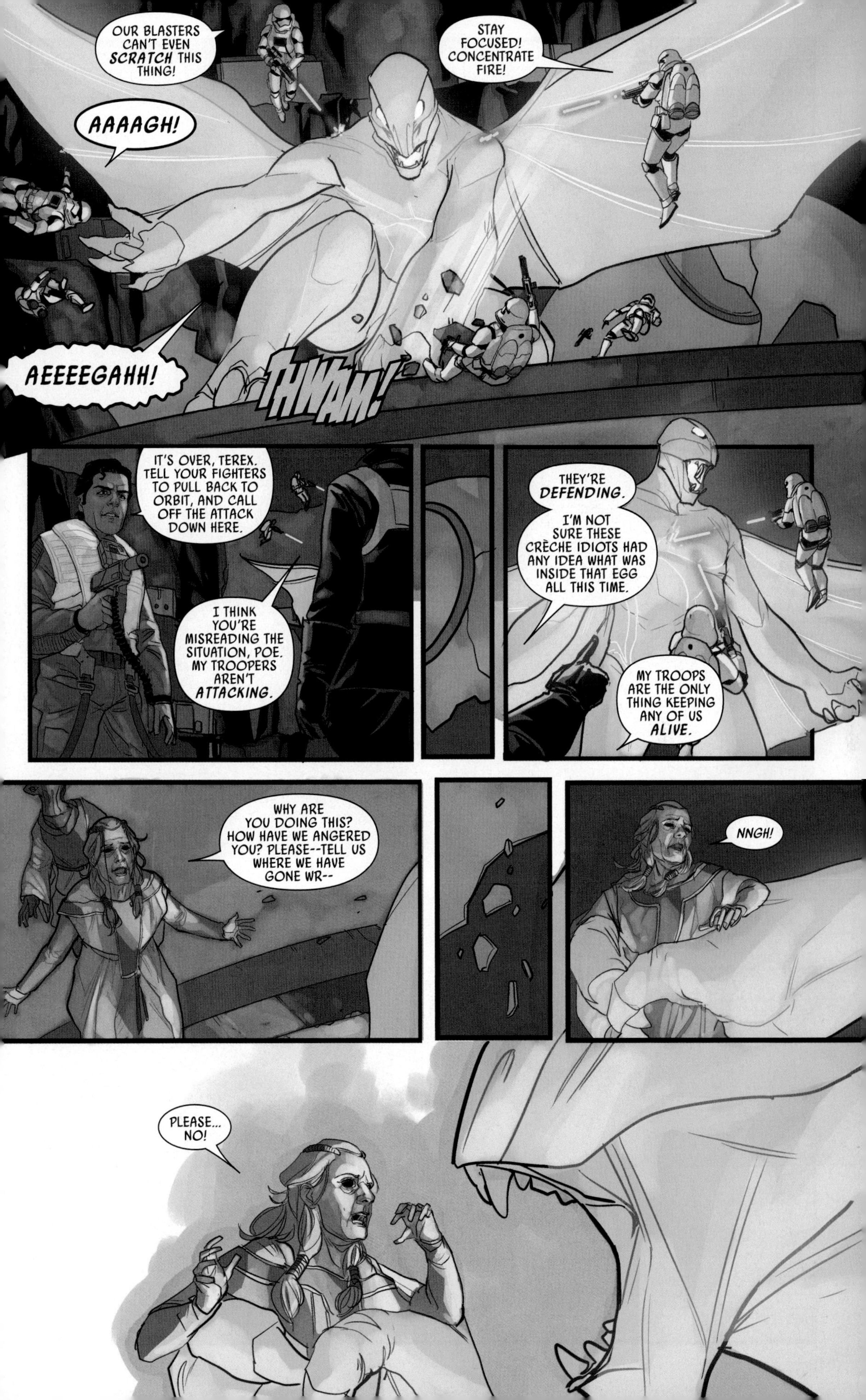
OUR BLASTERS CAN'T EVEN SCRATCH THIS THING!
STAY FOCUSED! CONCENTRATE FIRE!
AAAAGH!
AEEEEGAHH!
THWAM!
IT'S OVER, TEREX. TELL YOUR FIGHTERS TO PULL BACK TO ORBIT, AND CALL OFF THE ATTACK DOWN HERE.
I THINK YOU'RE MISREADING THE SITUATION, POE. MY TROOPERS AREN'T ATTACKING.
THEY'RE DEFENDING.
I'M NOT SURE THESE CRÈCHE IDIOTS HAD ANY IDEA WHAT WAS INSIDE THAT EGG ALL THIS TIME.
MY TROOPS ARE THE ONLY THING KEEPING ANY OF US ALIVE.
WHY ARE YOU DOING THIS? HOW HAVE WE ANGERED YOU? PLEASE--TELL US WHERE WE HAVE GONE WR--
NNGH!
PLEASE... NO!

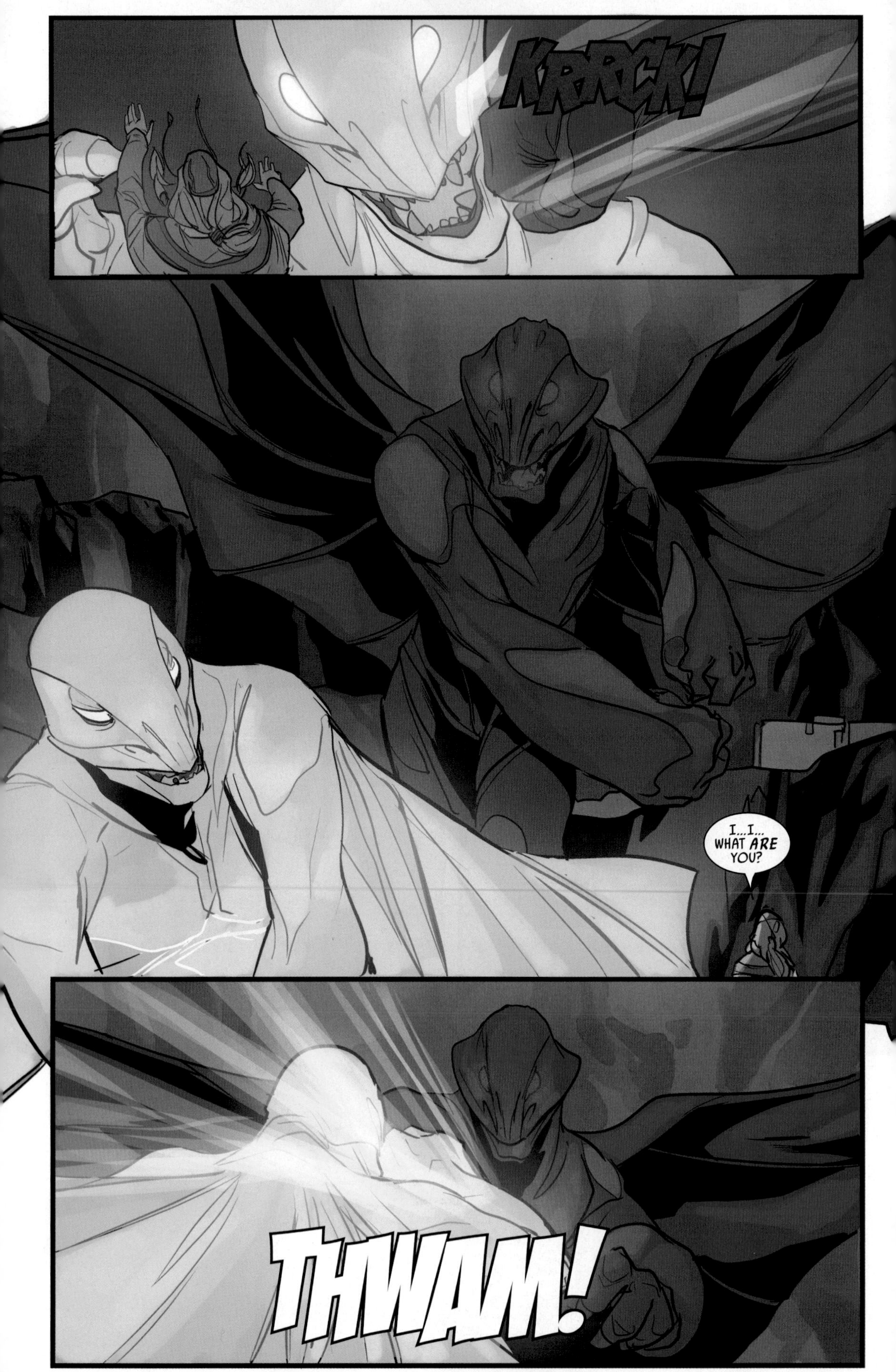
KRRCK!
I...I... WHAT ARE YOU?
THWAM!

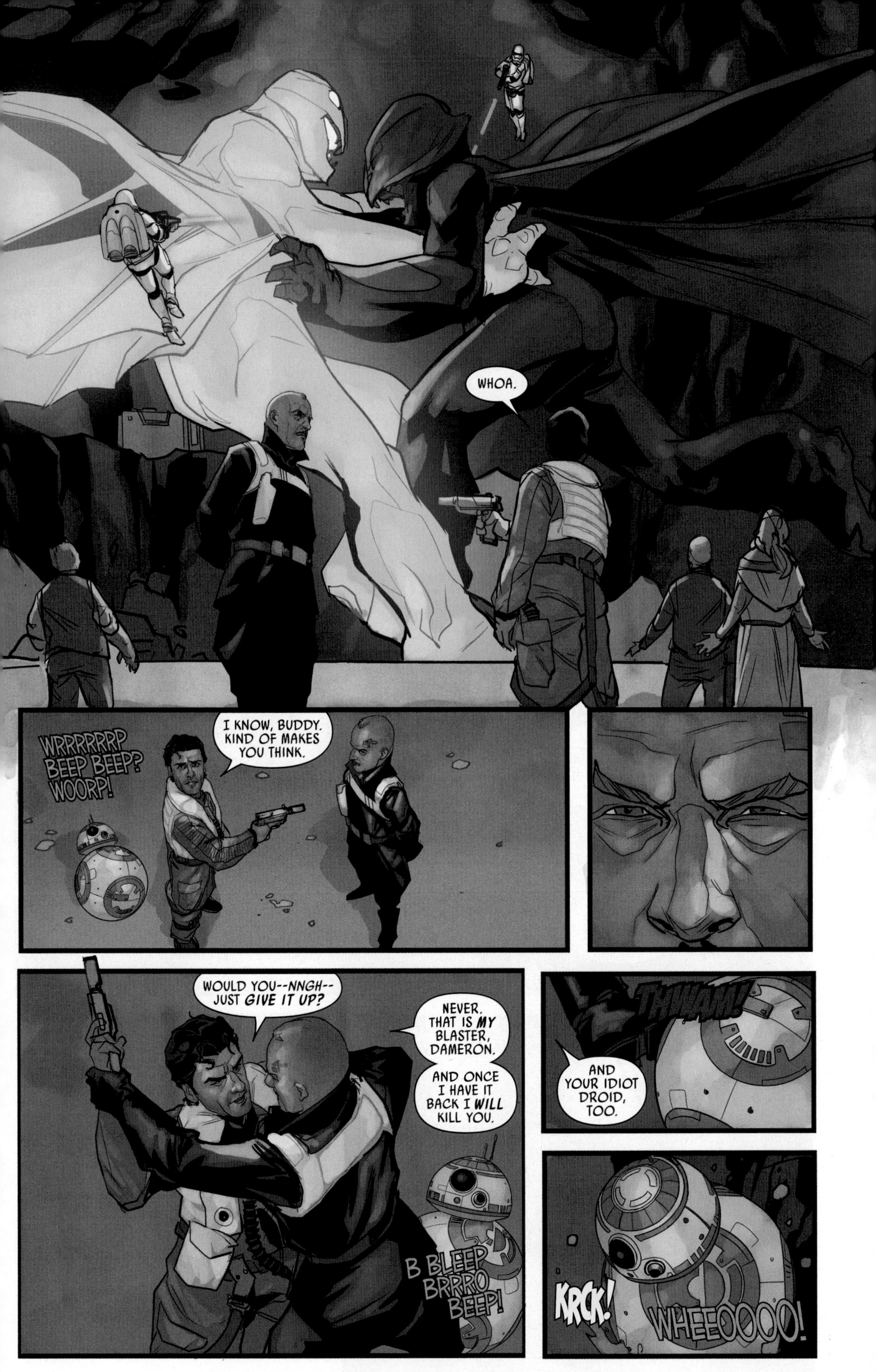
WHOA.
WRRRRRRP BEEP BEEP? WOORP!
I KNOW, BUDDY. KIND OF MAKES YOU THINK.
WOULD YOU--NNGH-- JUST GIVE IT UP?
NEVER. THAT IS MY BLASTER, DAMERON.
AND ONCE I HAVE IT BACK I WILL KILL YOU.
B BLEEP BRRRO BEEP!
THWAM!
AND YOUR IDIOT DROID, TOO.
KRCK!
WHEEOOOO!

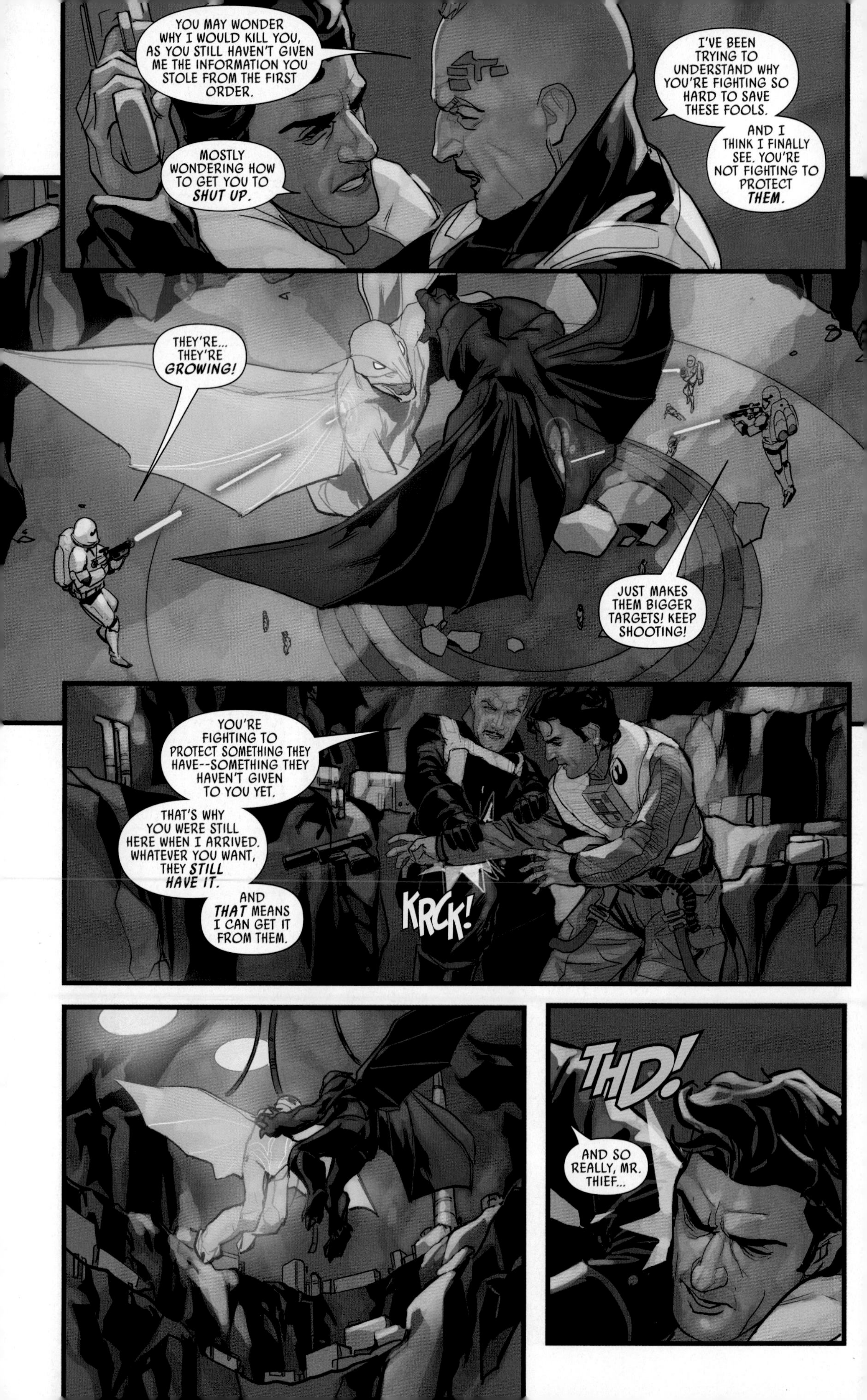
YOU MAY WONDER WHY I WOULD KILL YOU, AS YOU STILL HAVEN'T GIVEN ME THE INFORMATION YOU STOLE FROM THE FIRST ORDER.
MOSTLY WONDERING HOW TO GET YOU TO SHUT UP.
I'VE BEEN TRYING TO UNDERSTAND WHY YOU'RE FIGHTING SO HARD TO SAVE THESE FOOLS.
AND I THINK I FINALLY SEE. YOU'RE NOT FIGHTING TO PROTECT THEM.
THEY'RE... THEY'RE GROWING!
JUST MAKES THEM BIGGER TARGETS! KEEP SHOOTING!
YOU'RE FIGHTING TO PROTECT SOMETHING THEY HAVE--SOMETHING THEY HAVEN'T GIVEN TO YOU YET.
THAT'S WHY YOU WERE STILL HERE WHEN I ARRIVED. WHATEVER YOU WANT, THEY STILL HAVE IT.
AND THAT MEANS I CAN GET IT FROM THEM.
KRCK!
THD!
AND SO REALLY, MR. THIEF...

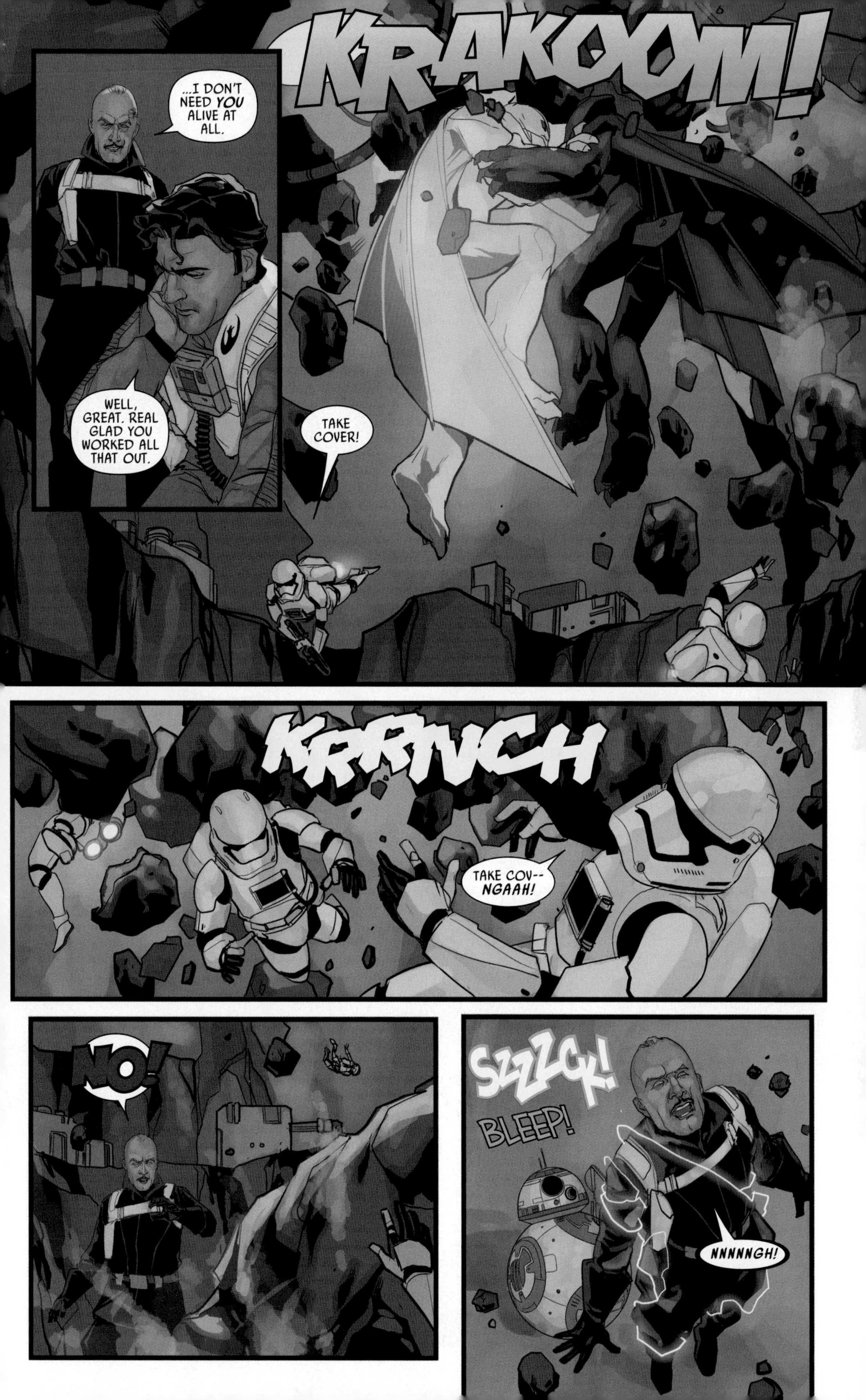
KRAKOOM!
...I DON'T NEED YOU ALIVE AT ALL.
WELL, GREAT. REAL GLAD YOU WORKED ALL THAT OUT.
TAKE COVER!
KRRNCH
TAKE COV-- NGAAH!
NO!
SZZZCK!
BLEEP!
NNNNNGH!

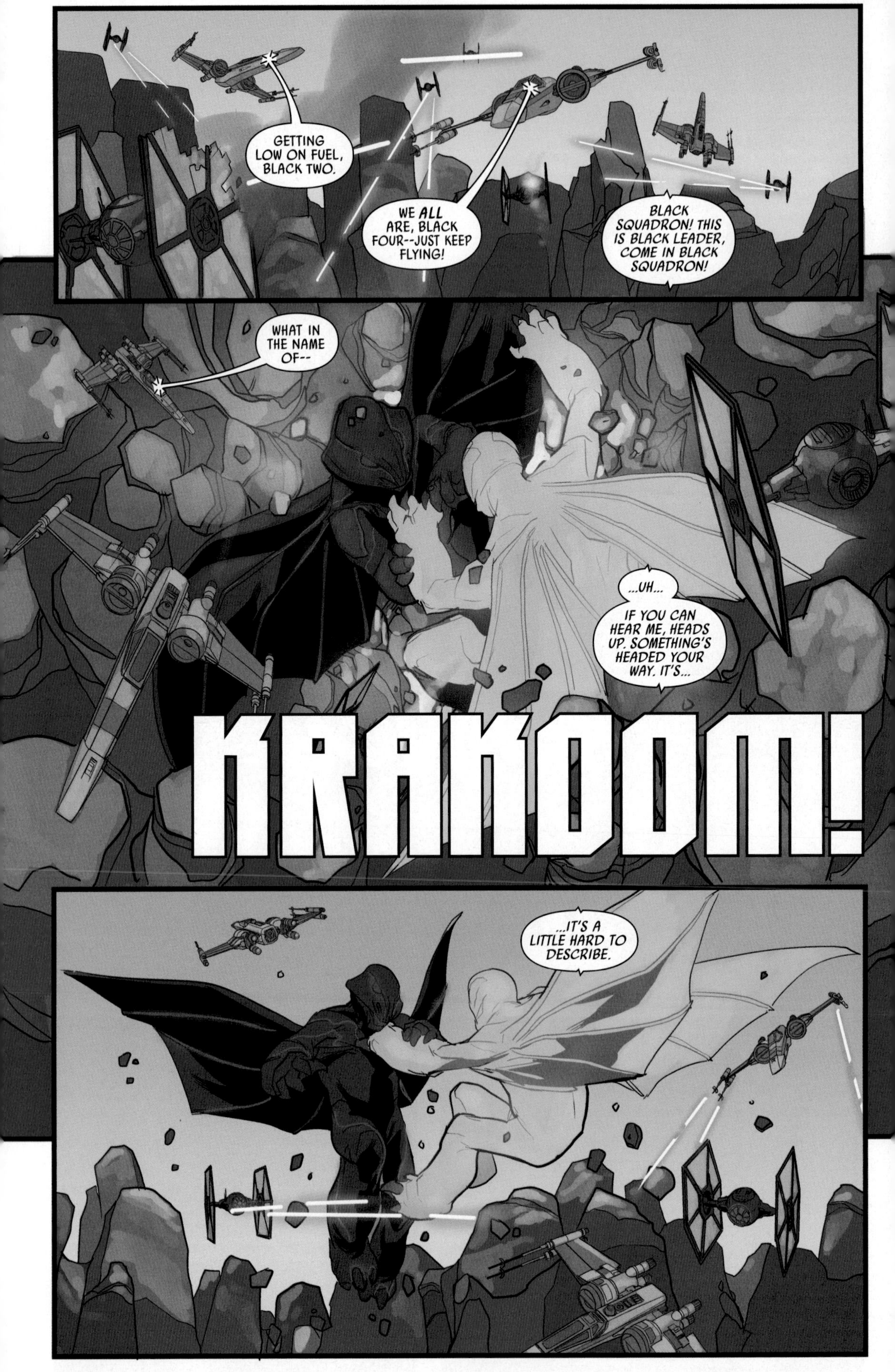
GETTING LOW ON FUEL, BLACK TWO.
WE ALL ARE, BLACK FOUR--JUST KEEP FLYING!
BLACK SQUADRON! THIS IS BLACK LEADER, COME IN BLACK SQUADRON!
WHAT IN THE NAME OF--
...UH...
IF YOU CAN HEAR ME, HEADS UP. SOMETHING'S HEADED YOUR WAY. IT'S...
KRAKOOM!
...IT'S A LITTLE HARD TO DESCRIBE.

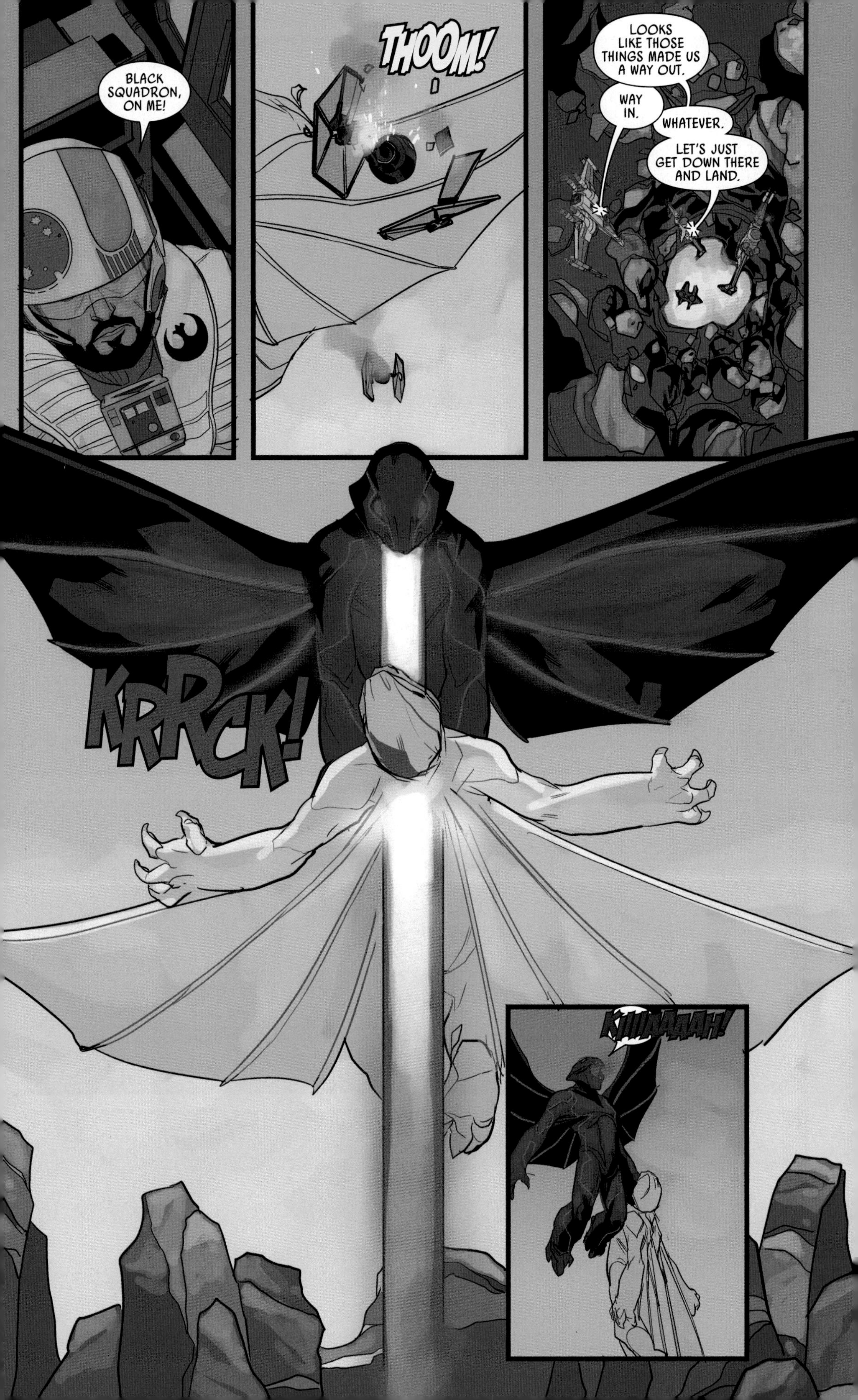
BLACK SQUADRON, ON ME!
THOOM!
LOOKS LIKE THOSE THINGS MADE US A WAY OUT.
WAY IN.
WHATEVER.
LET'S JUST GET DOWN THERE AND LAND.
KRRCK!
KIIIAAAAH!

AND WHAT WILL YOU DO NOW, DAMERON?

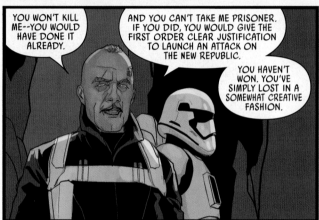

YOU WON'T KILL ME--YOU WOULD HAVE DONE IT ALREADY.

AND YOU CAN'T TAKE ME PRISONER. IF YOU DID, YOU WOULD GIVE THE FIRST ORDER CLEAR JUSTIFICATION TO LAUNCH AN ATTACK ON THE NEW REPUBLIC.

YOU HAVEN'T WON. YOU'VE SIMPLY LOST IN A SOMEWHAT CREATIVE FASHION.

YOU KNOW WHAT, MAN?

YOU'RE SORT OF A DRAG.

THIS PROBLEM IS EASILY SOLVED. TEREX CAN'T HAVE MANY TIES LEFT. ONCE WE REFUEL, WE CAN FLY UP AND TAKE OUT HIS CRUISER IN ORBIT ON OUR WAY HOME.

LET THE CRÈCHE DECIDE WHAT TO DO WITH HIM.

IT'S NO GOOD. THE FIRST ORDER WOULD SEND ANOTHER SHIP, MAYBE EVEN A STAR DESTROYER. THEY'D BURN THIS WHOLE PLANET LOOKING FOR HIM.

SO, WHAT... WE JUST LET HIM GO?

YES, WE WILL LET HIM GO. HE CAN'T HURT US ANYMORE.

THE SAVIOR... BORN.

IT WILL CARRY US FAR FROM HERE, TO WHEREVER OUR NEW LIFE WILL BEGIN.

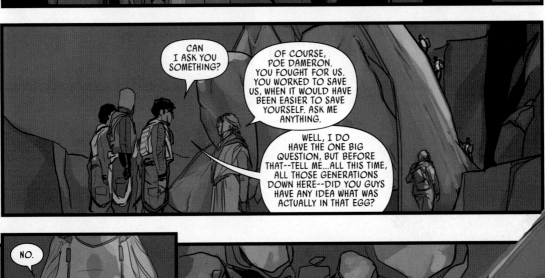

CAN I ASK YOU SOMETHING?

OF COURSE, POE DAMERON. YOU FOUGHT FOR US. YOU WORKED TO SAVE US, WHEN IT WOULD HAVE BEEN EASIER TO SAVE YOURSELF. ASK ME ANYTHING.

WELL, I DO HAVE THE ONE BIG QUESTION, BUT BEFORE THAT--TELL ME...ALL THIS TIME, ALL THOSE GENERATIONS DOWN HERE--DID YOU GUYS HAVE ANY IDEA WHAT WAS ACTUALLY IN THAT EGG?

NO.

"BUT THAT WAS NEVER THE POINT."

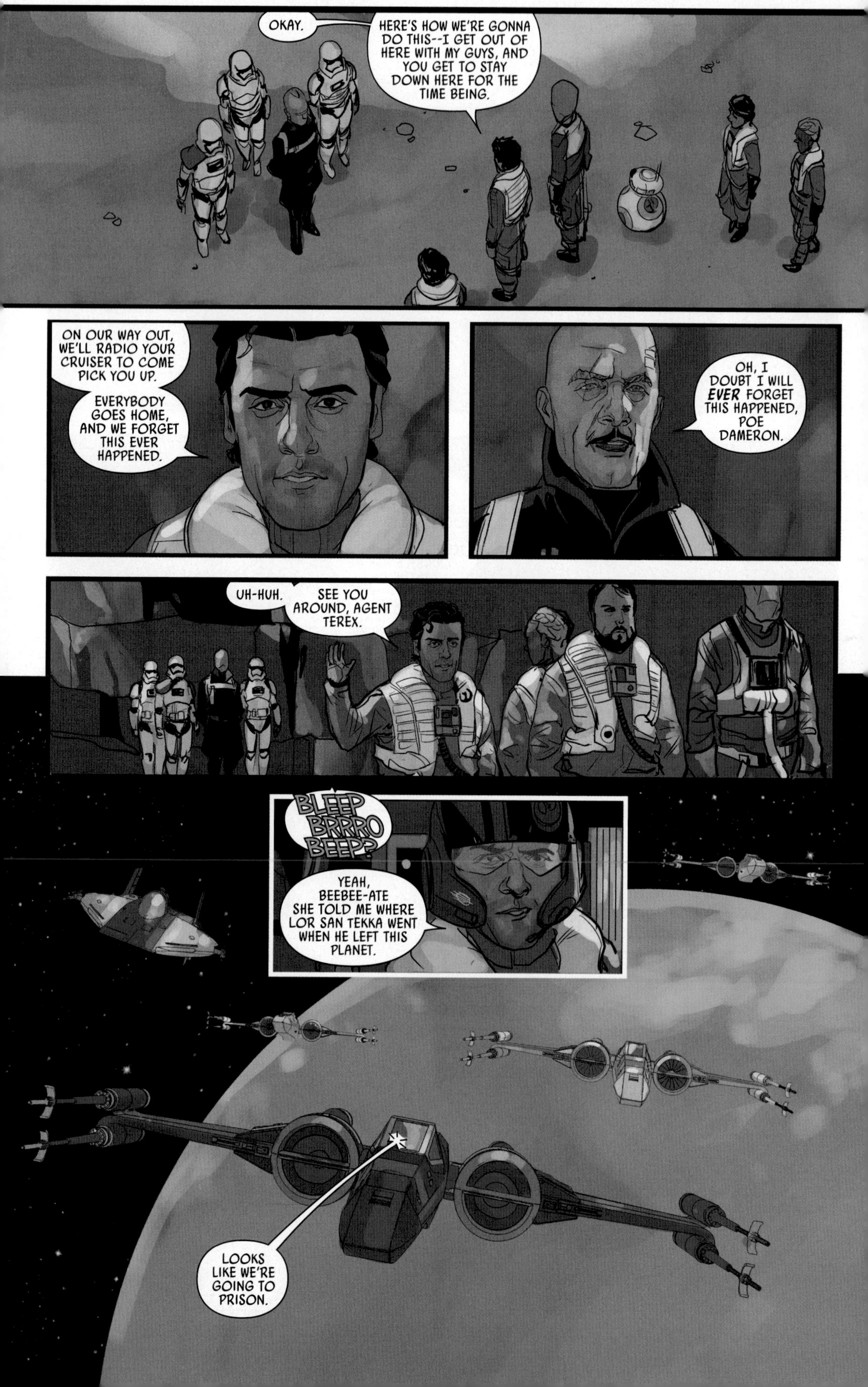
OKAY.
HERE'S HOW WE'RE GONNA DO THIS--I GET OUT OF HERE WITH MY GUYS, AND YOU GET TO STAY DOWN HERE FOR THE TIME BEING.
ON OUR WAY OUT, WE'LL RADIO YOUR CRUISER TO COME PICK YOU UP.
EVERYBODY GOES HOME, AND WE FORGET THIS EVER HAPPENED.
OH, I DOUBT I WILL *EVER* FORGET THIS HAPPENED, POE DAMERON.
UH-HUH.
SEE YOU AROUND, AGENT TEREX.
BLEEP BRRRO BEEP?
YEAH, BEEBEE-ATE SHE TOLD ME WHERE LOR SAN TEKKA WENT WHEN HE LEFT THIS PLANET.
LOOKS LIKE WE'RE GOING TO PRISON.

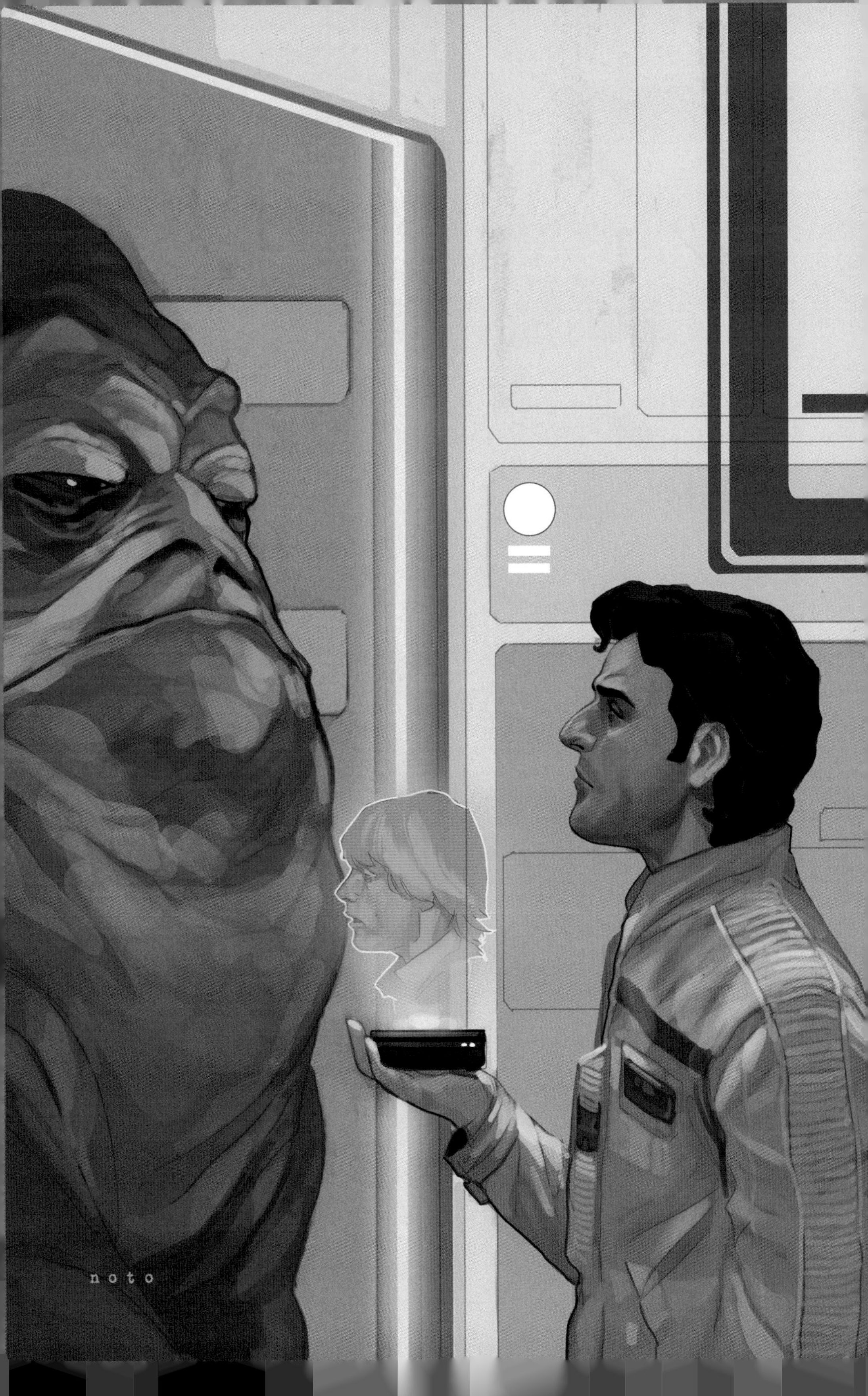
noto

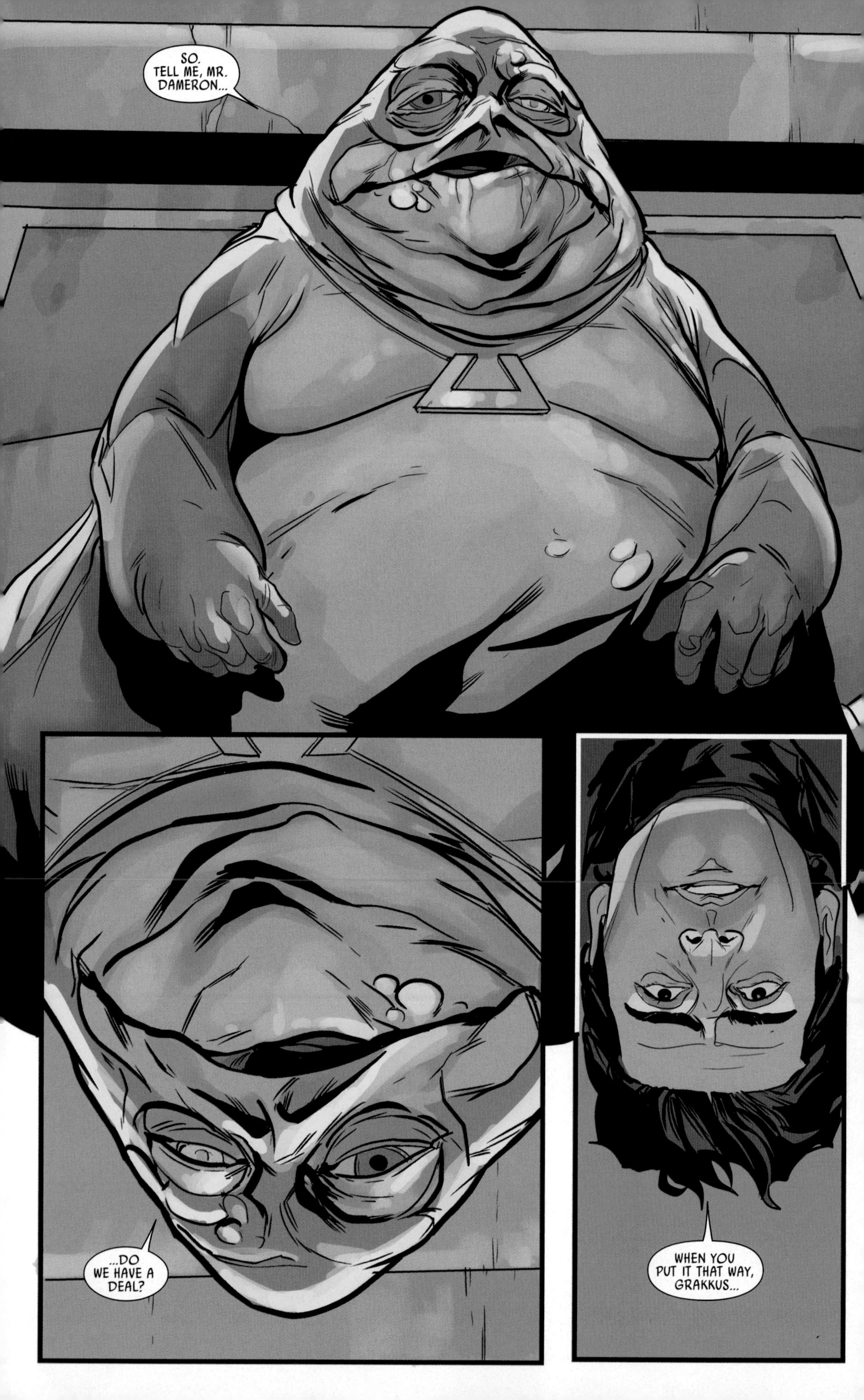
SO. TELL ME, MR. DAMERON...
...DO WE HAVE A DEAL?
WHEN YOU PUT IT THAT WAY, GRAKKUS...

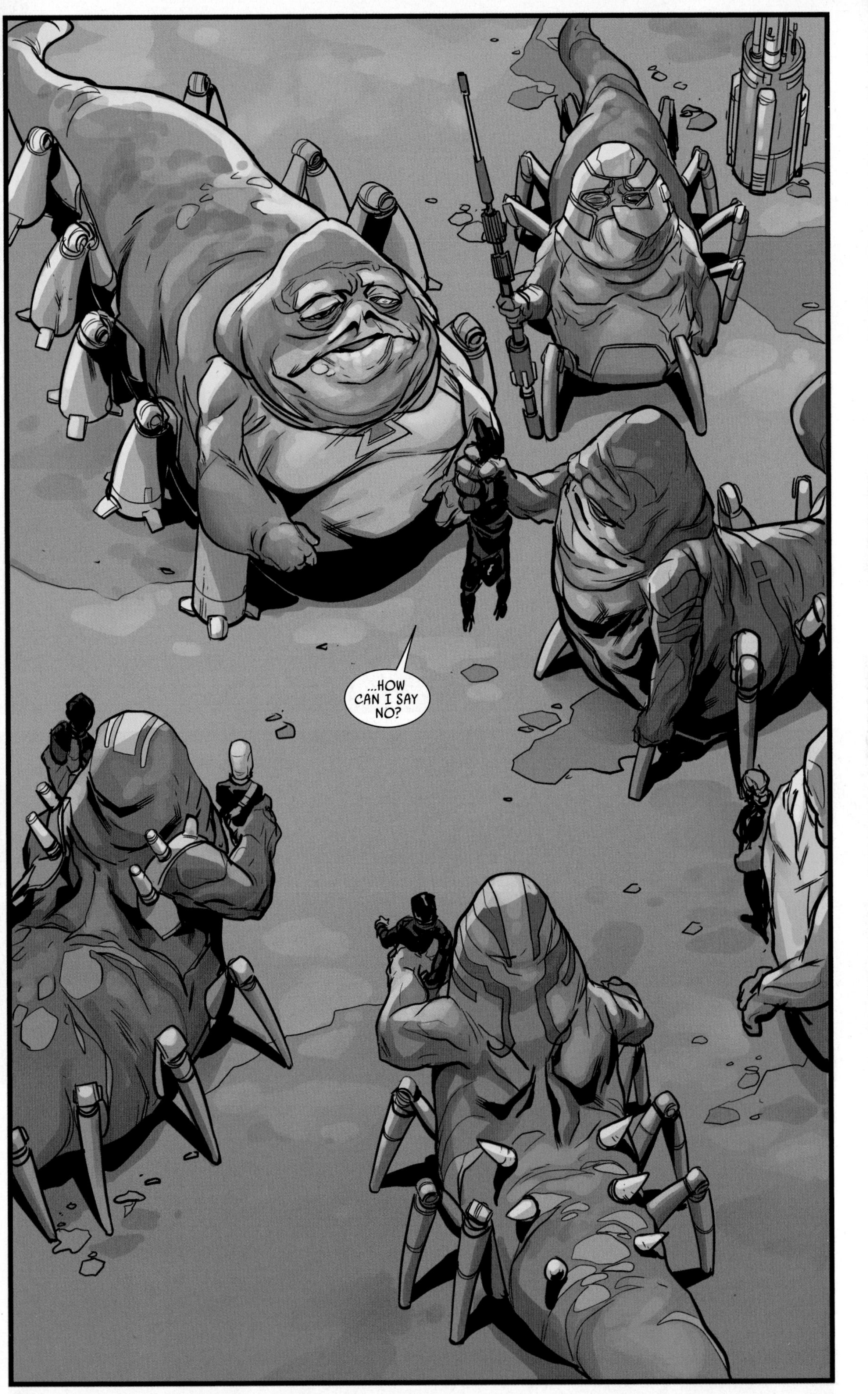
...HOW CAN I SAY NO?

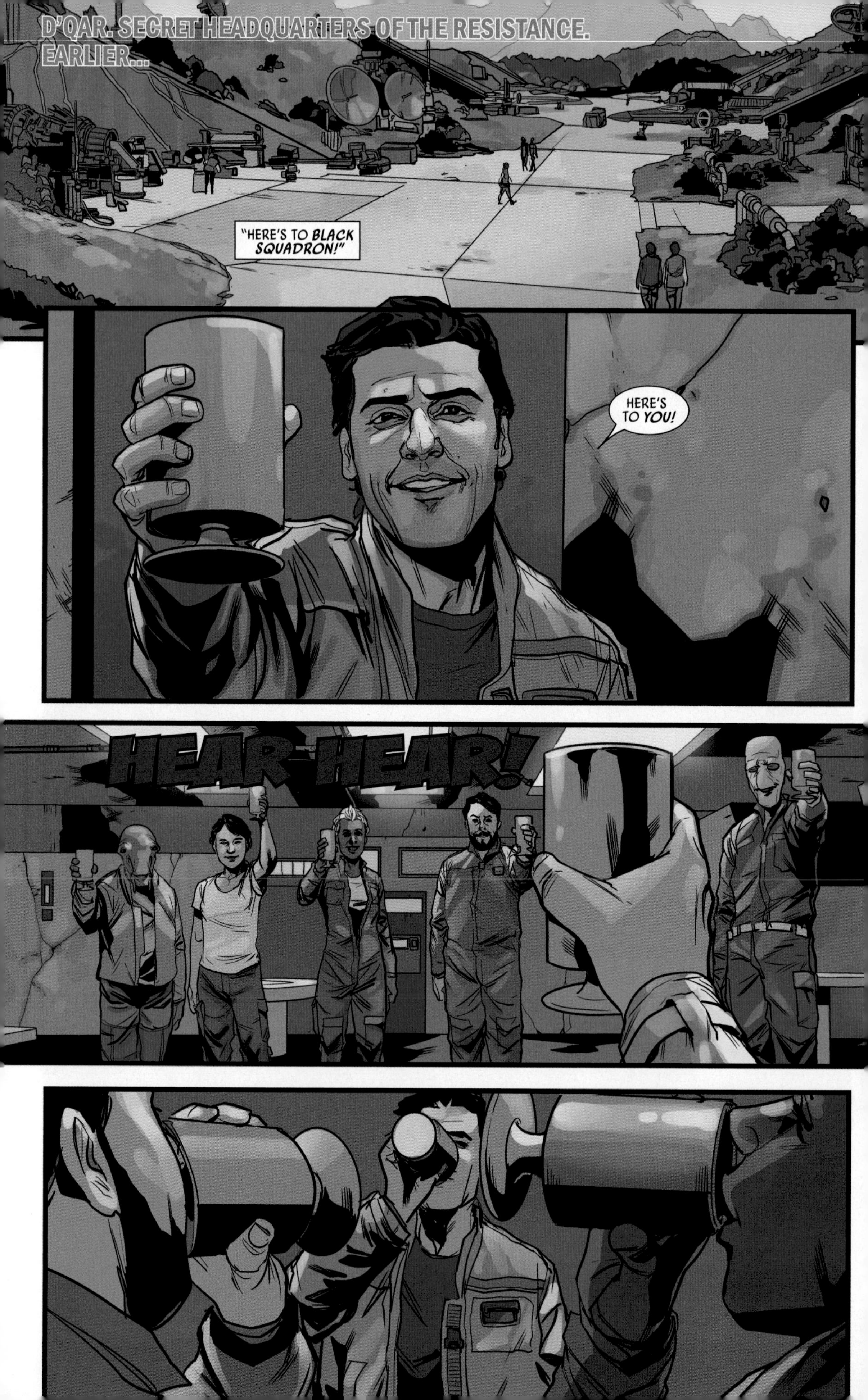
D'QAR. SECRET HEADQUARTERS OF THE RESISTANCE.
EARLIER...
"HERE'S TO BLACK SQUADRON!"
HERE'S TO YOU!
HEAR HEAR!

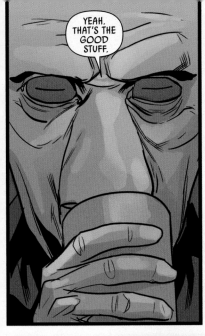

YEAH. THAT'S THE GOOD STUFF.

BY THE FORCE. I NEEDED THAT, POE.

YOU AND ME BOTH. ALL OF US. WE BARELY MADE IT THROUGH THAT EGG BUSINESS. TIME TO BLOW OFF A LITTLE STEAM.

AND TO *CELEBRATE*. WE SHOWED THE FIRST ORDER WHO WE *ARE*.

THAT'S ACTUALLY WHAT I WANTED TO TALK TO YOU ABOUT, L'ULO. I REVIEWED THE AFTER-ACTION REPORTS--YOU ESCALATED THE SITUATION. YOU COMPLETELY BLEW OFF THE RULES OF ENGAGEMENT.

YOU FIRED FIRST. YOU GAVE THE FIRST ORDER AN EXCUSE TO ATTACK US.

ABSOLUTELY. AND I'D DO IT AGAIN.

WE BOTH KNOW THAT'S WHERE THINGS ARE HEADED. EVERY TIE FIGHTER WE DESTROY NOW IS ONE LESS THAT CAN ATTACK US WHEN THINGS REALLY GET HOT.

WE HAVE TO FIGHT THEM EVERY CHANCE WE GET!

WHAT DO YOU THINK THIS *IS*, L'ULO?

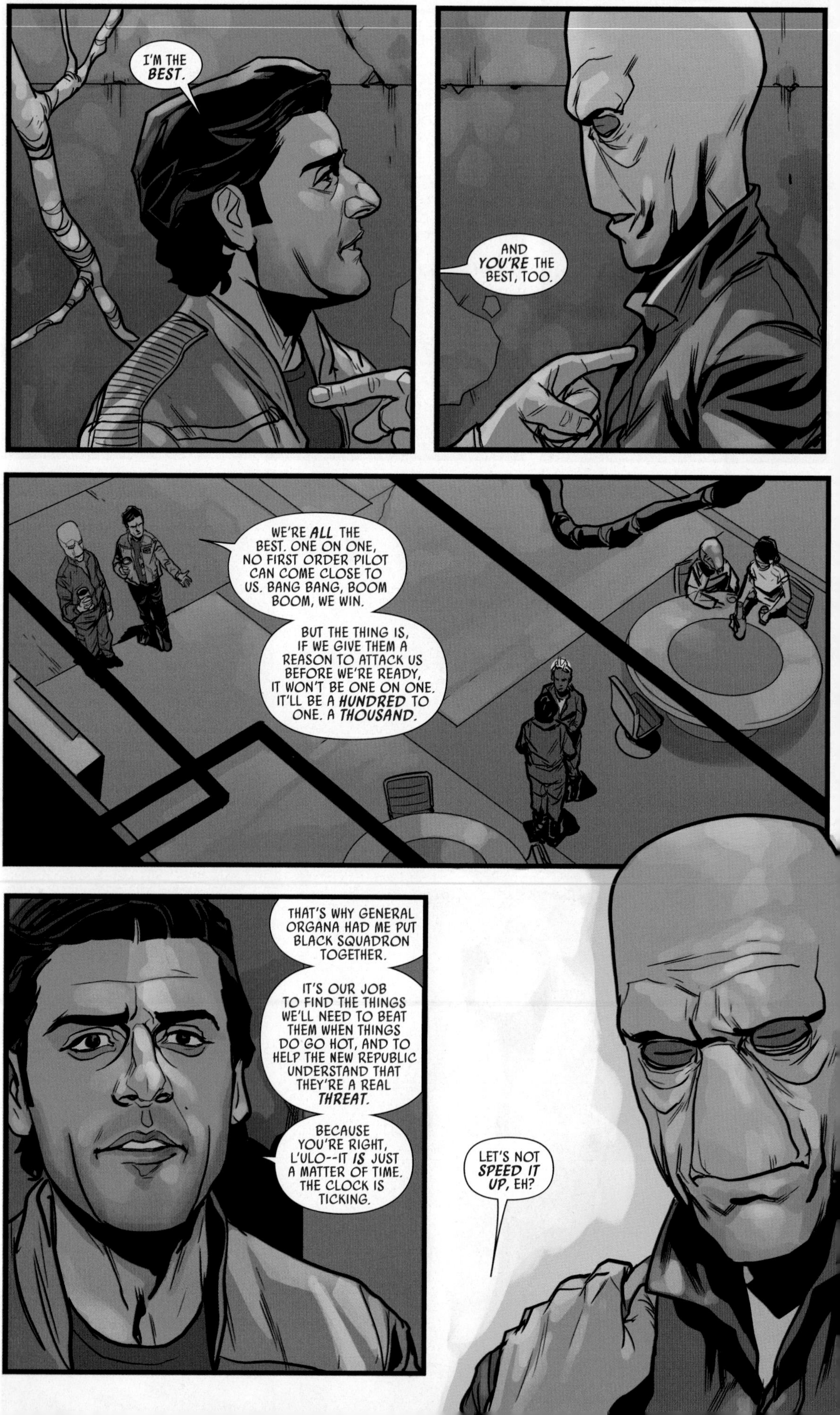
I'M THE BEST.
AND YOU'RE THE BEST, TOO.
WE'RE ALL THE BEST. ONE ON ONE, NO FIRST ORDER PILOT CAN COME CLOSE TO US. BANG BANG, BOOM BOOM, WE WIN.
BUT THE THING IS, IF WE GIVE THEM A REASON TO ATTACK US BEFORE WE'RE READY, IT WON'T BE ONE ON ONE. IT'LL BE A HUNDRED TO ONE. A THOUSAND.
THAT'S WHY GENERAL ORGANA HAD ME PUT BLACK SQUADRON TOGETHER.
IT'S OUR JOB TO FIND THE THINGS WE'LL NEED TO BEAT THEM WHEN THINGS DO GO HOT, AND TO HELP THE NEW REPUBLIC UNDERSTAND THAT THEY'RE A REAL THREAT.
BECAUSE YOU'RE RIGHT, L'ULO--IT IS JUST A MATTER OF TIME. THE CLOCK IS TICKING.
LET'S NOT SPEED IT UP, EH?

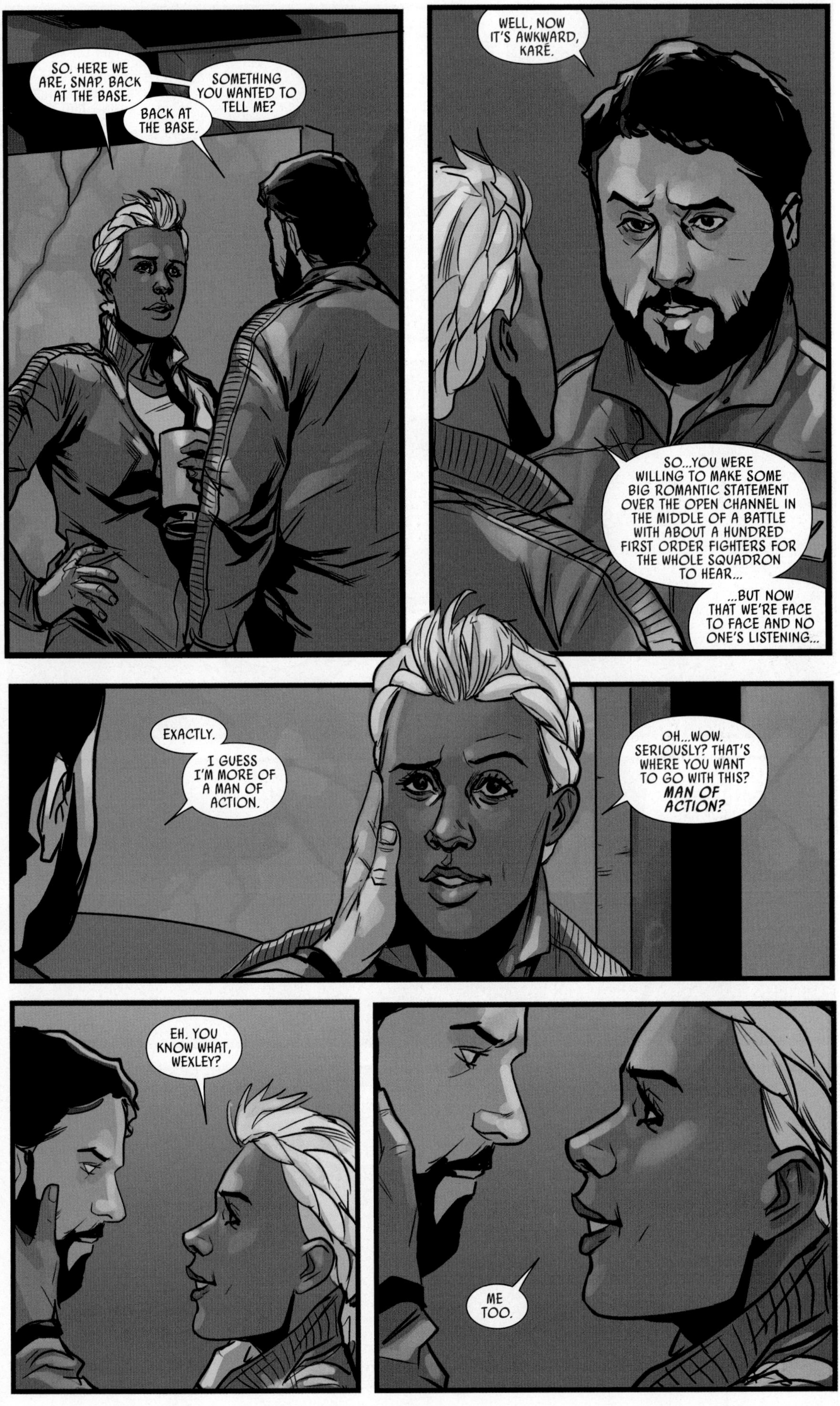
SO. HERE WE ARE, SNAP. BACK AT THE BASE.
BACK AT THE BASE.
SOMETHING YOU WANTED TO TELL ME?
WELL, NOW IT'S AWKWARD, KARÉ.
SO...YOU WERE WILLING TO MAKE SOME BIG ROMANTIC STATEMENT OVER THE OPEN CHANNEL IN THE MIDDLE OF A BATTLE WITH ABOUT A HUNDRED FIRST ORDER FIGHTERS FOR THE WHOLE SQUADRON TO HEAR...
...BUT NOW THAT WE'RE FACE TO FACE AND NO ONE'S LISTENING...
EXACTLY.
I GUESS I'M MORE OF A MAN OF ACTION.
OH...WOW. SERIOUSLY? THAT'S WHERE YOU WANT TO GO WITH THIS? *MAN OF ACTION?*
EH. YOU KNOW WHAT, WEXLEY?
ME TOO.

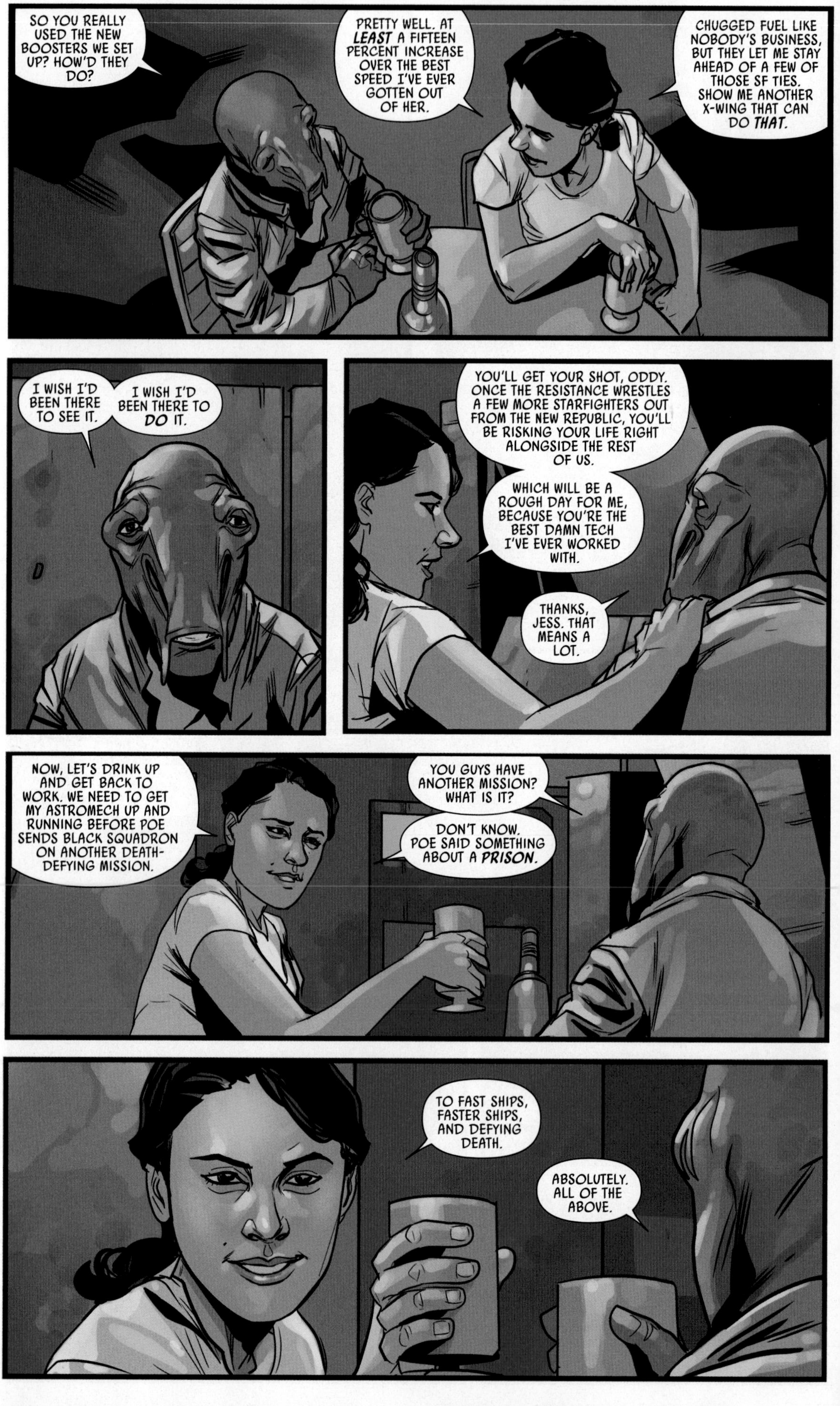
SO YOU REALLY USED THE NEW BOOSTERS WE SET UP? HOW'D THEY DO?
PRETTY WELL. AT *LEAST* A FIFTEEN PERCENT INCREASE OVER THE BEST SPEED I'VE EVER GOTTEN OUT OF HER.
CHUGGED FUEL LIKE NOBODY'S BUSINESS, BUT THEY LET ME STAY AHEAD OF A FEW OF THOSE SF TIES. SHOW ME ANOTHER X-WING THAT CAN DO *THAT.*
I WISH I'D BEEN THERE TO SEE IT.
I WISH I'D BEEN THERE TO *DO* IT.
YOU'LL GET YOUR SHOT, ODDY. ONCE THE RESISTANCE WRESTLES A FEW MORE STARFIGHTERS OUT FROM THE NEW REPUBLIC, YOU'LL BE RISKING YOUR LIFE RIGHT ALONGSIDE THE REST OF US.
WHICH WILL BE A ROUGH DAY FOR ME, BECAUSE YOU'RE THE BEST DAMN TECH I'VE EVER WORKED WITH.
THANKS, JESS. THAT MEANS A LOT.
NOW, LET'S DRINK UP AND GET BACK TO WORK. WE NEED TO GET MY ASTROMECH UP AND RUNNING BEFORE POE SENDS BLACK SQUADRON ON ANOTHER DEATH-DEFYING MISSION.
YOU GUYS HAVE ANOTHER MISSION? WHAT IS IT?
DON'T KNOW. POE SAID SOMETHING ABOUT A *PRISON.*
TO FAST SHIPS, FASTER SHIPS, AND DEFYING DEATH.
ABSOLUTELY. ALL OF THE ABOVE.

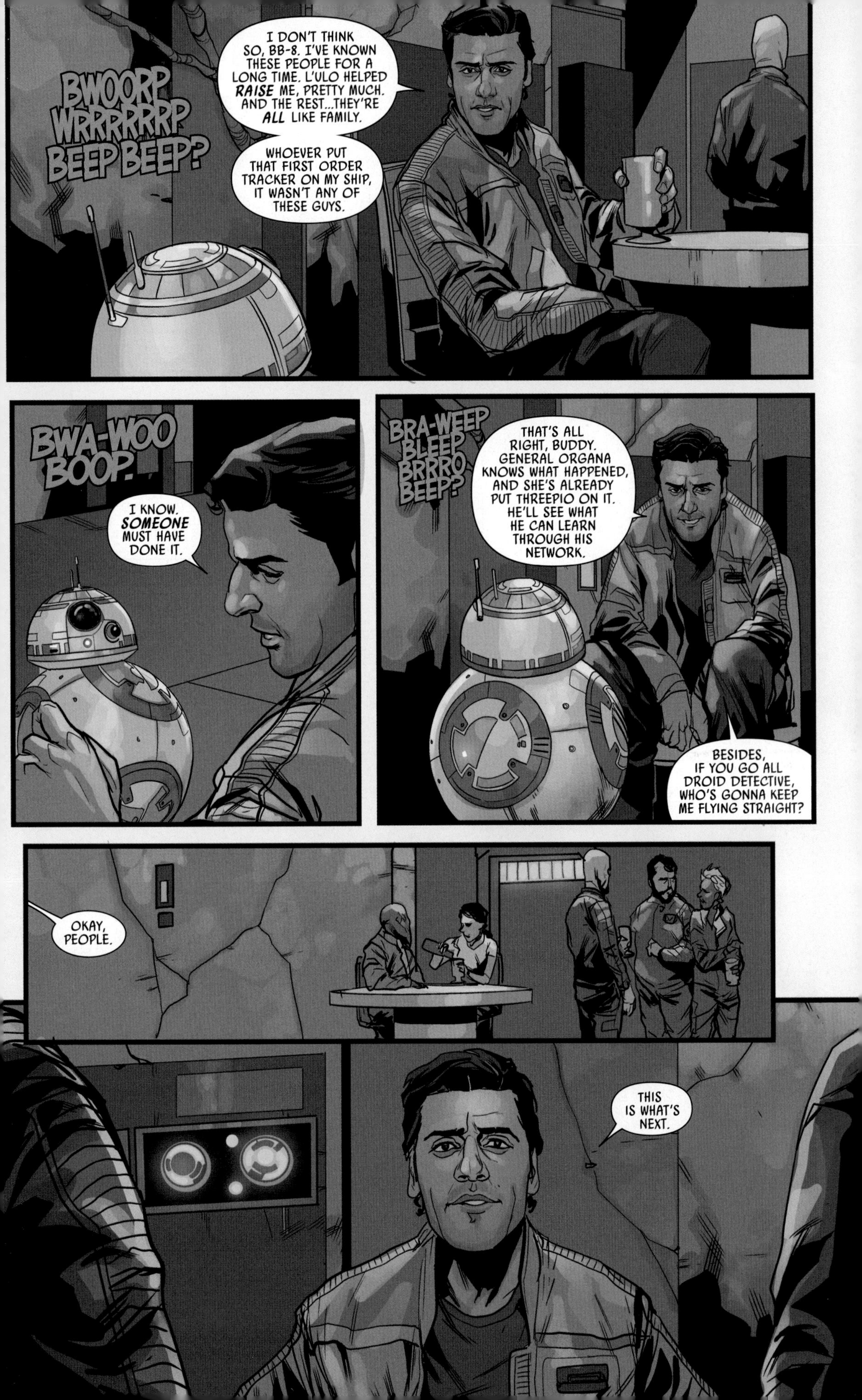
I DON'T THINK SO, BB-8. I'VE KNOWN THESE PEOPLE FOR A LONG TIME. L'ULO HELPED RAISE ME, PRETTY MUCH. AND THE REST...THEY'RE ALL LIKE FAMILY.
BWOORP WRRRRRRP BEEP BEEP?
WHOEVER PUT THAT FIRST ORDER TRACKER ON MY SHIP, IT WASN'T ANY OF THESE GUYS.
BWA-WOO BOOP.
I KNOW. SOMEONE MUST HAVE DONE IT.
BRA-WEEP BLEEP BRRRO BEEP?
THAT'S ALL RIGHT, BUDDY. GENERAL ORGANA KNOWS WHAT HAPPENED, AND SHE'S ALREADY PUT THREEPIO ON IT. HE'LL SEE WHAT HE CAN LEARN THROUGH HIS NETWORK.
BESIDES, IF YOU GO ALL DROID DETECTIVE, WHO'S GONNA KEEP ME FLYING STRAIGHT?
OKAY, PEOPLE.
THIS IS WHAT'S NEXT.

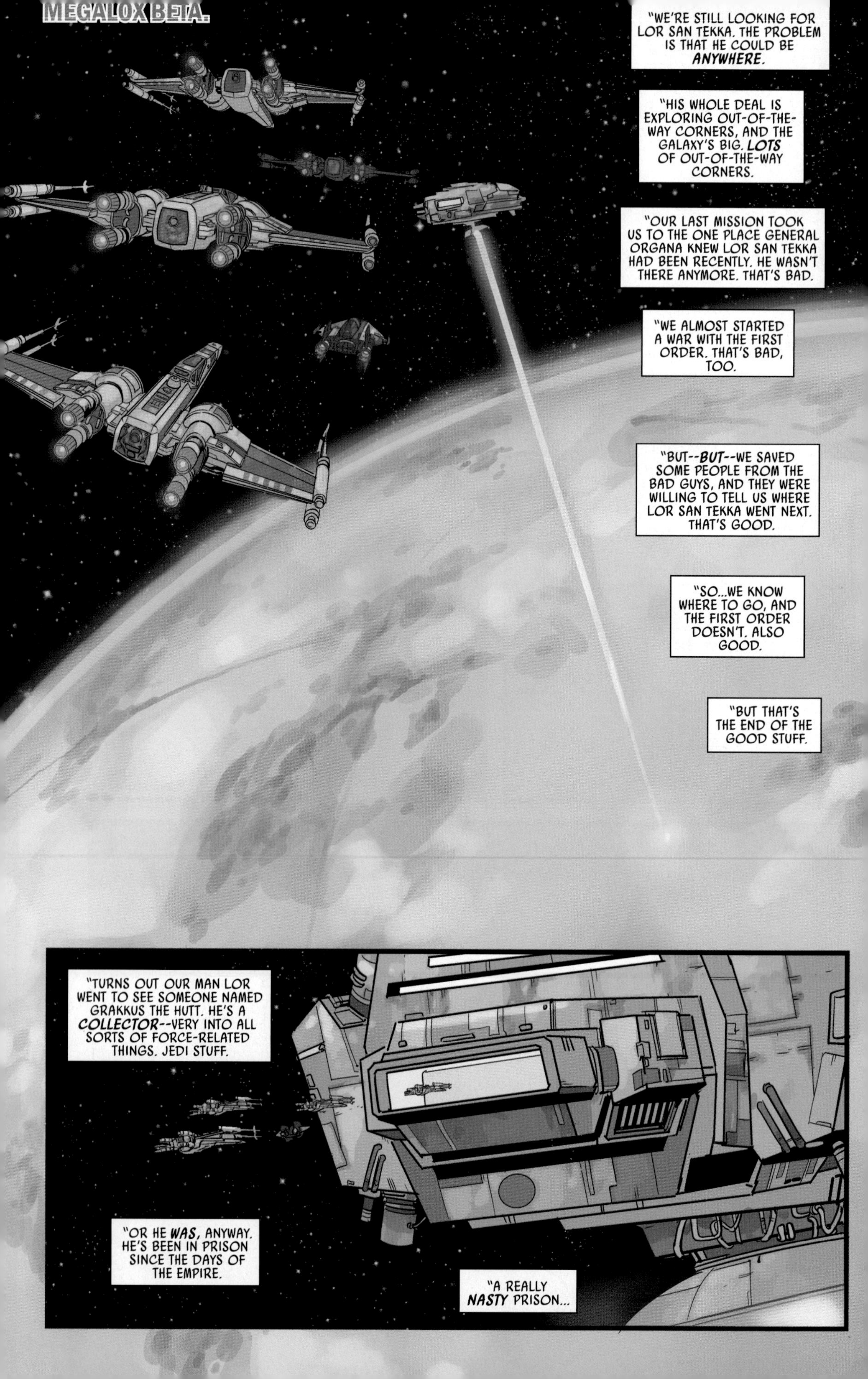

MEGALOX BETA.
"WE'RE STILL LOOKING FOR LOR SAN TEKKA. THE PROBLEM IS THAT HE COULD BE *ANYWHERE.*
"HIS WHOLE DEAL IS EXPLORING OUT-OF-THE-WAY CORNERS, AND THE GALAXY'S BIG. *LOTS* OF OUT-OF-THE-WAY CORNERS.
"OUR LAST MISSION TOOK US TO THE ONE PLACE GENERAL ORGANA KNEW LOR SAN TEKKA HAD BEEN RECENTLY. HE WASN'T THERE ANYMORE. THAT'S BAD.
"WE ALMOST STARTED A WAR WITH THE FIRST ORDER. THAT'S BAD, TOO.
"BUT--*BUT*--WE SAVED SOME PEOPLE FROM THE BAD GUYS, AND THEY WERE WILLING TO TELL US WHERE LOR SAN TEKKA WENT NEXT. THAT'S GOOD.
"SO...WE KNOW WHERE TO GO, AND THE FIRST ORDER DOESN'T. ALSO GOOD.
"BUT THAT'S THE END OF THE GOOD STUFF.
"TURNS OUT OUR MAN LOR WENT TO SEE SOMEONE NAMED GRAKKUS THE HUTT. HE'S A *COLLECTOR*--VERY INTO ALL SORTS OF FORCE-RELATED THINGS. JEDI STUFF.
"OR HE *WAS,* ANYWAY. HE'S BEEN IN PRISON SINCE THE DAYS OF THE EMPIRE.
"A REALLY *NASTY* PRISON...

"...FOR REALLY *NASTY* PEOPLE."

HELLO, WELCOME TO MEGALOX.

MY NAME IS WARDEN LUTA. EVERYTHING YOU SEE HERE IS MINE.

"THE PRISON'S PRIVATELY RUN--IT'S A *BUSINESS.* EVERYTHING'S FOR SALE-- EVEN *ACCESS.*

"THE MORE YOU PAY, THE FEWER QUESTIONS THEY ASK. AND FROM WHAT I UNDERSTAND, GENERAL ORGANA PAID A *LOT* TO GET US IN."

I'M *POE DAMERON.* AND AS FAR AS THIS PLACE GOES...YOU CAN KEEP IT, MA'AM. WE'RE JUST VISITING.

YES, I KNOW. I INTEND TO DO EVERYTHING I CAN TO MAKE SURE YOUR TIME HERE IS AS BRIEF AND PLEASANT AS POSSIBLE.

BRIEF? WHY'S THAT?

BECAUSE THE LONGER YOU STAY ON MEGALOX, THE LESS *PLEASANT* THINGS TEND TO BE.

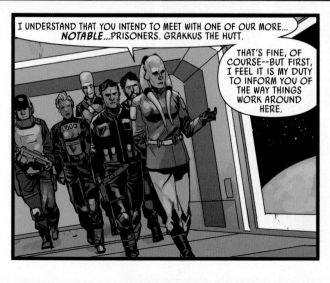

I UNDERSTAND THAT YOU INTEND TO MEET WITH ONE OF OUR MORE... *NOTABLE*...PRISONERS. GRAKKUS THE HUTT.

THAT'S FINE, OF COURSE--BUT FIRST, I FEEL IT IS MY DUTY TO INFORM YOU OF THE WAY THINGS WORK AROUND HERE.

OR MORE SPECIFICALLY, DOWN THERE.

THE ENORMOUS SIZE AND HIGH DENSITY OF THE PLANET GENERATE A GRAVITATIONAL FIELD TEN TIMES STANDARD.

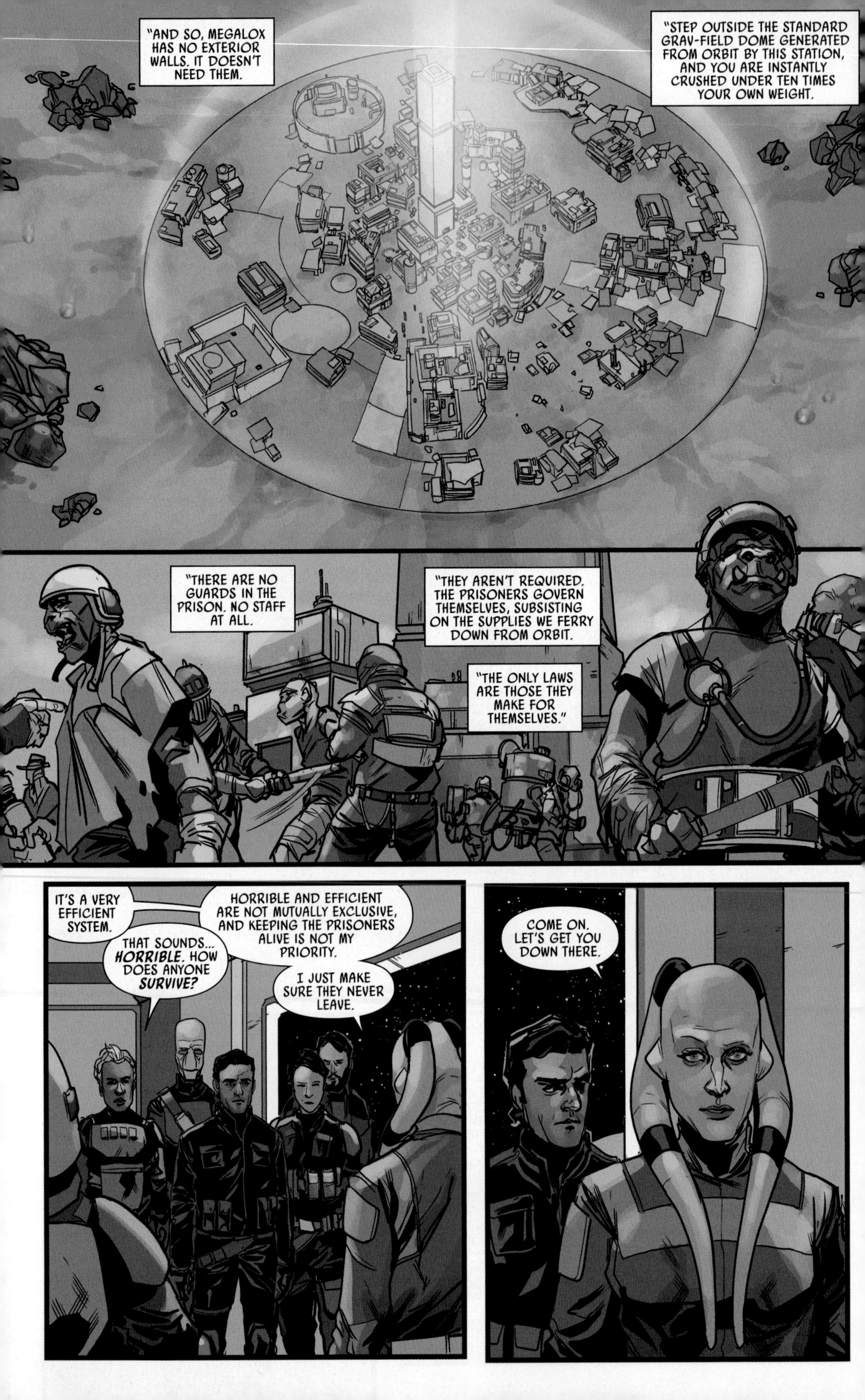

"AND SO, MEGALOX HAS NO EXTERIOR WALLS. IT DOESN'T NEED THEM.
"STEP OUTSIDE THE STANDARD GRAV-FIELD DOME GENERATED FROM ORBIT BY THIS STATION, AND YOU ARE INSTANTLY CRUSHED UNDER TEN TIMES YOUR OWN WEIGHT.
"THERE ARE NO GUARDS IN THE PRISON. NO STAFF AT ALL.
"THEY AREN'T REQUIRED. THE PRISONERS GOVERN THEMSELVES, SUBSISTING ON THE SUPPLIES WE FERRY DOWN FROM ORBIT.
"THE ONLY LAWS ARE THOSE THEY MAKE FOR THEMSELVES."
IT'S A VERY EFFICIENT SYSTEM.
THAT SOUNDS... HORRIBLE. HOW DOES ANYONE SURVIVE?
HORRIBLE AND EFFICIENT ARE NOT MUTUALLY EXCLUSIVE, AND KEEPING THE PRISONERS ALIVE IS NOT MY PRIORITY.
I JUST MAKE SURE THEY NEVER LEAVE.
COME ON. LET'S GET YOU DOWN THERE.

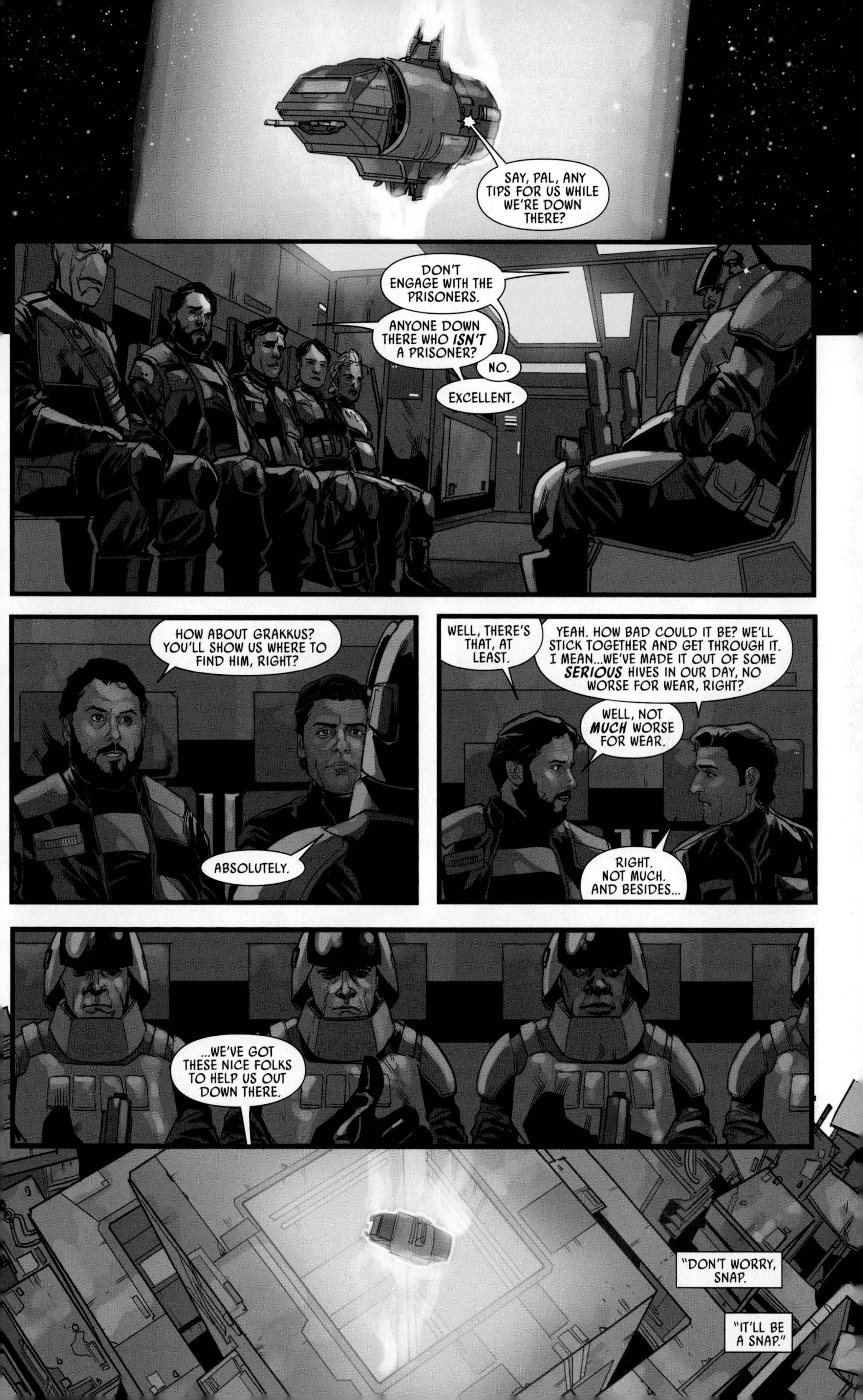
SAY, PAL, ANY TIPS FOR US WHILE WE'RE DOWN THERE?
DON'T ENGAGE WITH THE PRISONERS.
ANYONE DOWN THERE WHO ISN'T A PRISONER?
NO.
EXCELLENT.
HOW ABOUT GRAKKUS? YOU'LL SHOW US WHERE TO FIND HIM, RIGHT?
ABSOLUTELY.
WELL, THERE'S THAT, AT LEAST.
YEAH. HOW BAD COULD IT BE? WE'LL STICK TOGETHER AND GET THROUGH IT. I MEAN...WE'VE MADE IT OUT OF SOME SERIOUS HIVES IN OUR DAY, NO WORSE FOR WEAR, RIGHT?
WELL, NOT MUCH WORSE FOR WEAR.
RIGHT. NOT MUCH. AND BESIDES...
...WE'VE GOT THESE NICE FOLKS TO HELP US OUT DOWN THERE.
"DON'T WORRY, SNAP.
"IT'LL BE A SNAP."

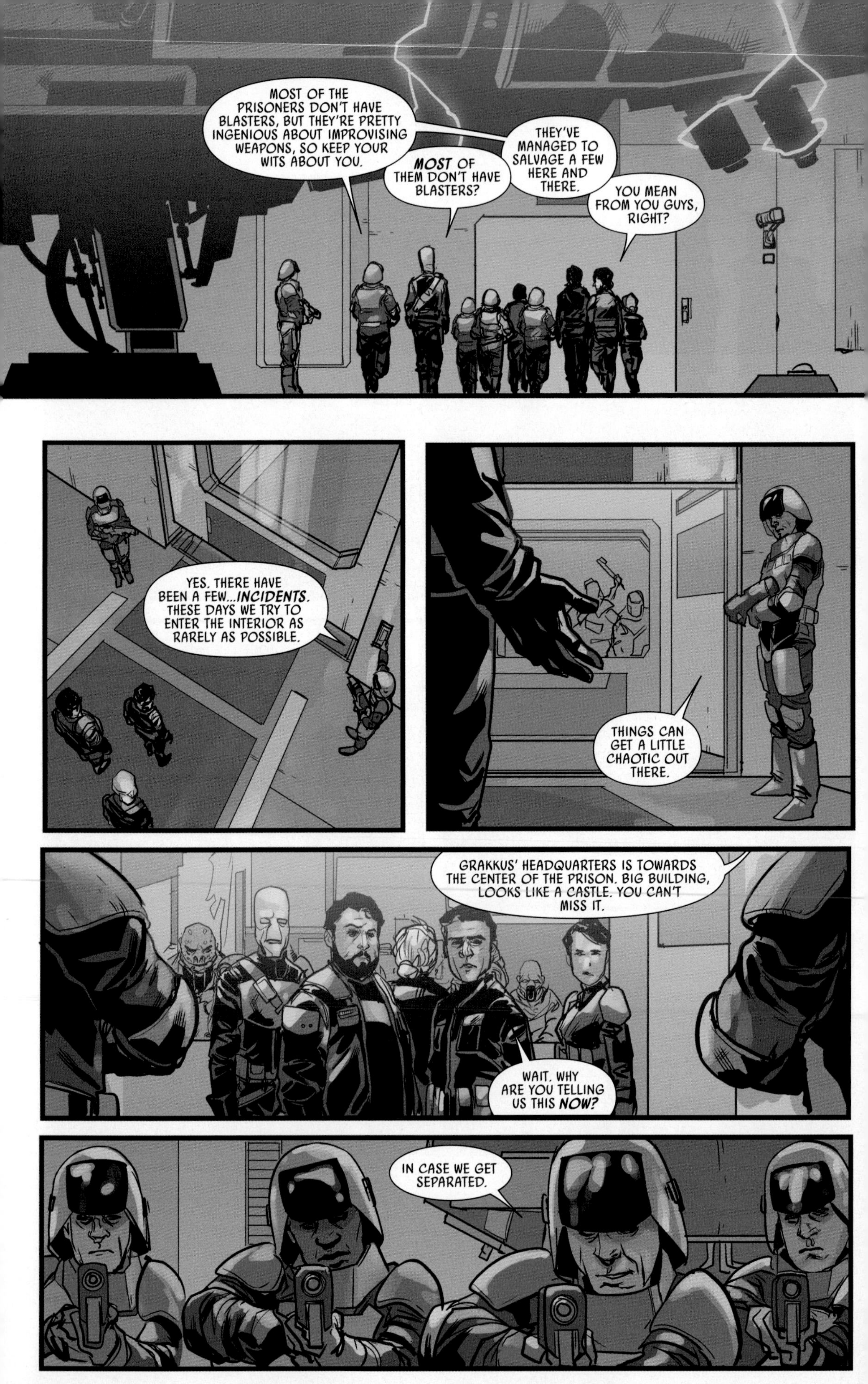
MOST OF THE PRISONERS DON'T HAVE BLASTERS, BUT THEY'RE PRETTY INGENIOUS ABOUT IMPROVISING WEAPONS, SO KEEP YOUR WITS ABOUT YOU.
MOST OF THEM DON'T HAVE BLASTERS?
THEY'VE MANAGED TO SALVAGE A FEW HERE AND THERE.
YOU MEAN FROM YOU GUYS, RIGHT?
YES. THERE HAVE BEEN A FEW...INCIDENTS. THESE DAYS WE TRY TO ENTER THE INTERIOR AS RARELY AS POSSIBLE.
THINGS CAN GET A LITTLE CHAOTIC OUT THERE.
GRAKKUS' HEADQUARTERS IS TOWARDS THE CENTER OF THE PRISON. BIG BUILDING, LOOKS LIKE A CASTLE. YOU CAN'T MISS IT.
WAIT. WHY ARE YOU TELLING US THIS NOW?
IN CASE WE GET SEPARATED.

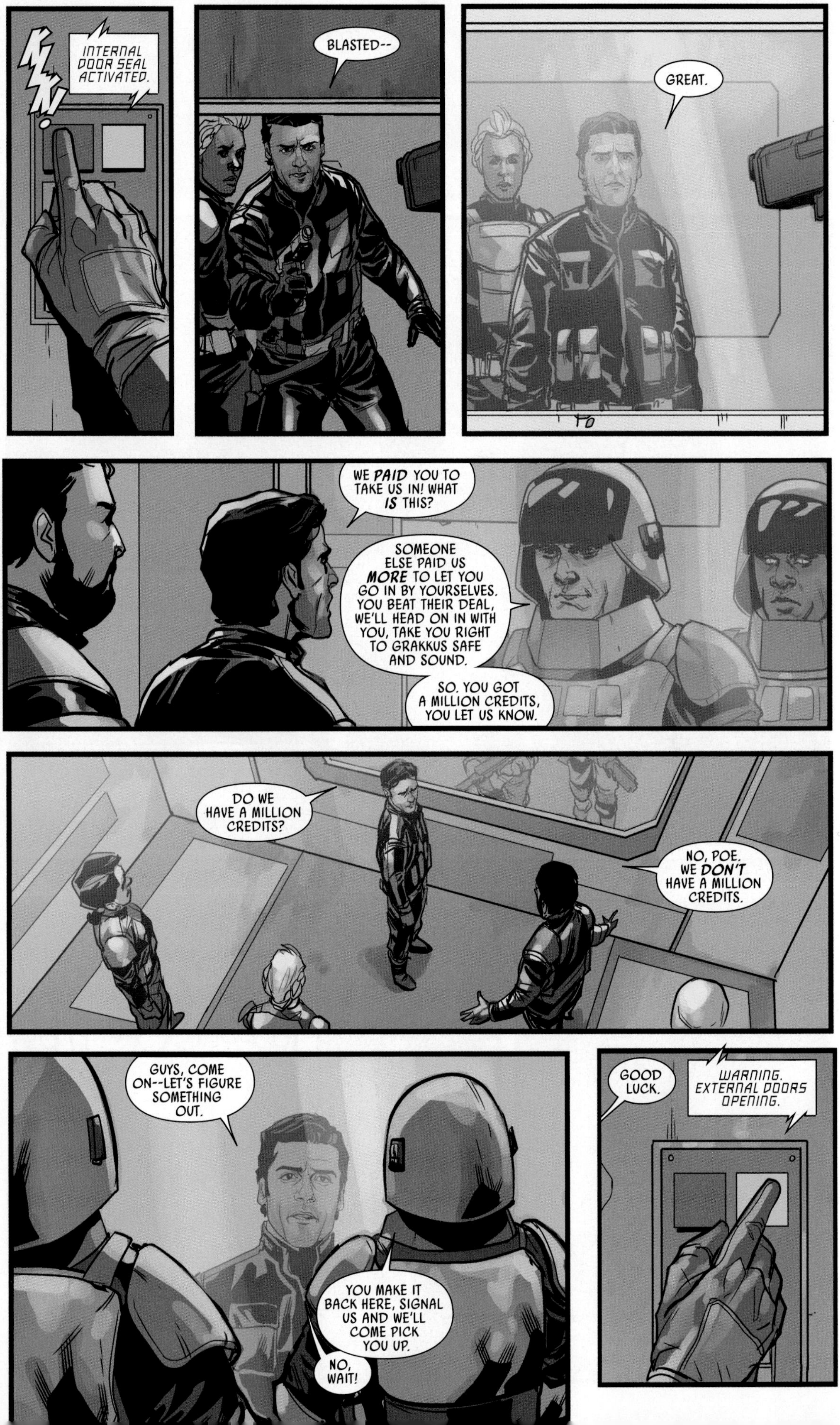
KLIK!
INTERNAL DOOR SEAL ACTIVATED.
BLASTED--
GREAT.
WE PAID YOU TO TAKE US IN! WHAT IS THIS?
SOMEONE ELSE PAID US MORE TO LET YOU GO IN BY YOURSELVES. YOU BEAT THEIR DEAL, WE'LL HEAD ON IN WITH YOU, TAKE YOU RIGHT TO GRAKKUS SAFE AND SOUND.
SO. YOU GOT A MILLION CREDITS, YOU LET US KNOW.
DO WE HAVE A MILLION CREDITS?
NO, POE. WE DON'T HAVE A MILLION CREDITS.
GUYS, COME ON--LET'S FIGURE SOMETHING OUT.
YOU MAKE IT BACK HERE, SIGNAL US AND WE'LL COME PICK YOU UP.
NO, WAIT!
GOOD LUCK.
WARNING. EXTERNAL DOORS OPENING.

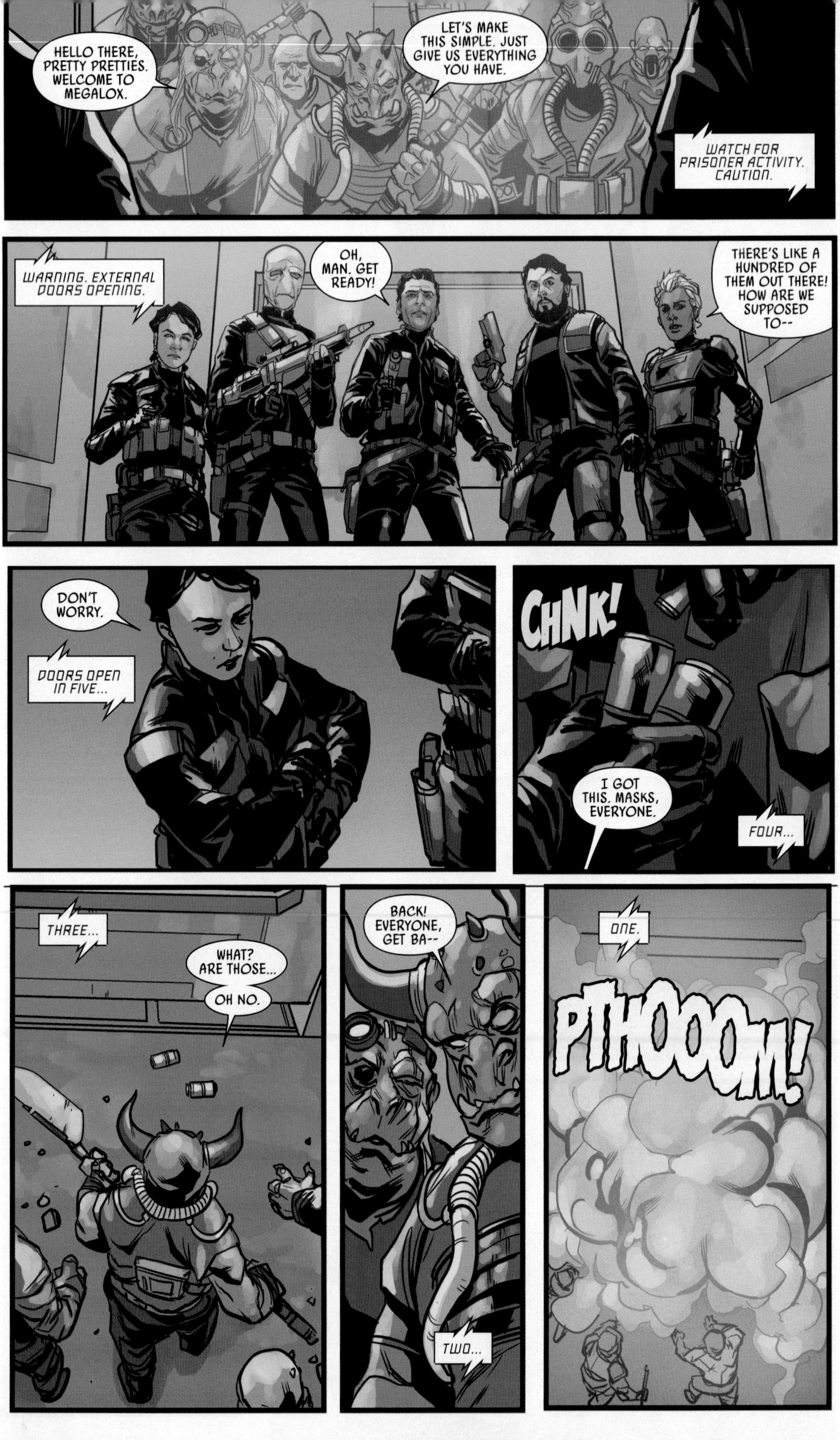
HELLO THERE, PRETTY PRETTIES. WELCOME TO MEGALOX.
LET'S MAKE THIS SIMPLE. JUST GIVE US EVERYTHING YOU HAVE.
WATCH FOR PRISONER ACTIVITY. CAUTION.
WARNING. EXTERNAL DOORS OPENING.
OH, MAN. GET READY!
THERE'S LIKE A HUNDRED OF THEM OUT THERE! HOW ARE WE SUPPOSED TO--
DON'T WORRY.
DOORS OPEN IN FIVE...
CHNK!
I GOT THIS. MASKS, EVERYONE.
FOUR...
THREE...
WHAT? ARE THOSE...
OH NO.
BACK! EVERYONE, GET BA--
TWO...
ONE.
PTHOOOM!

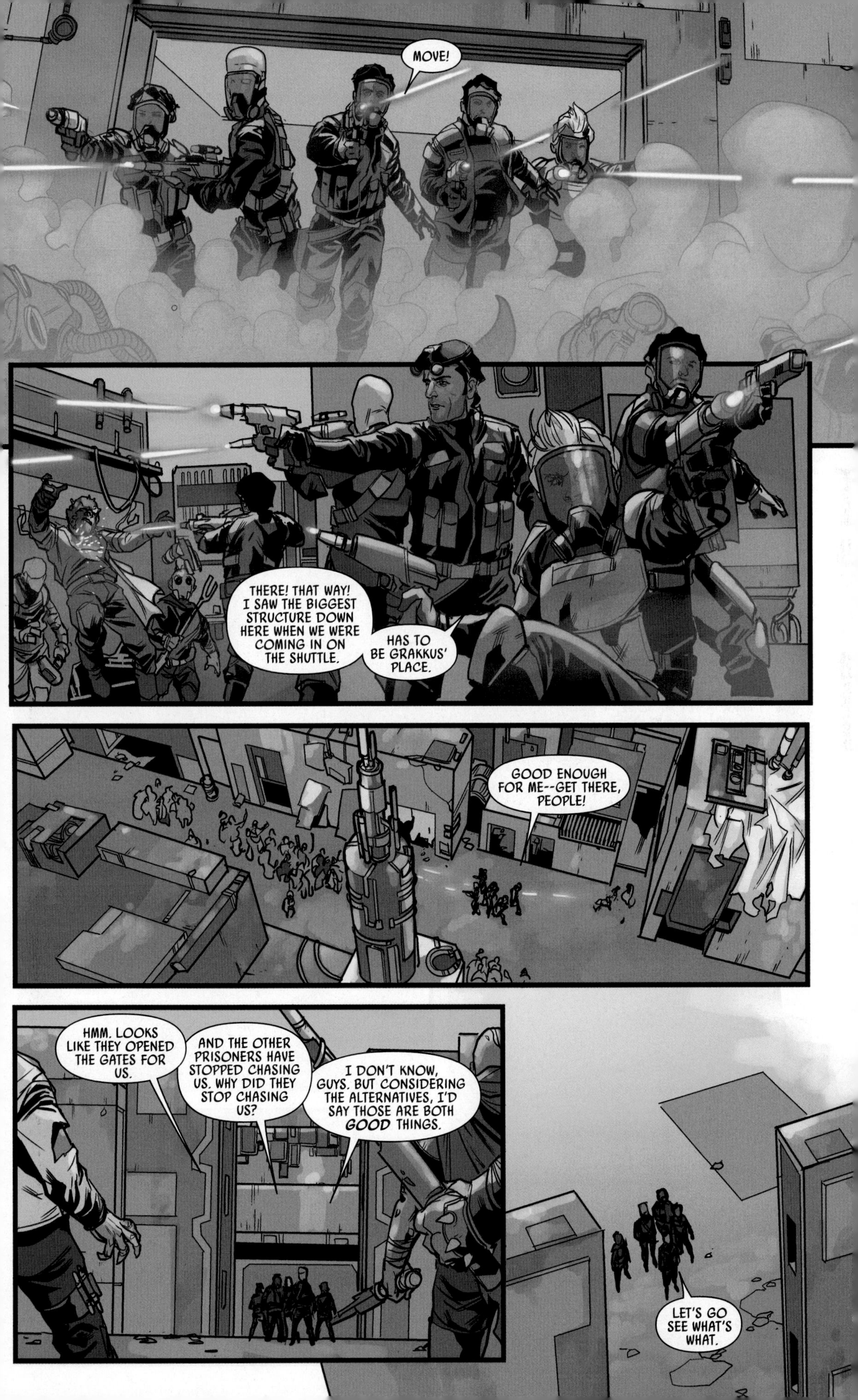
MOVE!
THERE! THAT WAY! I SAW THE BIGGEST STRUCTURE DOWN HERE WHEN WE WERE COMING IN ON THE SHUTTLE.
HAS TO BE GRAKKUS' PLACE.
GOOD ENOUGH FOR ME--GET THERE, PEOPLE!
HMM. LOOKS LIKE THEY OPENED THE GATES FOR US.
AND THE OTHER PRISONERS HAVE STOPPED CHASING US. WHY DID THEY STOP CHASING US?
I DON'T KNOW, GUYS. BUT CONSIDERING THE ALTERNATIVES, I'D SAY THOSE ARE BOTH *GOOD* THINGS.
LET'S GO SEE WHAT'S WHAT.

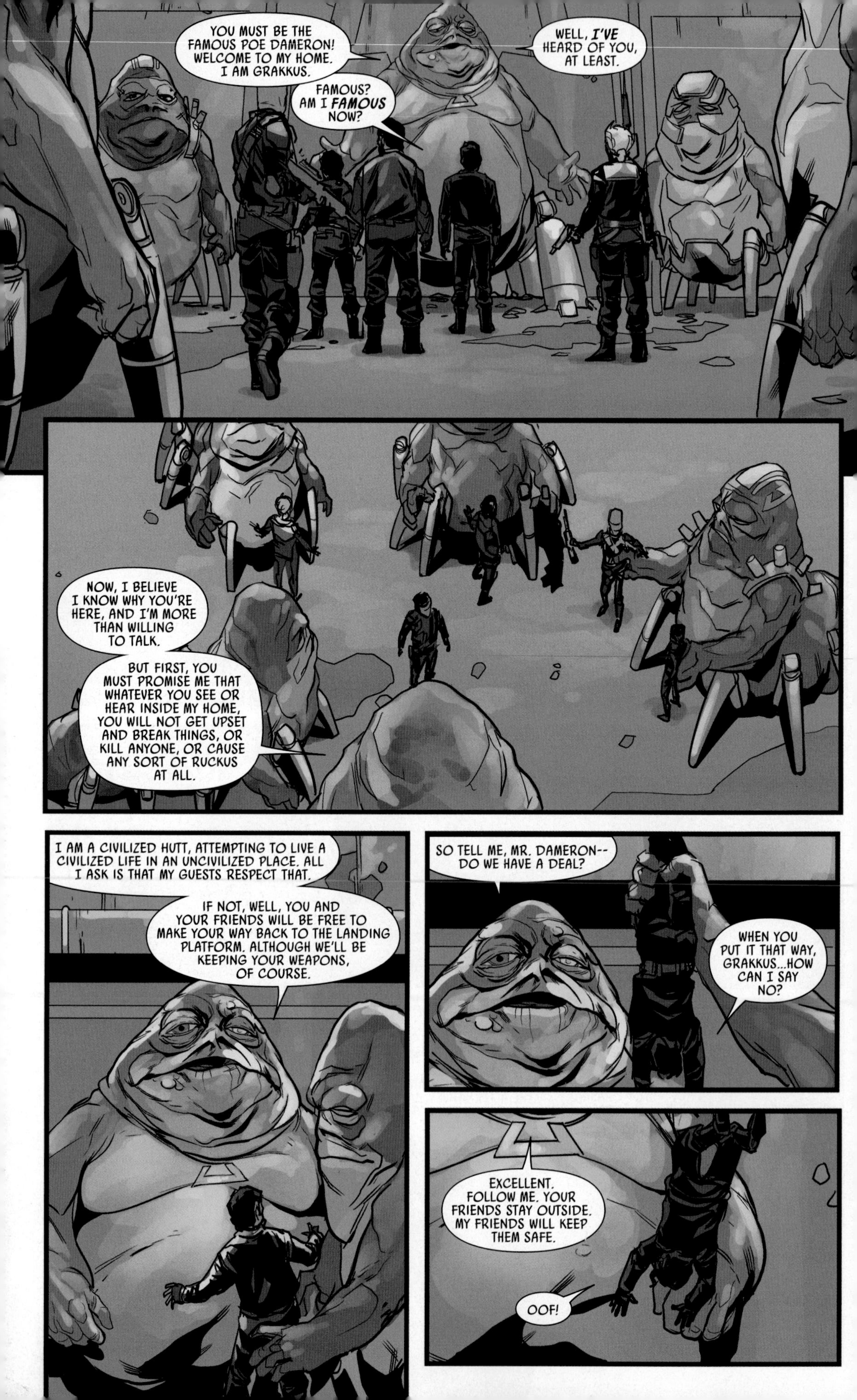
YOU MUST BE THE FAMOUS POE DAMERON! WELCOME TO MY HOME. I AM GRAKKUS.
FAMOUS? AM I FAMOUS NOW?
WELL, I'VE HEARD OF YOU, AT LEAST.
NOW, I BELIEVE I KNOW WHY YOU'RE HERE, AND I'M MORE THAN WILLING TO TALK.
BUT FIRST, YOU MUST PROMISE ME THAT WHATEVER YOU SEE OR HEAR INSIDE MY HOME, YOU WILL NOT GET UPSET AND BREAK THINGS, OR KILL ANYONE, OR CAUSE ANY SORT OF RUCKUS AT ALL.
I AM A CIVILIZED HUTT, ATTEMPTING TO LIVE A CIVILIZED LIFE IN AN UNCIVILIZED PLACE. ALL I ASK IS THAT MY GUESTS RESPECT THAT.
IF NOT, WELL, YOU AND YOUR FRIENDS WILL BE FREE TO MAKE YOUR WAY BACK TO THE LANDING PLATFORM. ALTHOUGH WE'LL BE KEEPING YOUR WEAPONS, OF COURSE.
SO TELL ME, MR. DAMERON-- DO WE HAVE A DEAL?
WHEN YOU PUT IT THAT WAY, GRAKKUS...HOW CAN I SAY NO?
EXCELLENT. FOLLOW ME. YOUR FRIENDS STAY OUTSIDE. MY FRIENDS WILL KEEP THEM SAFE.
OOF!

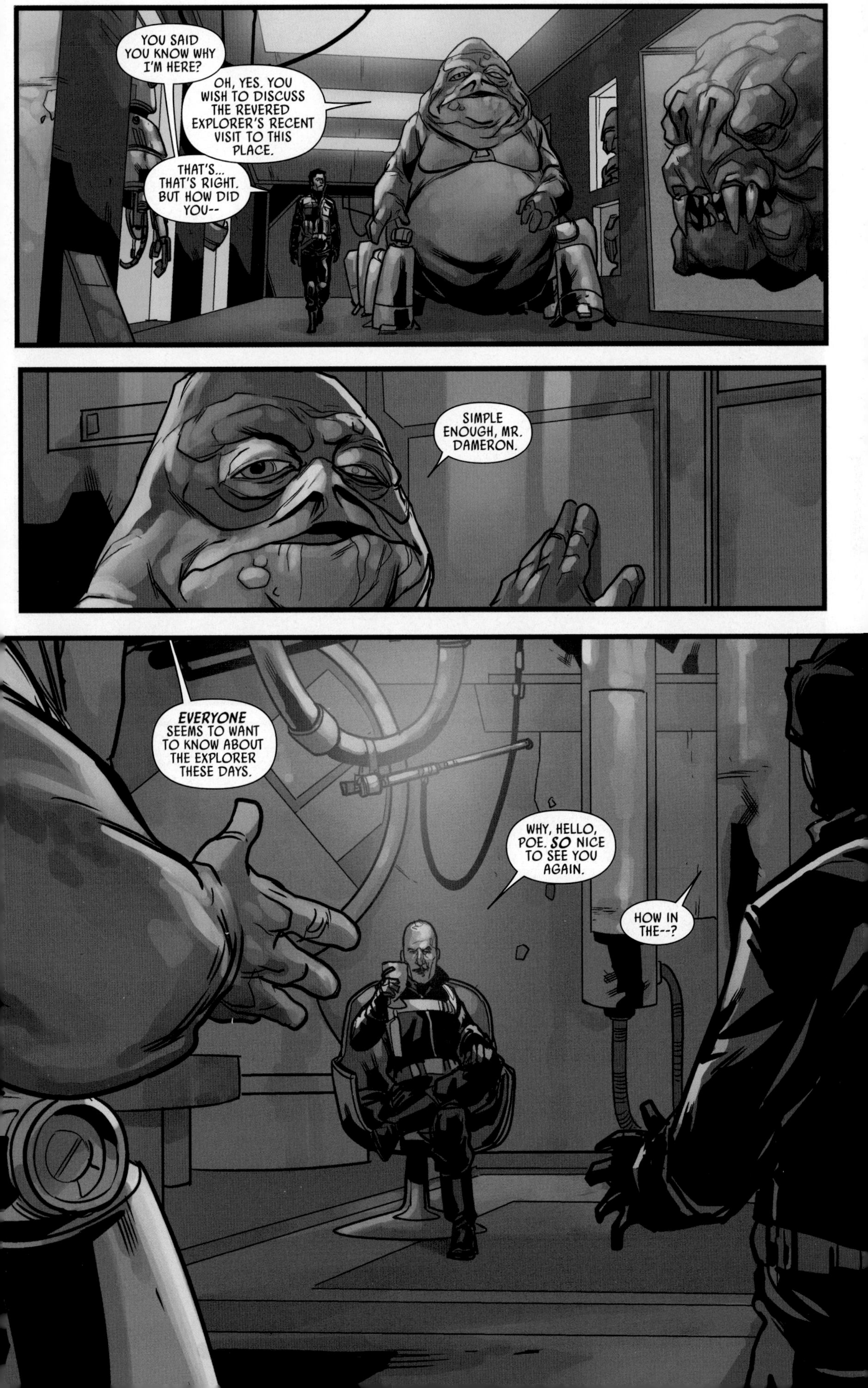

YOU SAID YOU KNOW WHY I'M HERE?
OH, YES. YOU WISH TO DISCUSS THE REVERED EXPLORER'S RECENT VISIT TO THIS PLACE.
THAT'S... THAT'S RIGHT. BUT HOW DID YOU--
SIMPLE ENOUGH, MR. DAMERON.
EVERYONE SEEMS TO WANT TO KNOW ABOUT THE EXPLORER THESE DAYS.
WHY, HELLO, POE. SO NICE TO SEE YOU AGAIN.
HOW IN THE--?

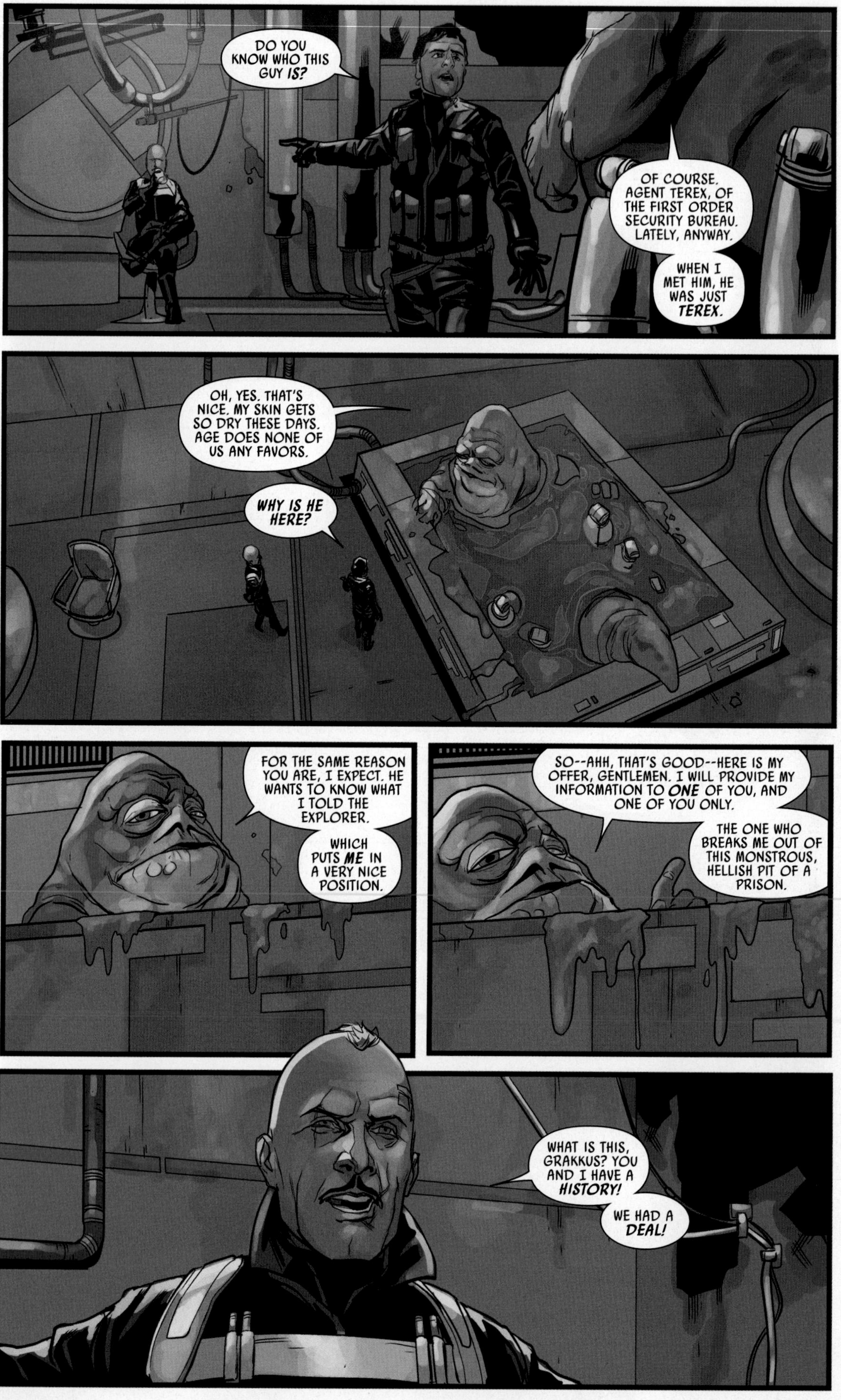

DO YOU KNOW WHO THIS GUY IS?
OF COURSE. AGENT TEREX, OF THE FIRST ORDER SECURITY BUREAU. LATELY, ANYWAY.
WHEN I MET HIM, HE WAS JUST TEREX.
OH, YES. THAT'S NICE. MY SKIN GETS SO DRY THESE DAYS. AGE DOES NONE OF US ANY FAVORS.
WHY IS HE HERE?
FOR THE SAME REASON YOU ARE, I EXPECT. HE WANTS TO KNOW WHAT I TOLD THE EXPLORER.
WHICH PUTS ME IN A VERY NICE POSITION.
SO--AHH, THAT'S GOOD--HERE IS MY OFFER, GENTLEMEN. I WILL PROVIDE MY INFORMATION TO ONE OF YOU, AND ONE OF YOU ONLY.
THE ONE WHO BREAKS ME OUT OF THIS MONSTROUS, HELLISH PIT OF A PRISON.
WHAT IS THIS, GRAKKUS? YOU AND I HAVE A HISTORY!
WE HAD A DEAL!

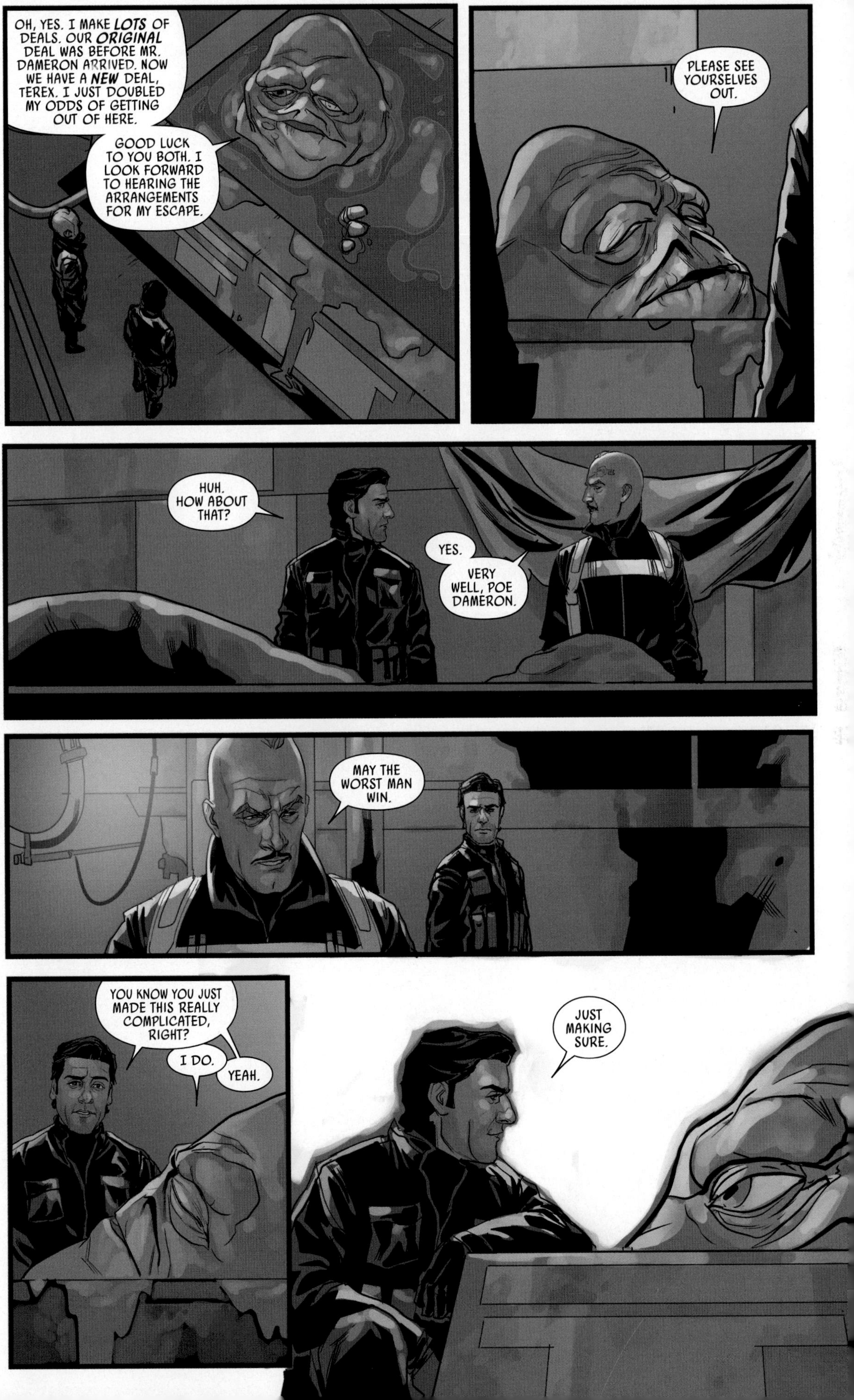
OH, YES. I MAKE LOTS OF DEALS. OUR ORIGINAL DEAL WAS BEFORE MR. DAMERON ARRIVED. NOW WE HAVE A NEW DEAL, TEREX. I JUST DOUBLED MY ODDS OF GETTING OUT OF HERE.
GOOD LUCK TO YOU BOTH. I LOOK FORWARD TO HEARING THE ARRANGEMENTS FOR MY ESCAPE.
PLEASE SEE YOURSELVES OUT.
HUH. HOW ABOUT THAT?
YES.
VERY WELL, POE DAMERON.
MAY THE WORST MAN WIN.
YOU KNOW YOU JUST MADE THIS REALLY COMPLICATED, RIGHT?
I DO.
YEAH.
JUST MAKING SURE.

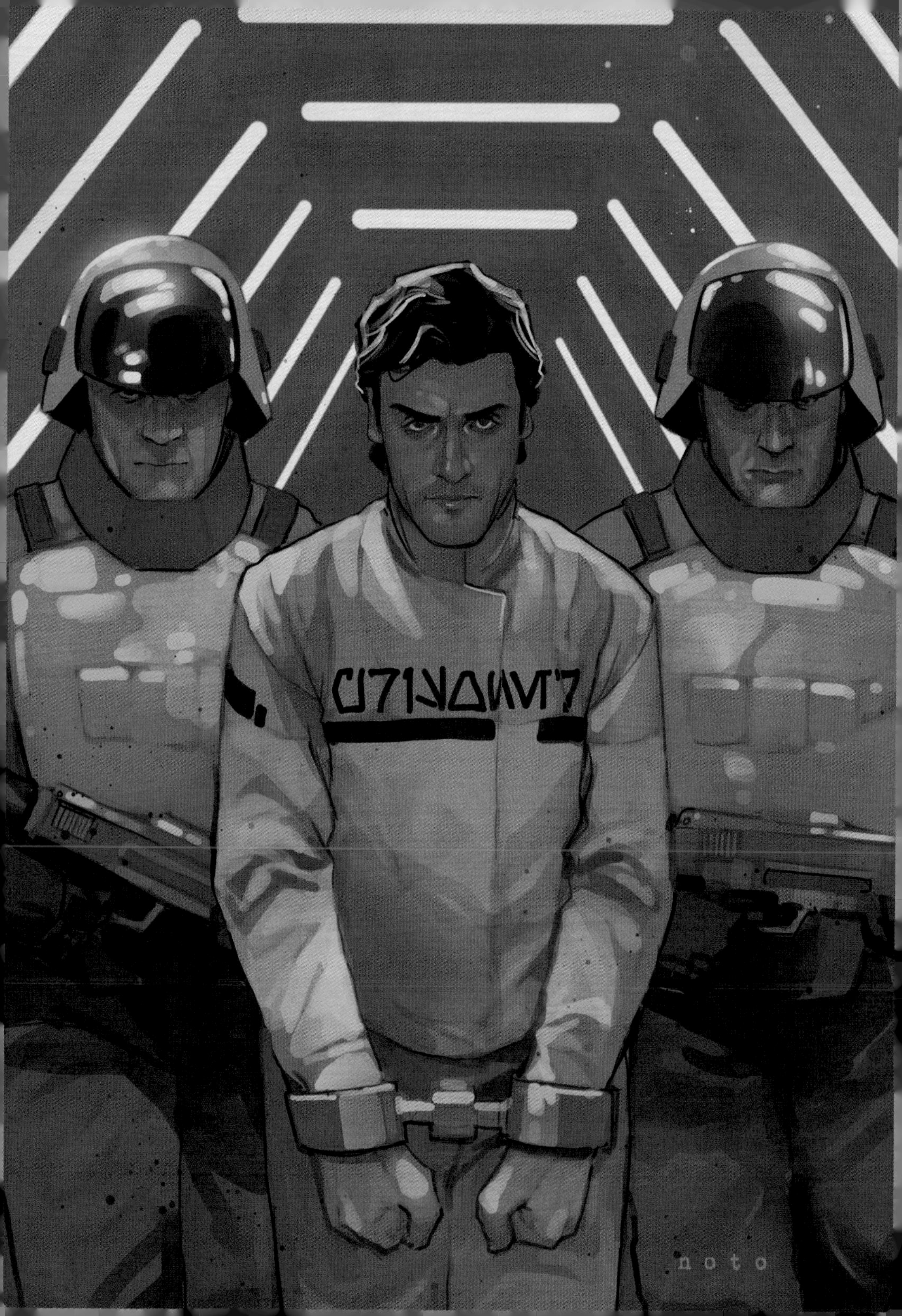
noto

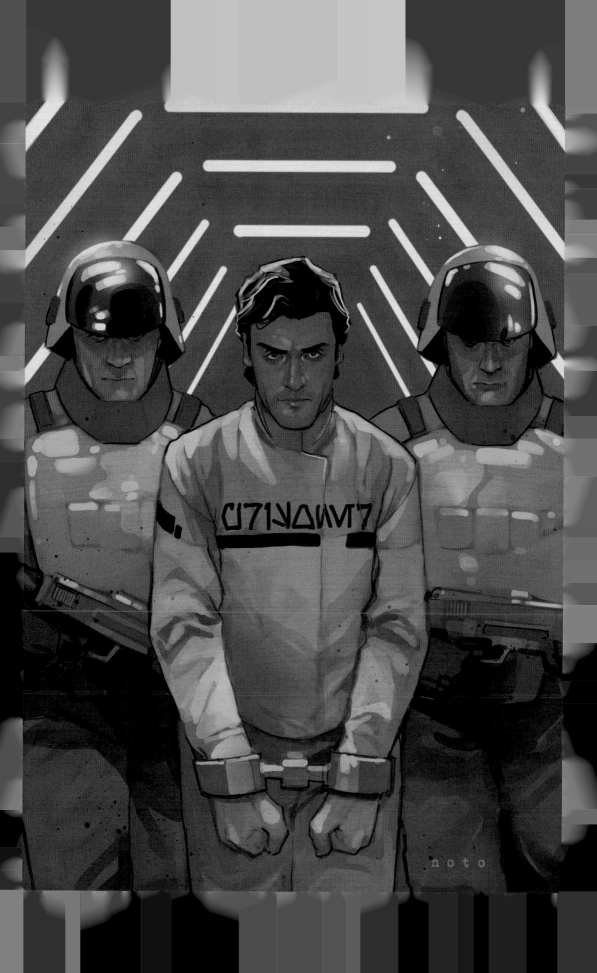

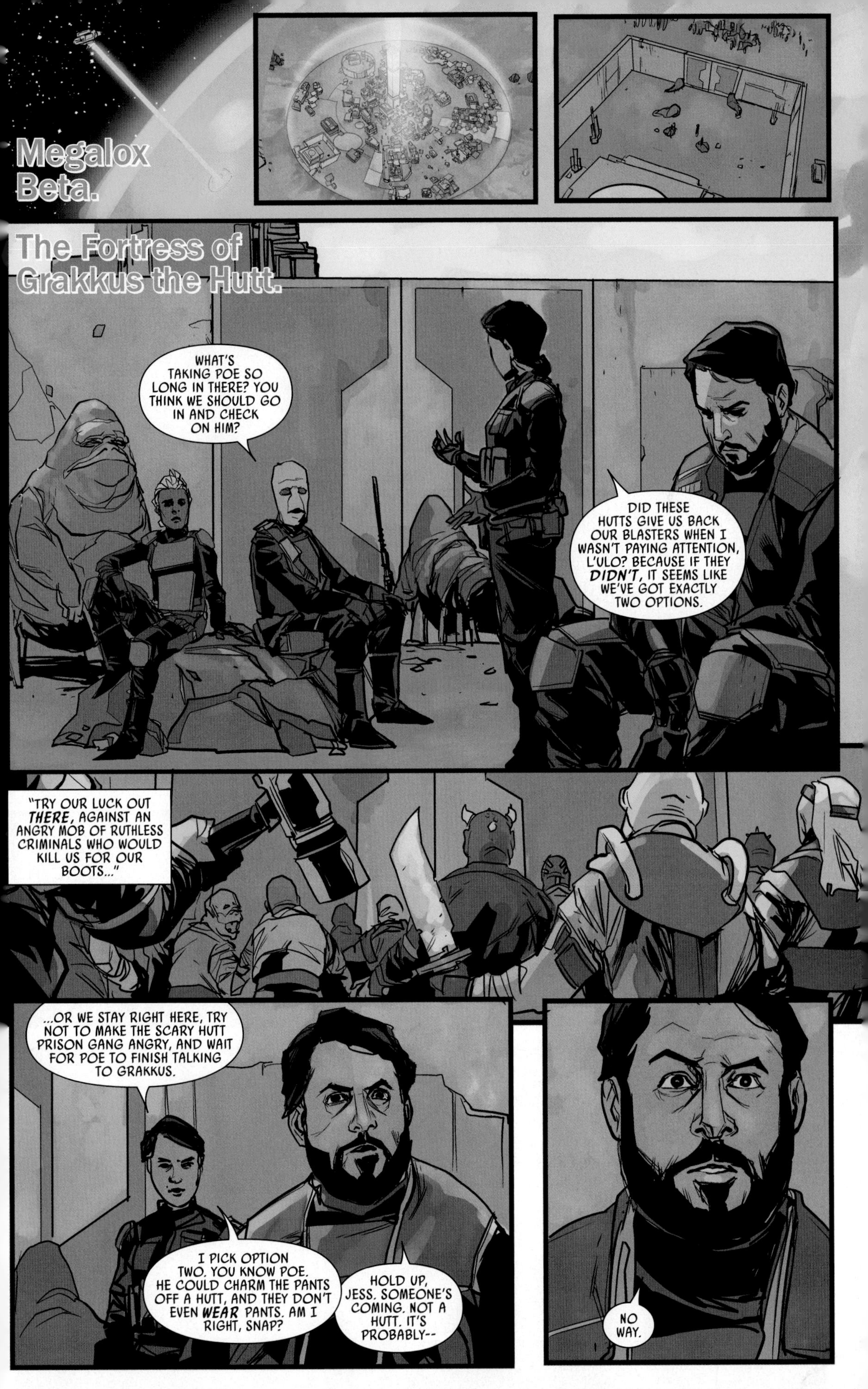
Megalox Beta.
The Fortress of Grakkus the Hutt.
WHAT'S TAKING POE SO LONG IN THERE? YOU THINK WE SHOULD GO IN AND CHECK ON HIM?
DID THESE HUTTS GIVE US BACK OUR BLASTERS WHEN I WASN'T PAYING ATTENTION, L'ULO? BECAUSE IF THEY *DIDN'T*, IT SEEMS LIKE WE'VE GOT EXACTLY TWO OPTIONS.
"TRY OUR LUCK OUT *THERE*, AGAINST AN ANGRY MOB OF RUTHLESS CRIMINALS WHO WOULD KILL US FOR OUR BOOTS..."
...OR WE STAY RIGHT HERE, TRY NOT TO MAKE THE SCARY HUTT PRISON GANG ANGRY, AND WAIT FOR POE TO FINISH TALKING TO GRAKKUS.
I PICK OPTION TWO. YOU KNOW POE. HE COULD CHARM THE PANTS OFF A HUTT, AND THEY DON'T EVEN *WEAR* PANTS. AM I RIGHT, SNAP?
HOLD UP, JESS. SOMEONE'S COMING. NOT A HUTT. IT'S PROBABLY--
NO WAY.

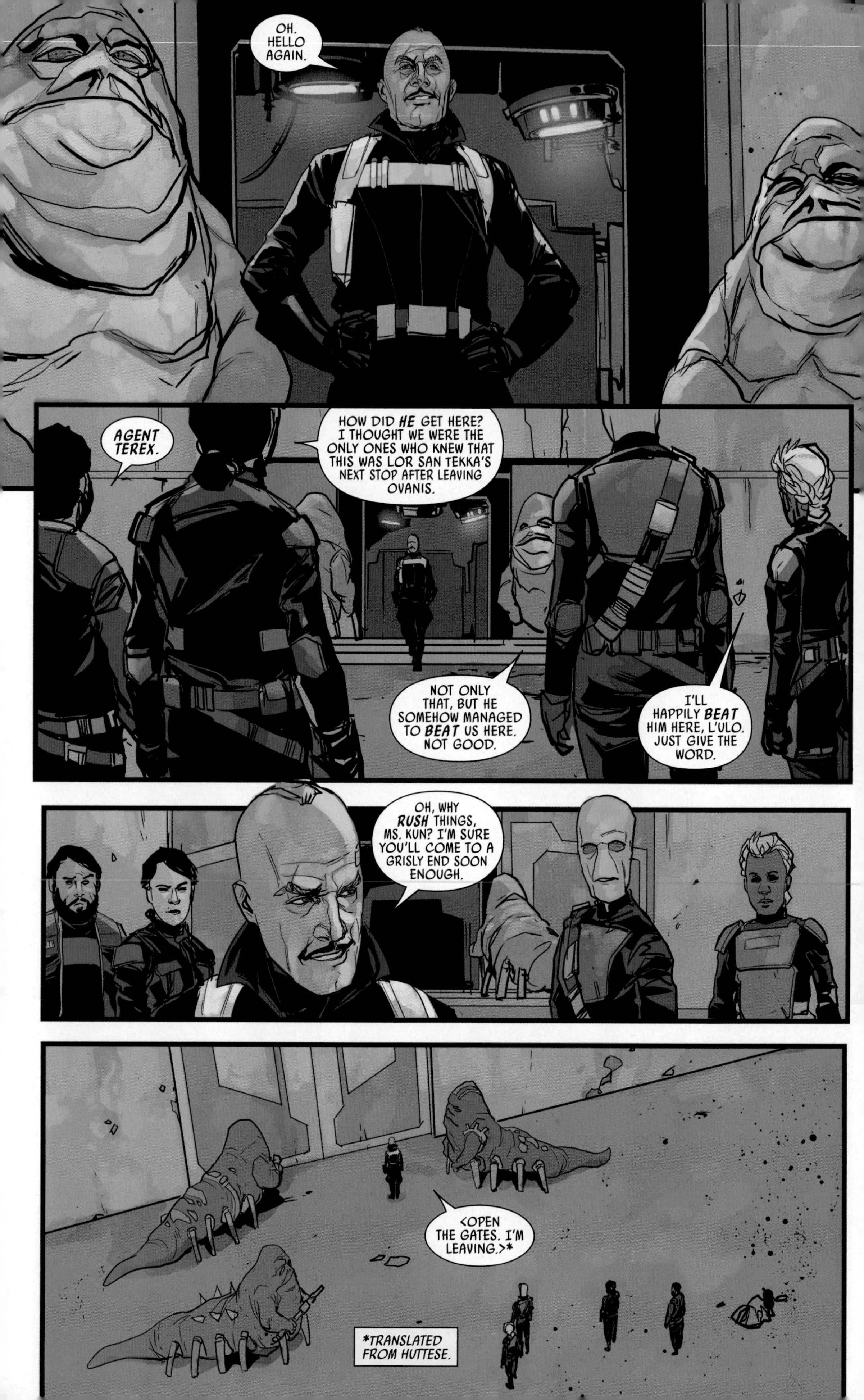
OH. HELLO AGAIN.
AGENT TEREX.
HOW DID HE GET HERE? I THOUGHT WE WERE THE ONLY ONES WHO KNEW THAT THIS WAS LOR SAN TEKKA'S NEXT STOP AFTER LEAVING OVANIS.
NOT ONLY THAT, BUT HE SOMEHOW MANAGED TO BEAT US HERE. NOT GOOD.
I'LL HAPPILY BEAT HIM HERE, L'ULO. JUST GIVE THE WORD.
OH, WHY RUSH THINGS, MS. KUN? I'M SURE YOU'LL COME TO A GRISLY END SOON ENOUGH.
<OPEN THE GATES. I'M LEAVING.>*
*TRANSLATED FROM HUTTESE.

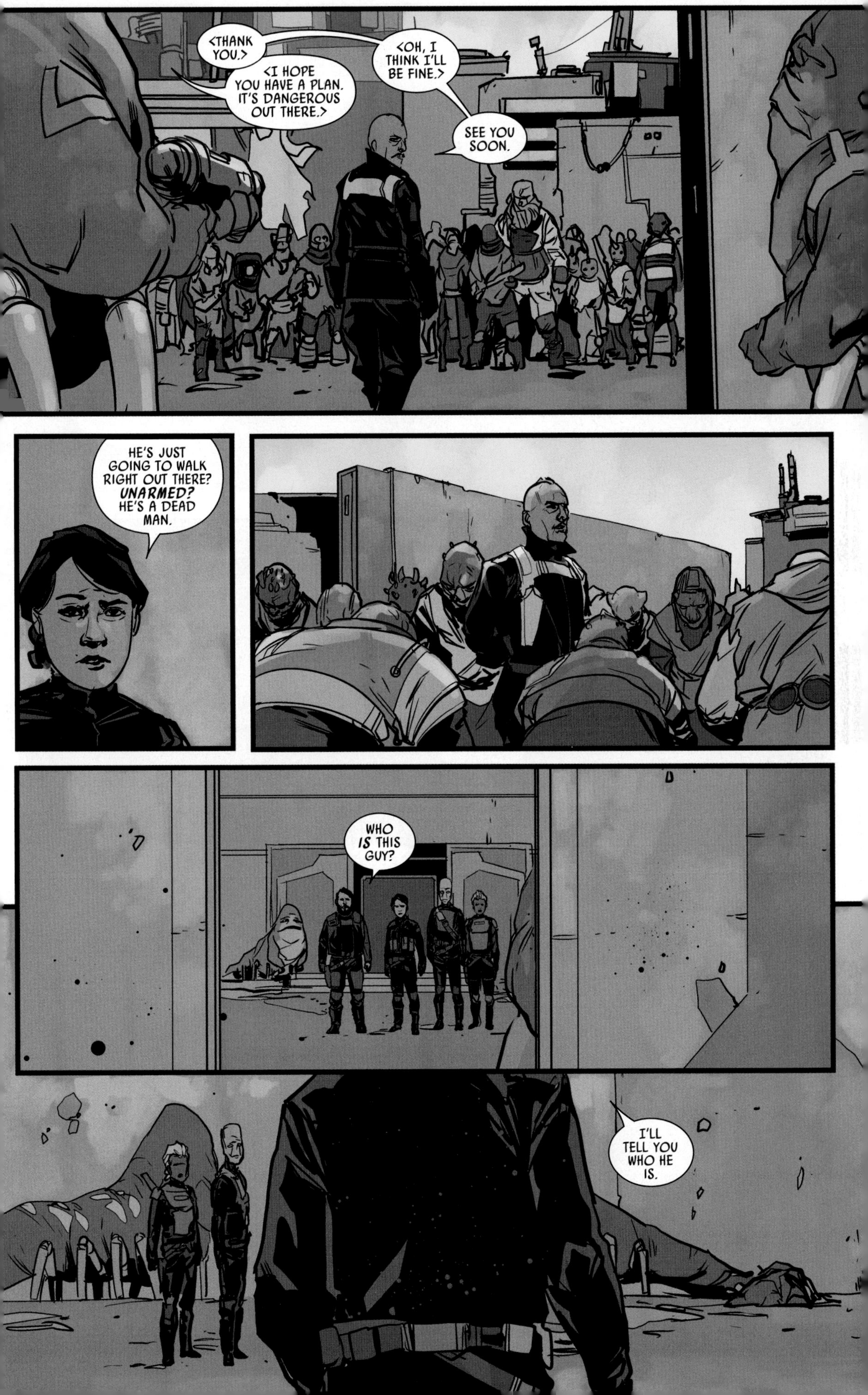
<THANK YOU.>
<I HOPE YOU HAVE A PLAN. IT'S DANGEROUS OUT THERE.>
<OH, I THINK I'LL BE FINE.>
SEE YOU SOON.
HE'S JUST GOING TO WALK RIGHT OUT THERE? UNARMED? HE'S A DEAD MAN.
WHO IS THIS GUY?
I'LL TELL YOU WHO HE IS.

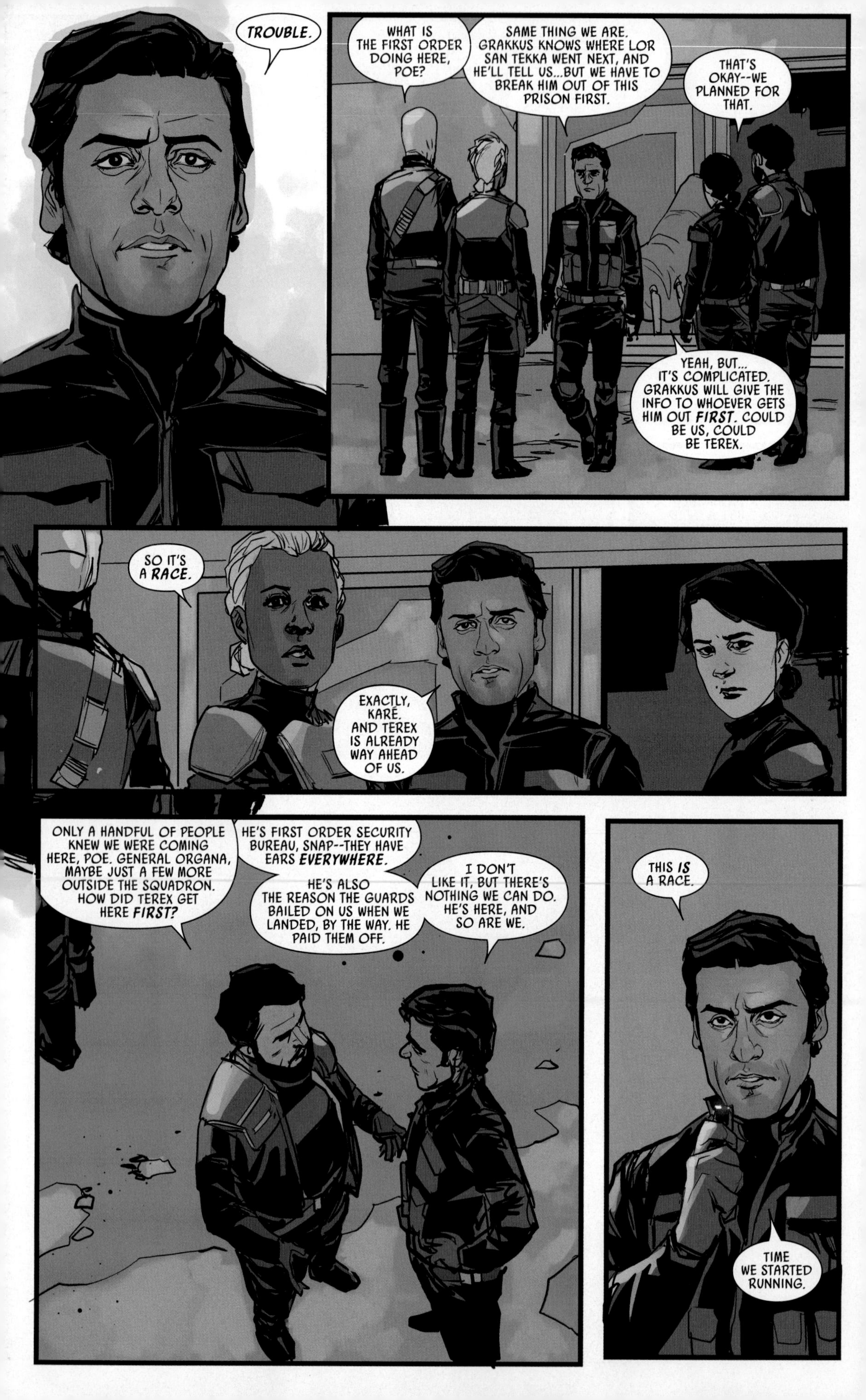
TROUBLE.
WHAT IS THE FIRST ORDER DOING HERE, POE?
SAME THING WE ARE. GRAKKUS KNOWS WHERE LOR SAN TEKKA WENT NEXT, AND HE'LL TELL US...BUT WE HAVE TO BREAK HIM OUT OF THIS PRISON FIRST.
THAT'S OKAY--WE PLANNED FOR THAT.
YEAH, BUT... IT'S COMPLICATED. GRAKKUS WILL GIVE THE INFO TO WHOEVER GETS HIM OUT FIRST. COULD BE US, COULD BE TEREX.
SO IT'S A RACE.
EXACTLY, KARÉ. AND TEREX IS ALREADY WAY AHEAD OF US.
ONLY A HANDFUL OF PEOPLE KNEW WE WERE COMING HERE, POE. GENERAL ORGANA, MAYBE JUST A FEW MORE OUTSIDE THE SQUADRON. HOW DID TEREX GET HERE FIRST?
HE'S FIRST ORDER SECURITY BUREAU, SNAP--THEY HAVE EARS EVERYWHERE.
HE'S ALSO THE REASON THE GUARDS BAILED ON US WHEN WE LANDED, BY THE WAY. HE PAID THEM OFF.
I DON'T LIKE IT, BUT THERE'S NOTHING WE CAN DO. HE'S HERE, AND SO ARE WE.
THIS IS A RACE.
TIME WE STARTED RUNNING.

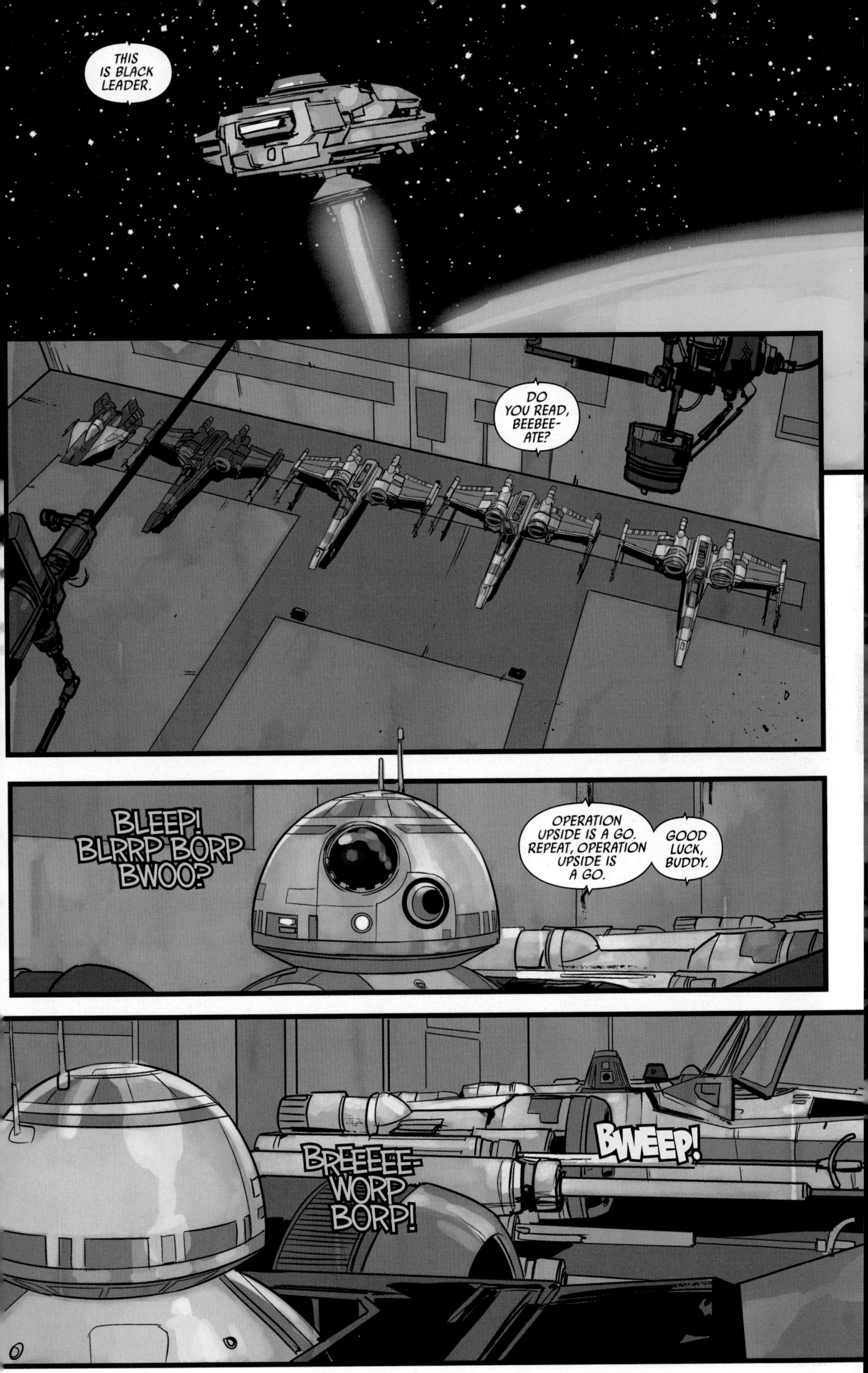
THIS IS BLACK LEADER.
DO YOU READ, BEEBEE-ATE?
BLEEP! BLRRP BORP BWOO?
OPERATION UPSIDE IS A GO. REPEAT, OPERATION UPSIDE IS A GO.
GOOD LUCK, BUDDY.
BREEEEE-WORP BORP!
BWEEP!

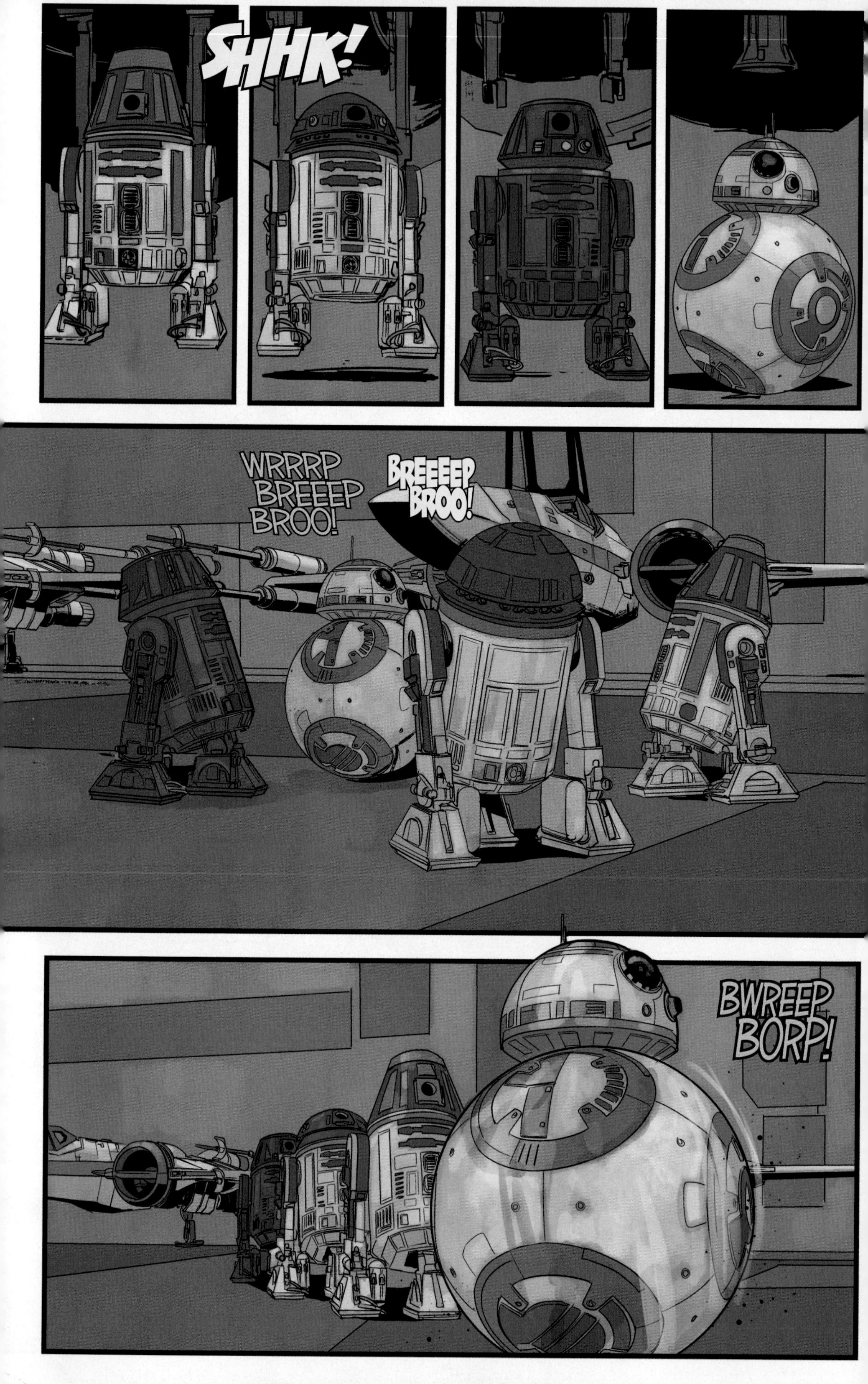
SHHK!
WRRRP BREEEP BROO!
BREEEEP BROO!
BWREEP BORP!

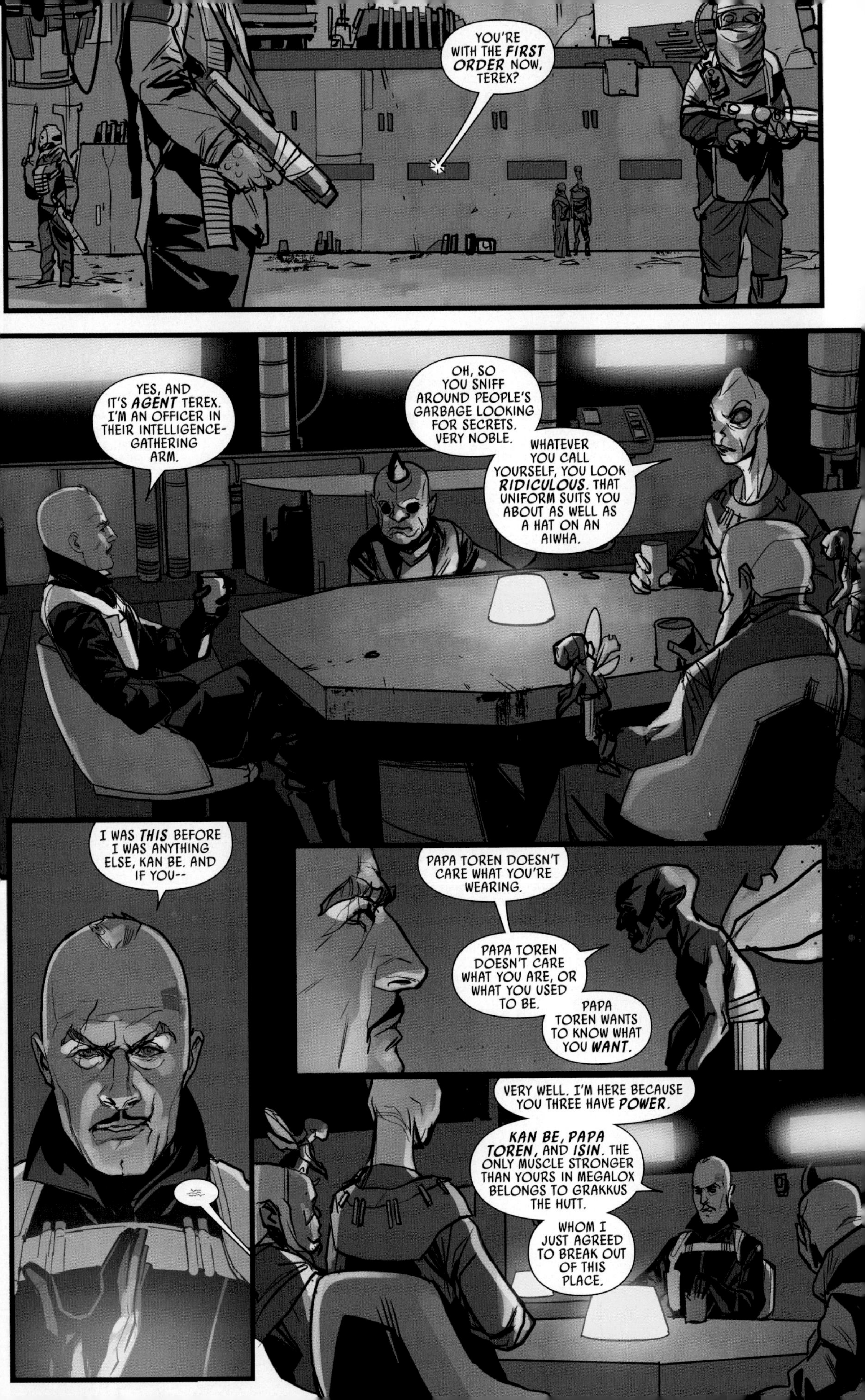
YOU'RE WITH THE FIRST ORDER NOW, TEREX?
YES, AND IT'S AGENT TEREX. I'M AN OFFICER IN THEIR INTELLIGENCE-GATHERING ARM.
OH, SO YOU SNIFF AROUND PEOPLE'S GARBAGE LOOKING FOR SECRETS. VERY NOBLE.
WHATEVER YOU CALL YOURSELF, YOU LOOK RIDICULOUS. THAT UNIFORM SUITS YOU ABOUT AS WELL AS A HAT ON AN AIWHA.
I WAS THIS BEFORE I WAS ANYTHING ELSE, KAN BE. AND IF YOU--
PAPA TOREN DOESN'T CARE WHAT YOU'RE WEARING.
PAPA TOREN DOESN'T CARE WHAT YOU ARE, OR WHAT YOU USED TO BE.
PAPA TOREN WANTS TO KNOW WHAT YOU WANT.
VERY WELL. I'M HERE BECAUSE YOU THREE HAVE POWER.
KAN BE, PAPA TOREN, AND ISIN. THE ONLY MUSCLE STRONGER THAN YOURS IN MEGALOX BELONGS TO GRAKKUS THE HUTT.
WHOM I JUST AGREED TO BREAK OUT OF THIS PLACE.

YOU'RE GOING TO GET GRAKKUS OUT? YOU REALLY THINK YOU SHOULD RUB THAT IN OUR *FACES?*

PAPA TOREN SAYS WE SHOULD CUT HIM UP AND DROP HIM IN THE STEWPOTS.

HE SAYS THERE'S NEVER ENOUGH FOOD DOWN HERE AS IT IS.

RELAX, ALL OF YOU.

I TOLD GRAKKUS I'D GET HIM OUT, BUT I'M TELLING *YOU* THAT I HAVE NO INTENTION OF DOING THAT.

GRAKKUS AND I HAD A DEAL, AND HE *BROKE* IT WHEN AN EXTRAORDINARILY FRUSTRATING MAN NAMED POE DAMERON CAME ALONG TO OFFER HIM ANOTHER OPTION.

SO-- HERE'S MY *NEW* PLAN.

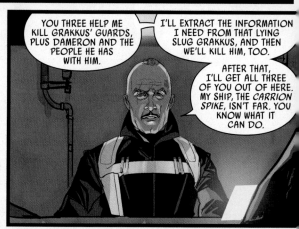

YOU THREE HELP ME KILL GRAKKUS' GUARDS, PLUS DAMERON AND THE PEOPLE HE HAS WITH HIM.

I'LL EXTRACT THE INFORMATION I NEED FROM THAT LYING SLUG GRAKKUS, AND THEN WE'LL KILL HIM, TOO.

AFTER THAT, I'LL GET ALL THREE OF YOU OUT OF HERE. MY SHIP, THE *CARRION SPIKE,* ISN'T FAR. YOU KNOW WHAT IT CAN DO.

YOU ALL KNOW WHAT *I* CAN DO, TOO. NOT SUCH A BAD THING TO HAVE AGENT TEREX IN YOUR DEBT.

SO, MY FRIENDS. WHAT DO YOU SAY?

THNK

TIME TO KILL.

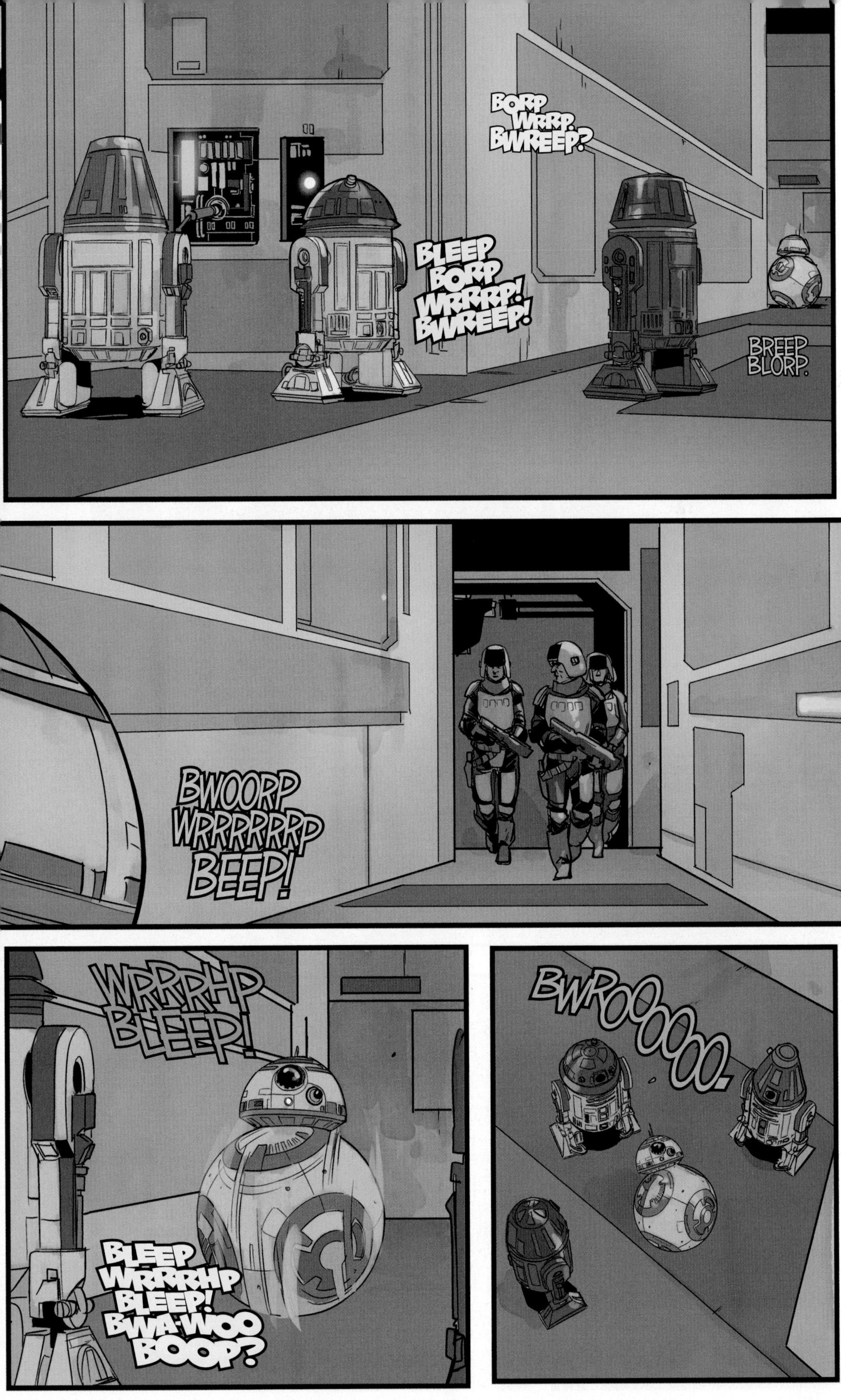
BLEEP BORP WRRRP! BWREEP!
BORP WRRP. BWREEP?
BREEP BLORP.
BWOORP WRRRRRRP BEEP!
WRRRHP BLEEP!
BLEEP WRRRHP BLEEP! BWA-WOO BOOP?
BWROOOOOO.

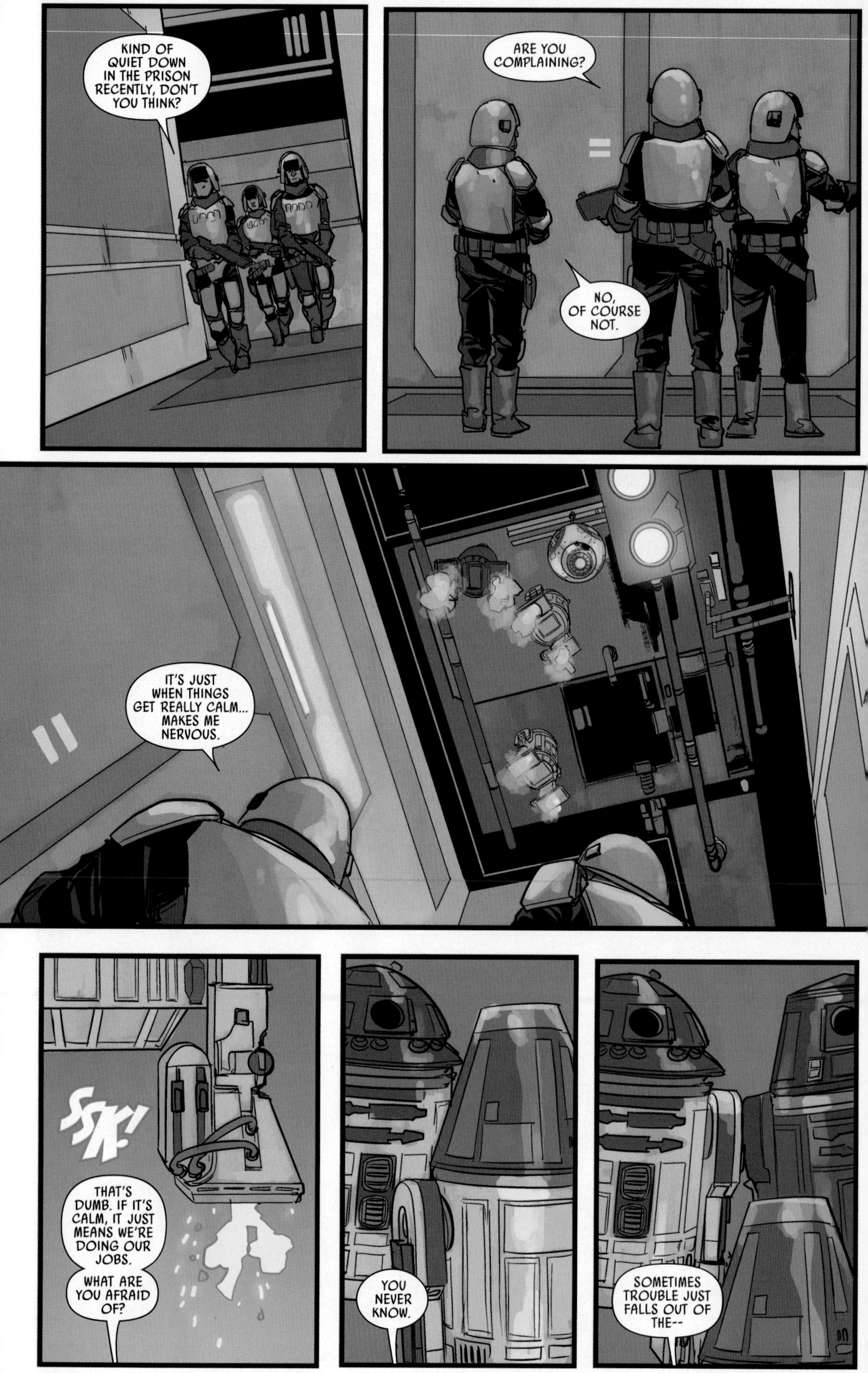
KIND OF QUIET DOWN IN THE PRISON RECENTLY, DON'T YOU THINK?
ARE YOU COMPLAINING?
NO, OF COURSE NOT.
IT'S JUST WHEN THINGS GET REALLY CALM... MAKES ME NERVOUS.
SSK!
THAT'S DUMB. IF IT'S CALM, IT JUST MEANS WE'RE DOING OUR JOBS.
WHAT ARE YOU AFRAID OF?
YOU NEVER KNOW.
SOMETIMES TROUBLE JUST FALLS OUT OF THE--

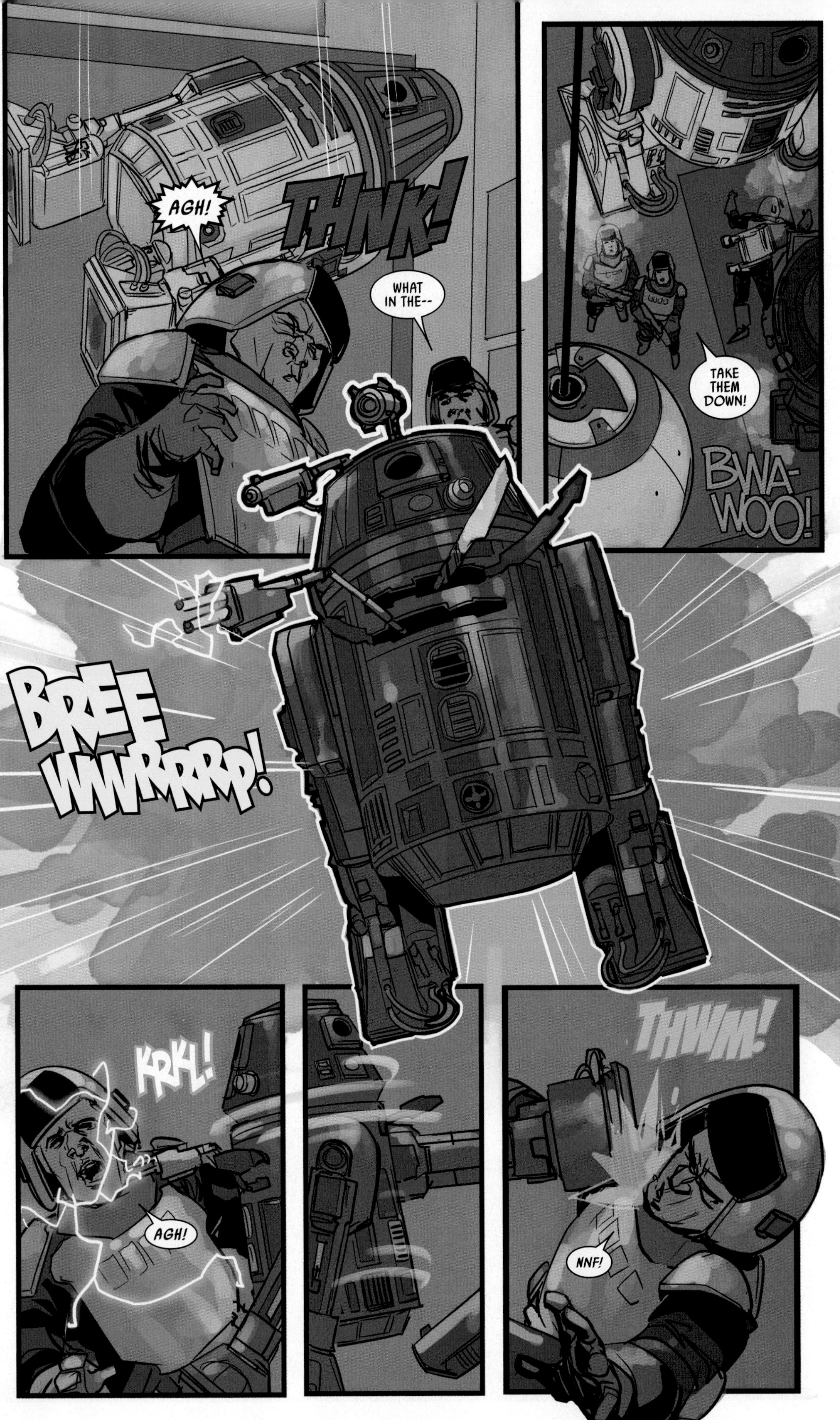
AGH!
THNK!
WHAT IN THE--
TAKE THEM DOWN!
BWA-WOO!
BREE WWRRRP!
KRKL!
AGH!
THWM!
NNF!

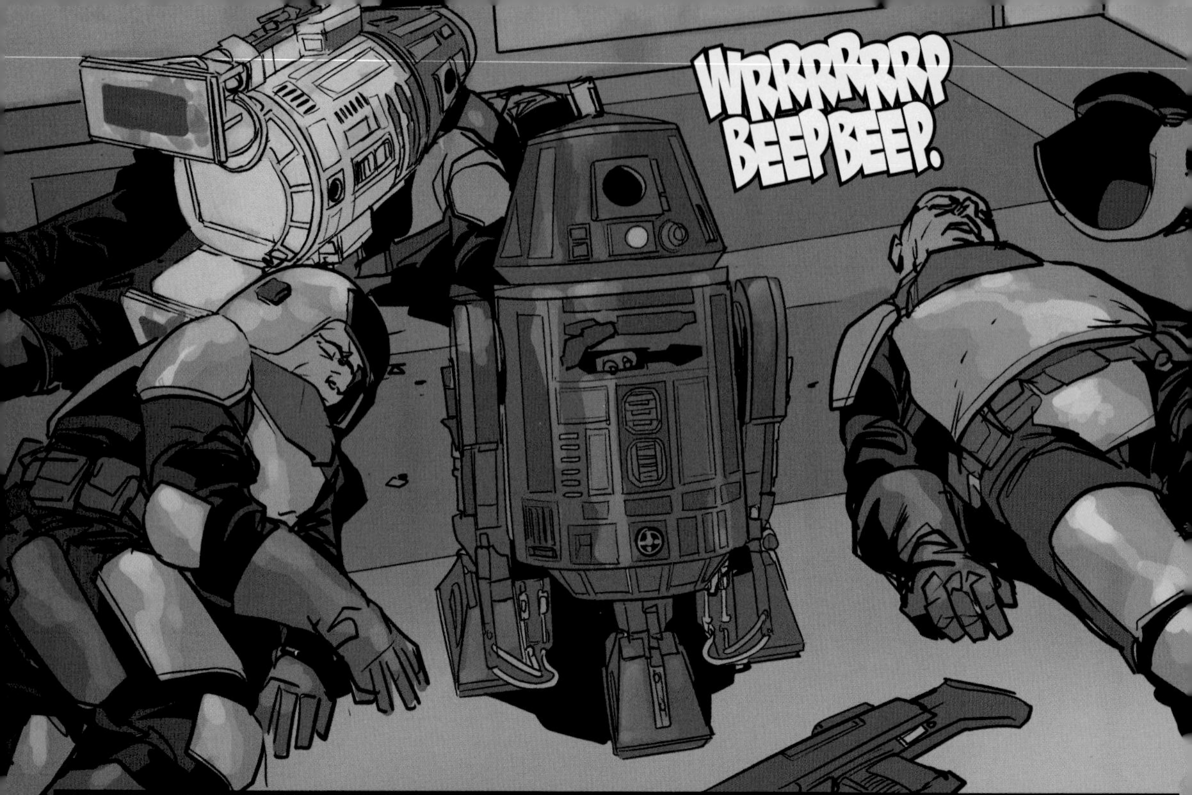
WRRRRRRP BEEP BEEP.
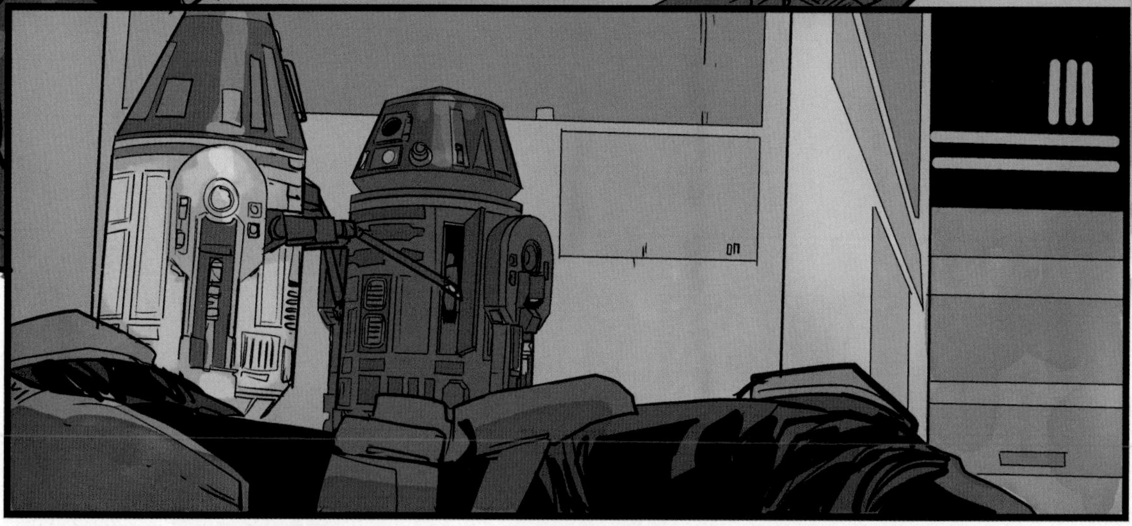
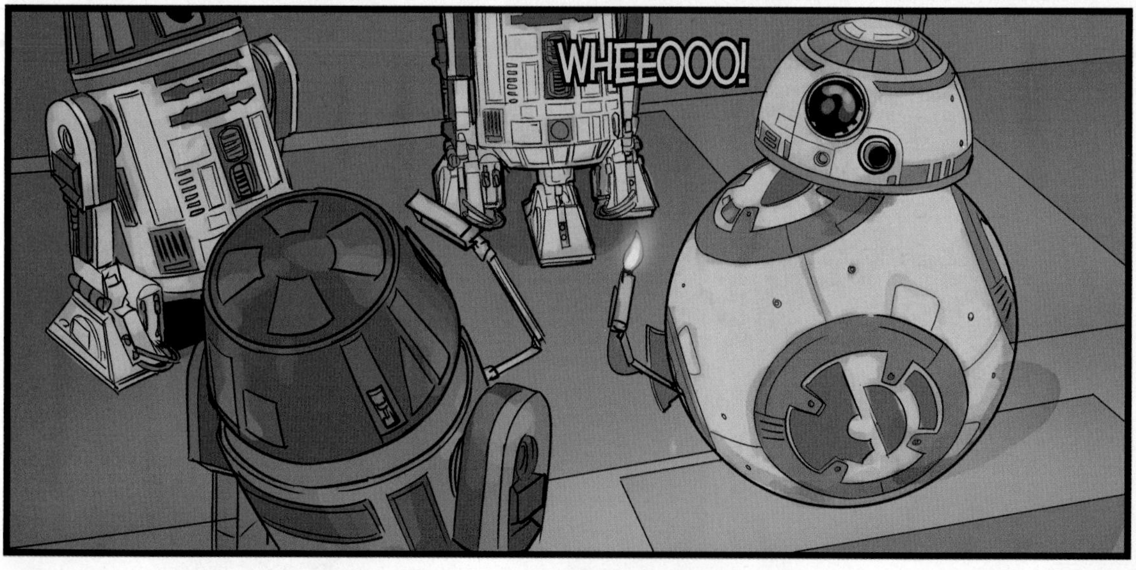
WHEEOOO!

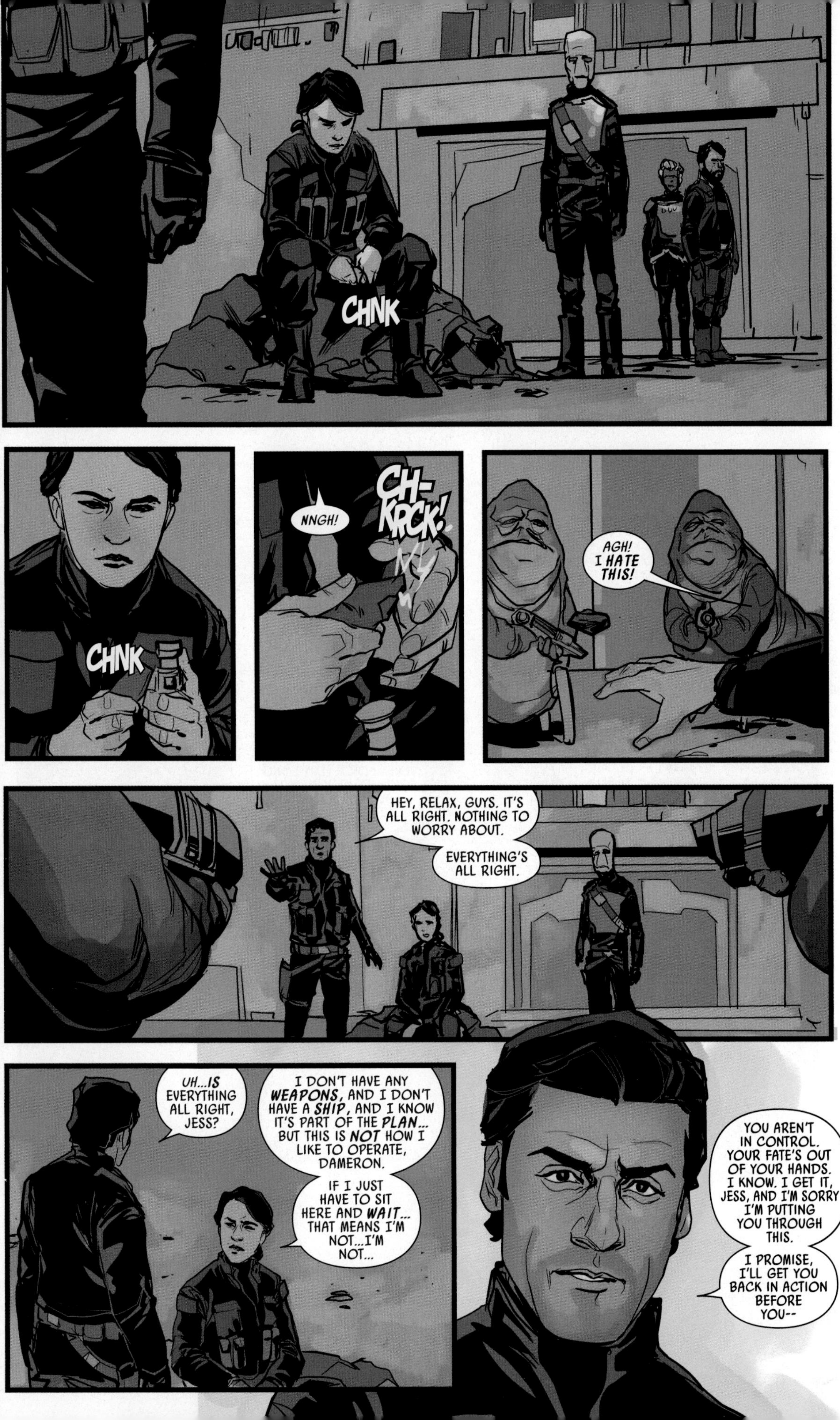
CHNK
CHNK
NNGH!
CH-KRCK!
AGH! I HATE THIS!
HEY, RELAX, GUYS. IT'S ALL RIGHT. NOTHING TO WORRY ABOUT.
EVERYTHING'S ALL RIGHT.
UH...IS EVERYTHING ALL RIGHT, JESS?
I DON'T HAVE ANY WEAPONS, AND I DON'T HAVE A SHIP, AND I KNOW IT'S PART OF THE PLAN... BUT THIS IS NOT HOW I LIKE TO OPERATE, DAMERON.
IF I JUST HAVE TO SIT HERE AND WAIT... THAT MEANS I'M NOT...I'M NOT...
YOU AREN'T IN CONTROL. YOUR FATE'S OUT OF YOUR HANDS. I KNOW. I GET IT, JESS, AND I'M SORRY I'M PUTTING YOU THROUGH THIS.
I PROMISE, I'LL GET YOU BACK IN ACTION BEFORE YOU--

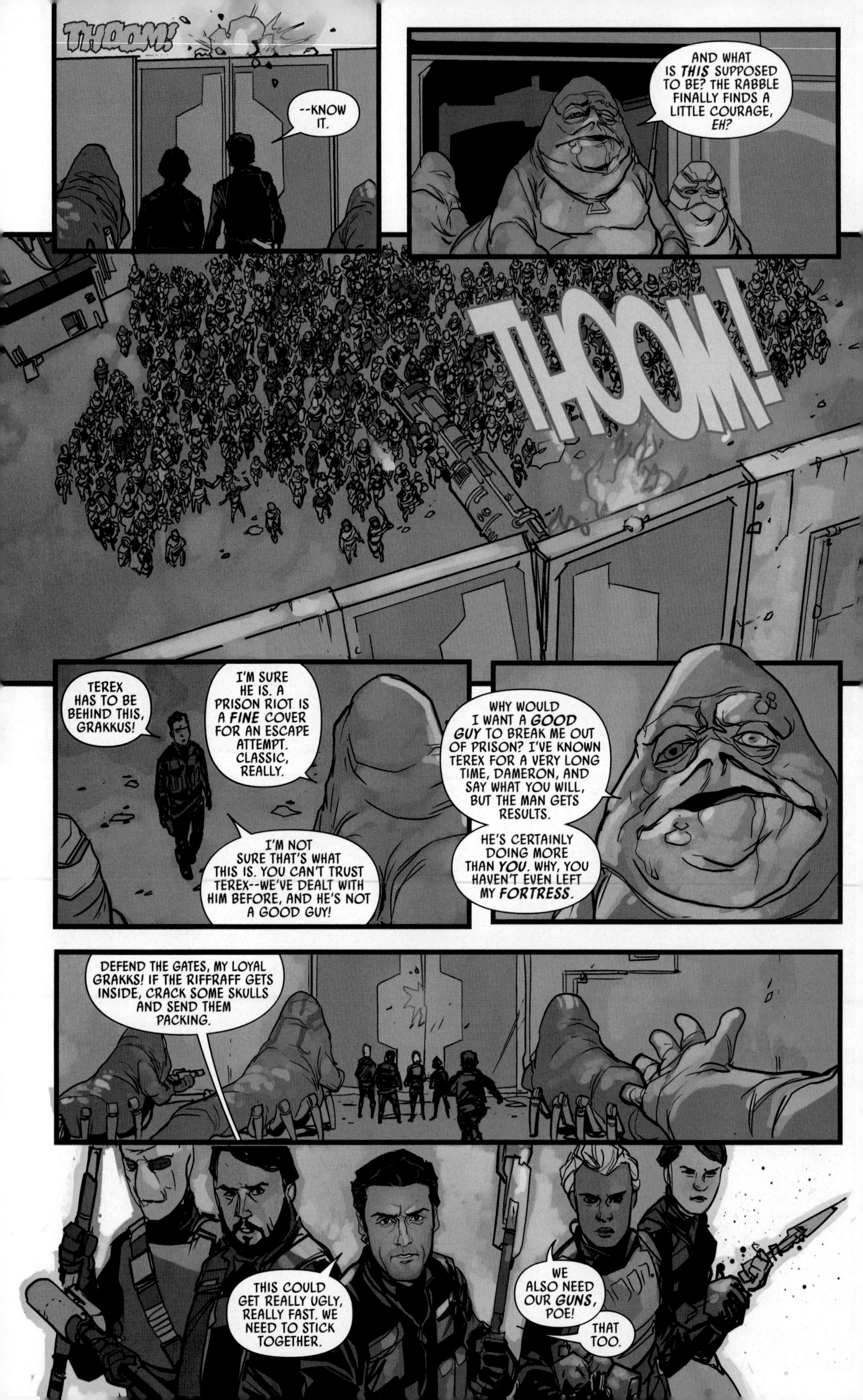
THOOM!
--KNOW IT.
AND WHAT IS THIS SUPPOSED TO BE? THE RABBLE FINALLY FINDS A LITTLE COURAGE, EH?
THOOM!
TEREX HAS TO BE BEHIND THIS, GRAKKUS!
I'M SURE HE IS. A PRISON RIOT IS A FINE COVER FOR AN ESCAPE ATTEMPT. CLASSIC, REALLY.
I'M NOT SURE THAT'S WHAT THIS IS. YOU CAN'T TRUST TEREX--WE'VE DEALT WITH HIM BEFORE, AND HE'S NOT A GOOD GUY!
WHY WOULD I WANT A GOOD GUY TO BREAK ME OUT OF PRISON? I'VE KNOWN TEREX FOR A VERY LONG TIME, DAMERON, AND SAY WHAT YOU WILL, BUT THE MAN GETS RESULTS.
HE'S CERTAINLY DOING MORE THAN YOU. WHY, YOU HAVEN'T EVEN LEFT MY FORTRESS.
DEFEND THE GATES, MY LOYAL GRAKKS! IF THE RIFFRAFF GETS INSIDE, CRACK SOME SKULLS AND SEND THEM PACKING.
THIS COULD GET REALLY UGLY, REALLY FAST. WE NEED TO STICK TOGETHER.
WE ALSO NEED OUR GUNS, POE!
THAT TOO.

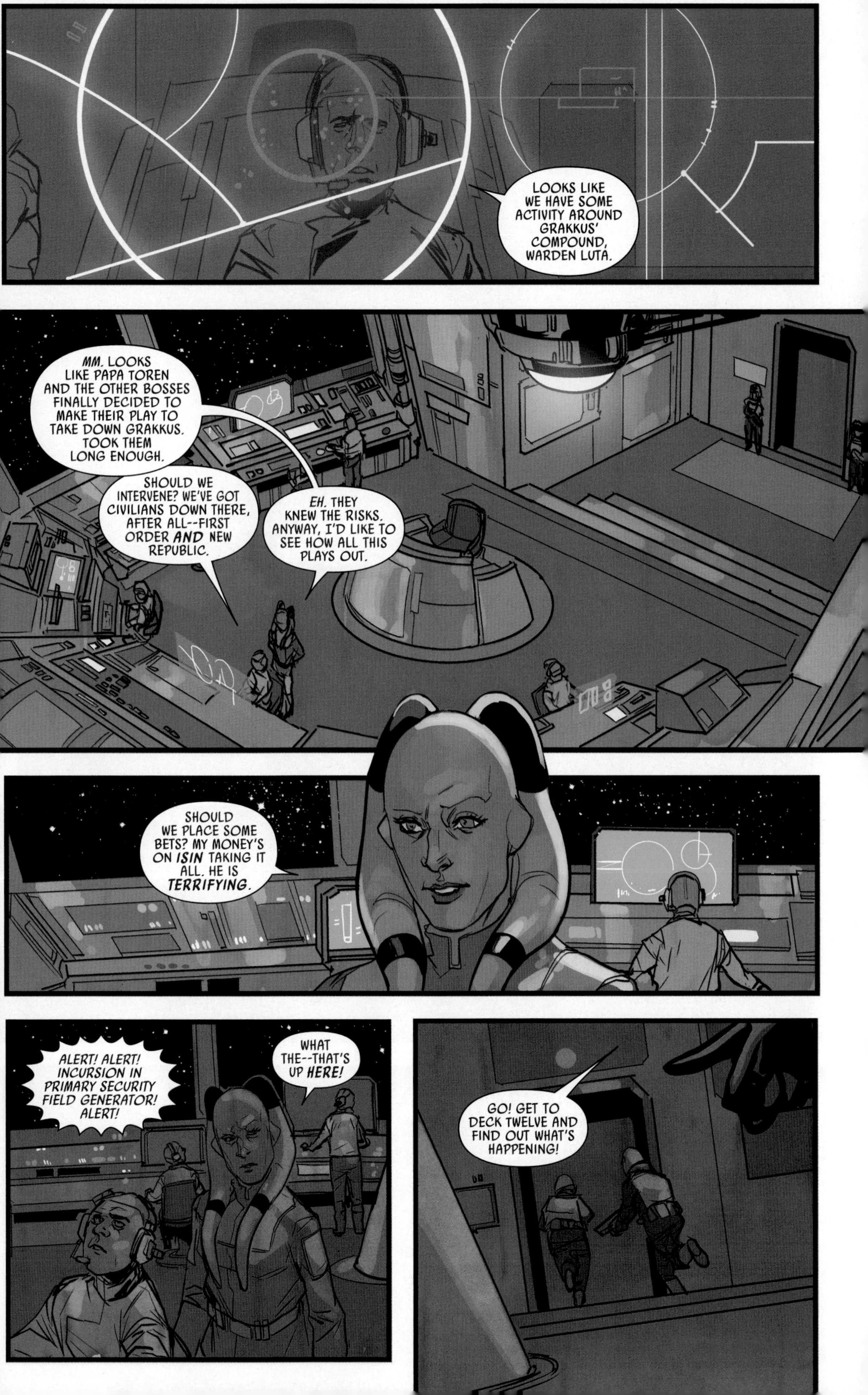
LOOKS LIKE WE HAVE SOME ACTIVITY AROUND GRAKKUS' COMPOUND, WARDEN LUTA.
MM. LOOKS LIKE PAPA TOREN AND THE OTHER BOSSES FINALLY DECIDED TO MAKE THEIR PLAY TO TAKE DOWN GRAKKUS. TOOK THEM LONG ENOUGH.
SHOULD WE INTERVENE? WE'VE GOT CIVILIANS DOWN THERE, AFTER ALL--FIRST ORDER AND NEW REPUBLIC.
EH. THEY KNEW THE RISKS. ANYWAY, I'D LIKE TO SEE HOW ALL THIS PLAYS OUT.
SHOULD WE PLACE SOME BETS? MY MONEY'S ON ISIN TAKING IT ALL. HE IS TERRIFYING.
ALERT! ALERT! INCURSION IN PRIMARY SECURITY FIELD GENERATOR! ALERT!
WHAT THE--THAT'S UP HERE!
GO! GET TO DECK TWELVE AND FIND OUT WHAT'S HAPPENING!

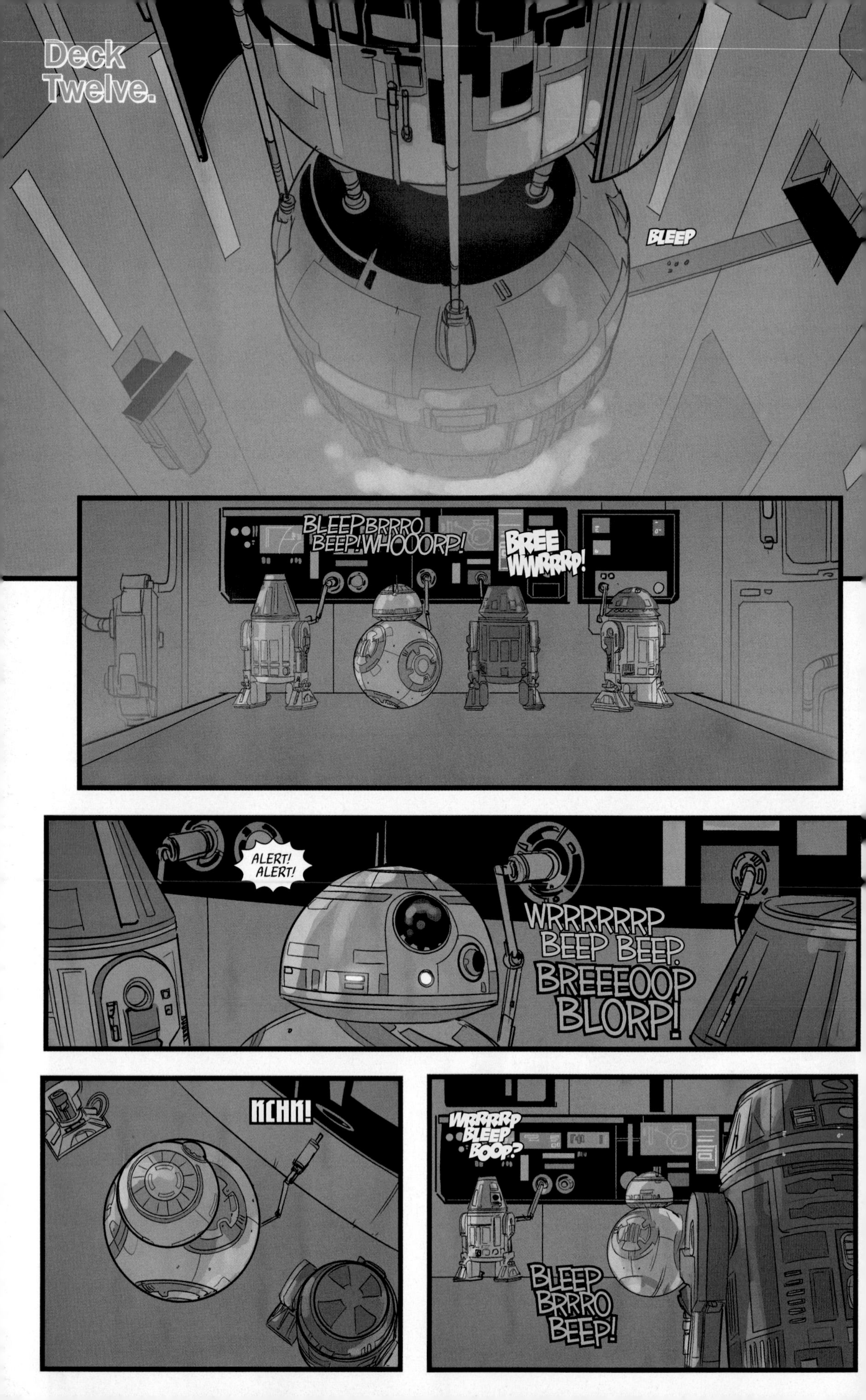
Deck Twelve.
BLEEP
BLEEP BRRRO BEEP! WHOOORP!
BREE WWRRRP!
ALERT! ALERT!
WRRRRRRP BEEP BEEP. BREEEOOP BLORP!
KCHK!
WRRRRP BLEEP BOOP?
BLEEP BRRRO BEEP!

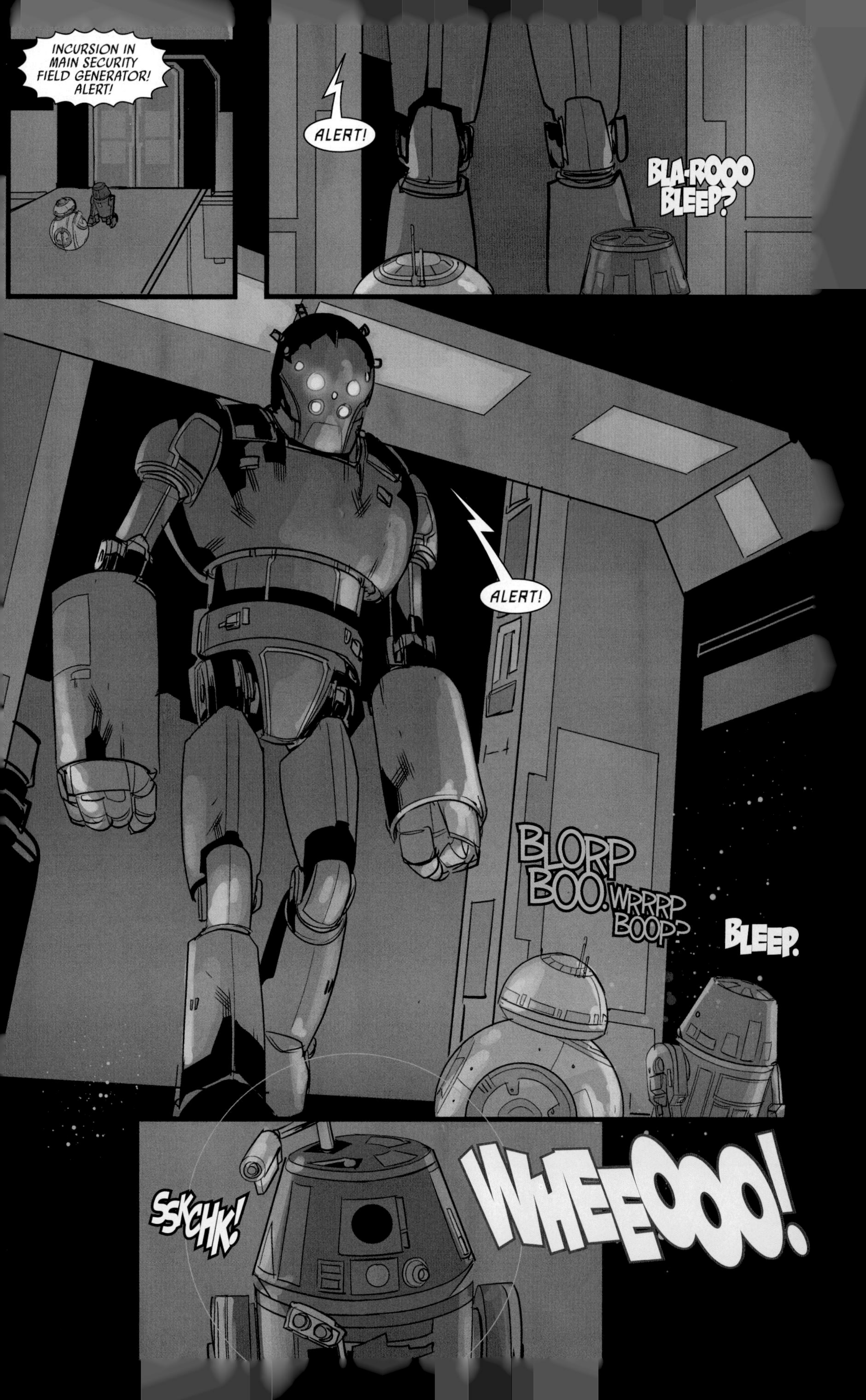
INCURSION IN MAIN SECURITY FIELD GENERATOR! ALERT!
ALERT!
BLA-ROOO BLEEP?
ALERT!
BLORP BOO.
WRRRP BOOP?
BLEEP.
SSKCHK!
WHEEOOO!

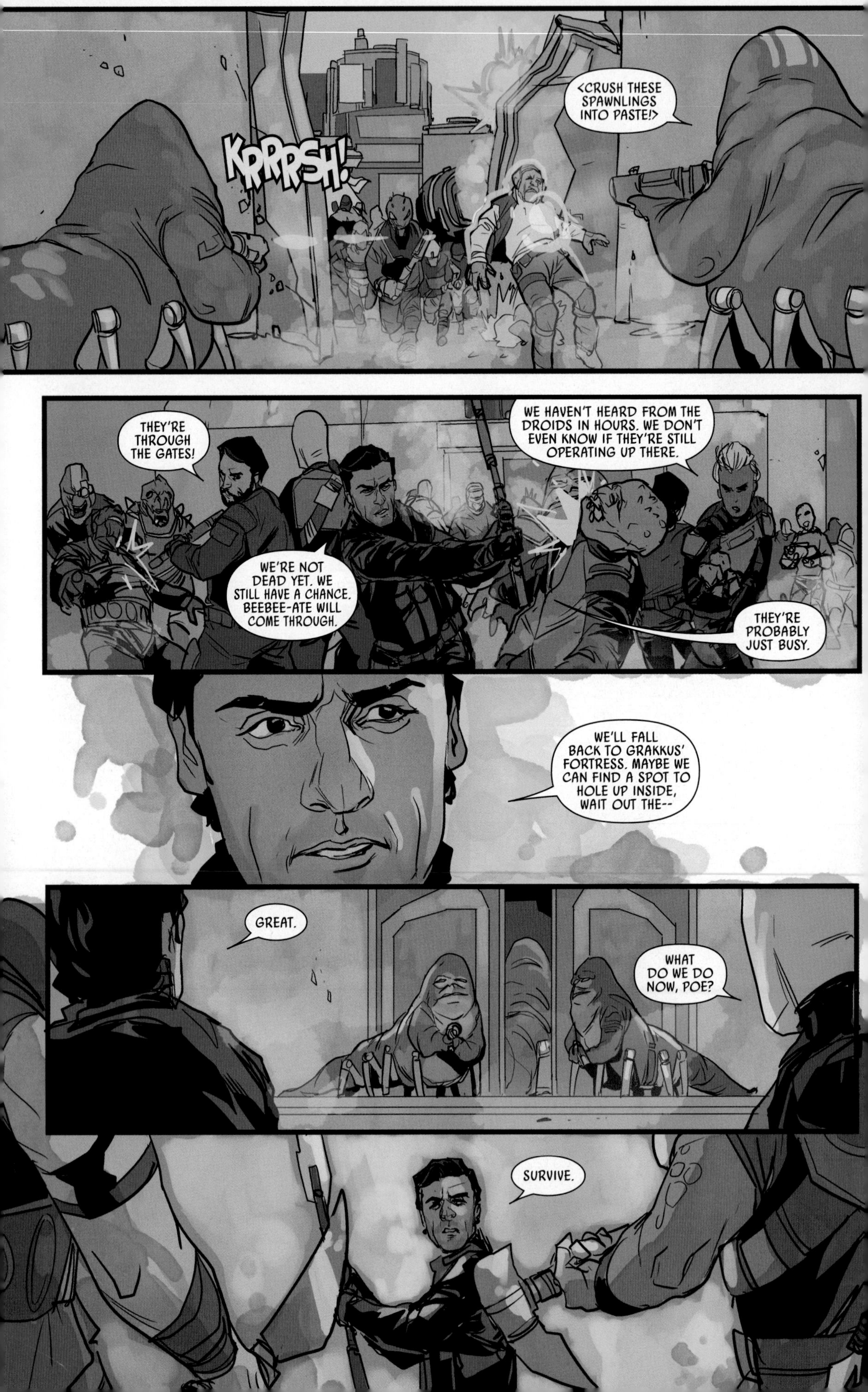
KRRRSH!
<CRUSH THESE SPAWNLINGS INTO PASTE!>
THEY'RE THROUGH THE GATES!
WE HAVEN'T HEARD FROM THE DROIDS IN HOURS. WE DON'T EVEN KNOW IF THEY'RE STILL OPERATING UP THERE.
WE'RE NOT DEAD YET. WE STILL HAVE A CHANCE. BEEBEE-ATE WILL COME THROUGH.
THEY'RE PROBABLY JUST BUSY.
WE'LL FALL BACK TO GRAKKUS' FORTRESS. MAYBE WE CAN FIND A SPOT TO HOLE UP INSIDE, WAIT OUT THE--
GREAT.
WHAT DO WE DO NOW, POE?
SURVIVE.

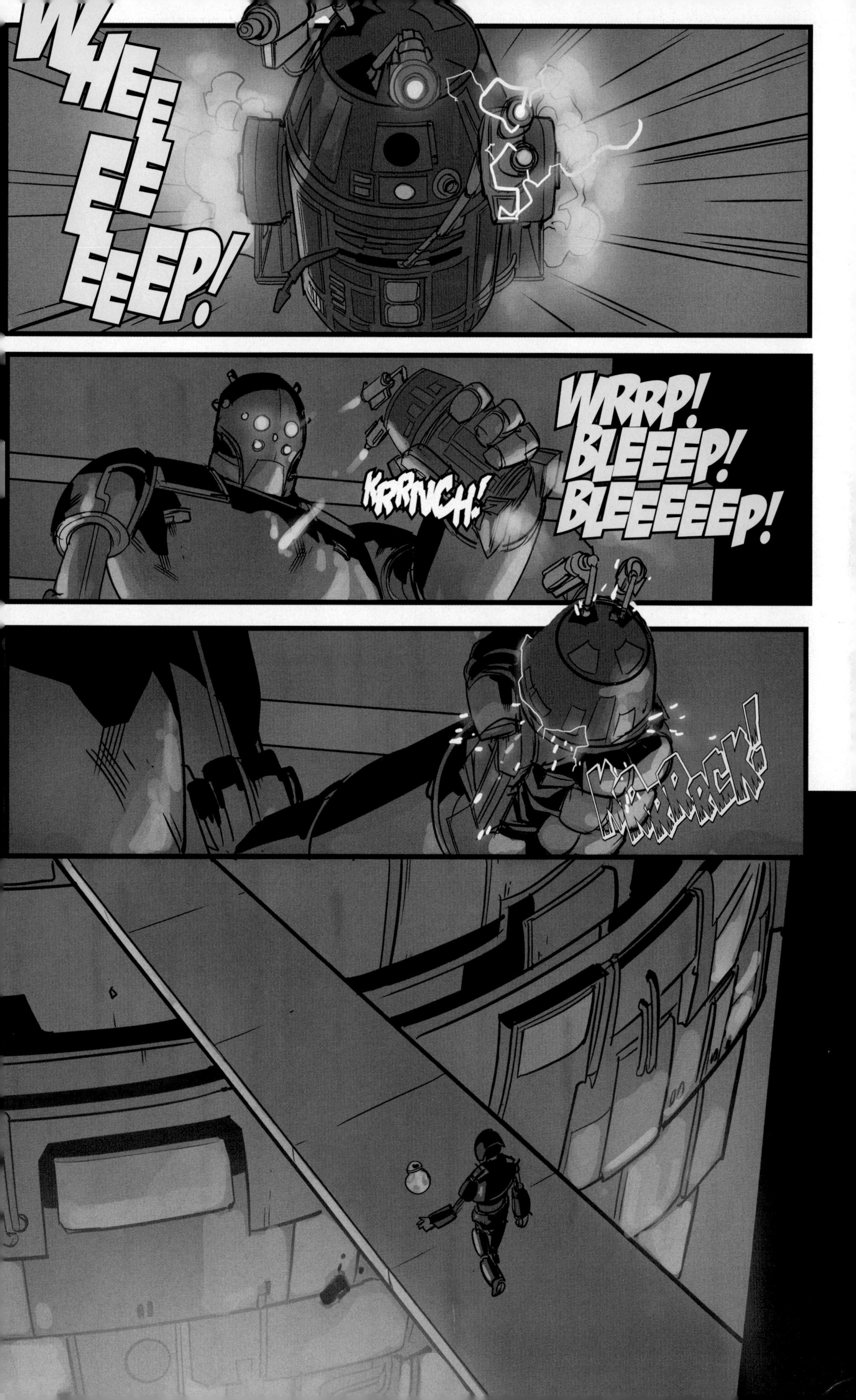
WHEEEEEEEEP!
KRRNCH!
WRRP! BLEEEP! BLEEEEEP!
KRRRCK!

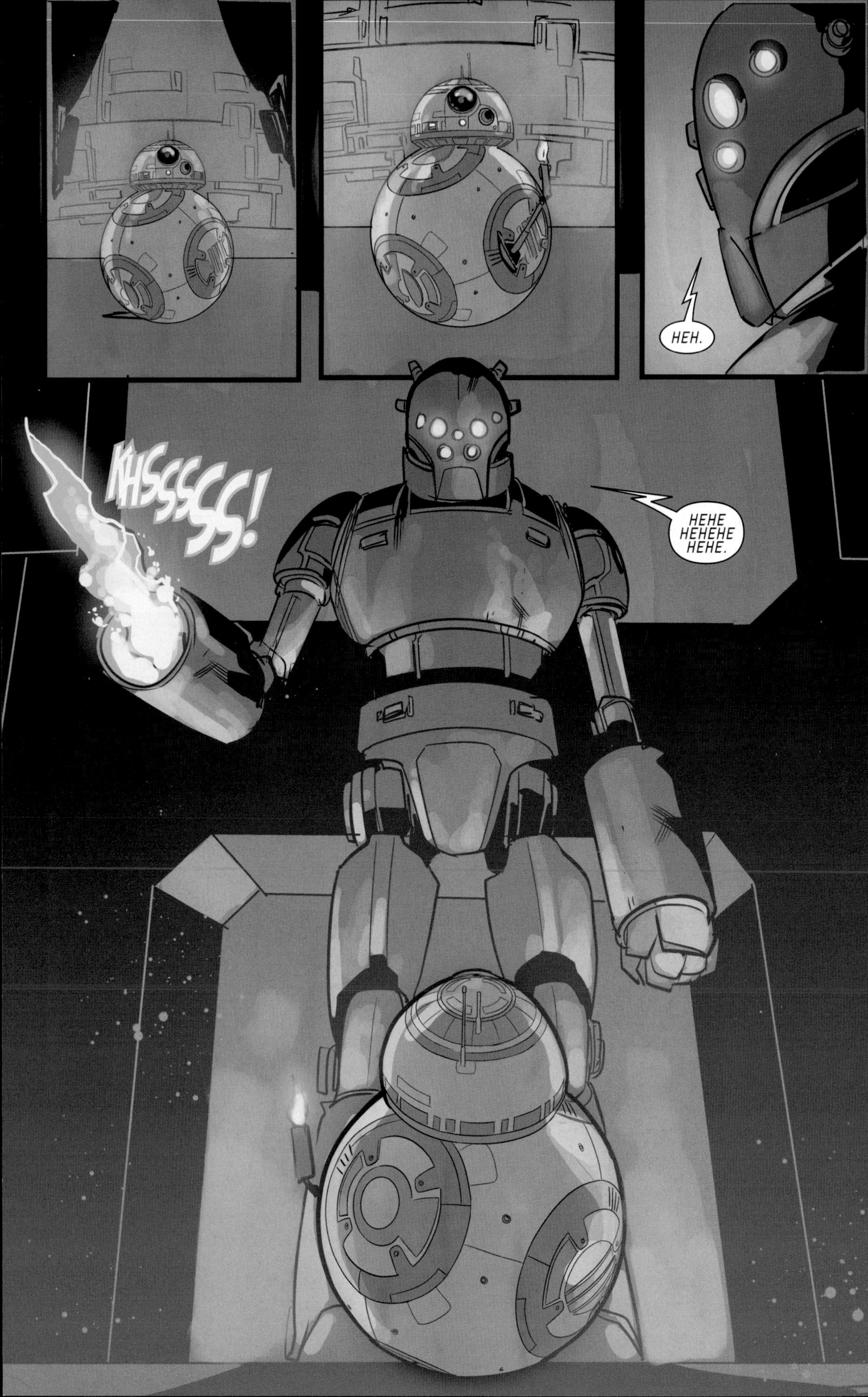
HEH.
KHSSSSSS!
HEHE HEHEHE HEHE.

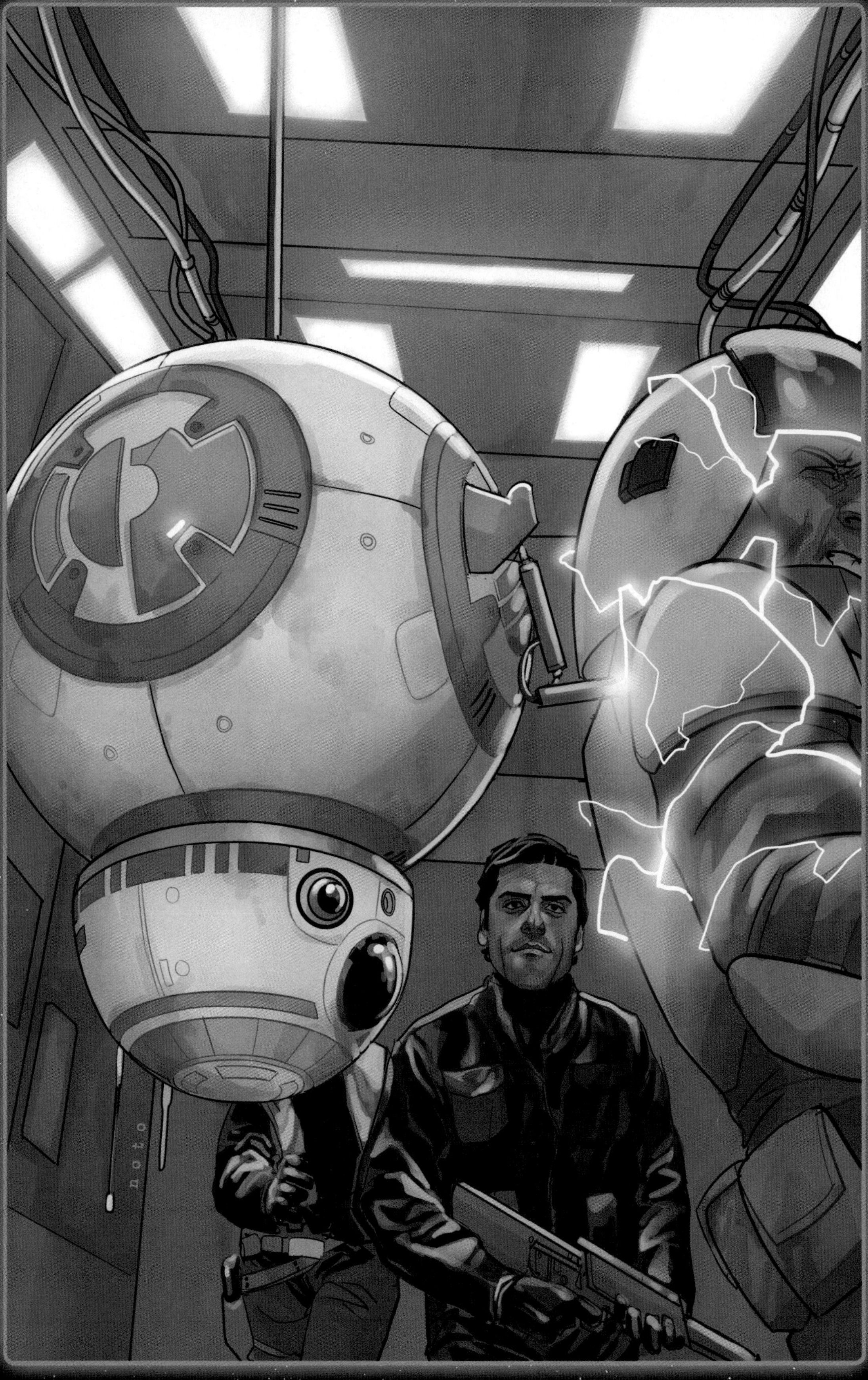
noto

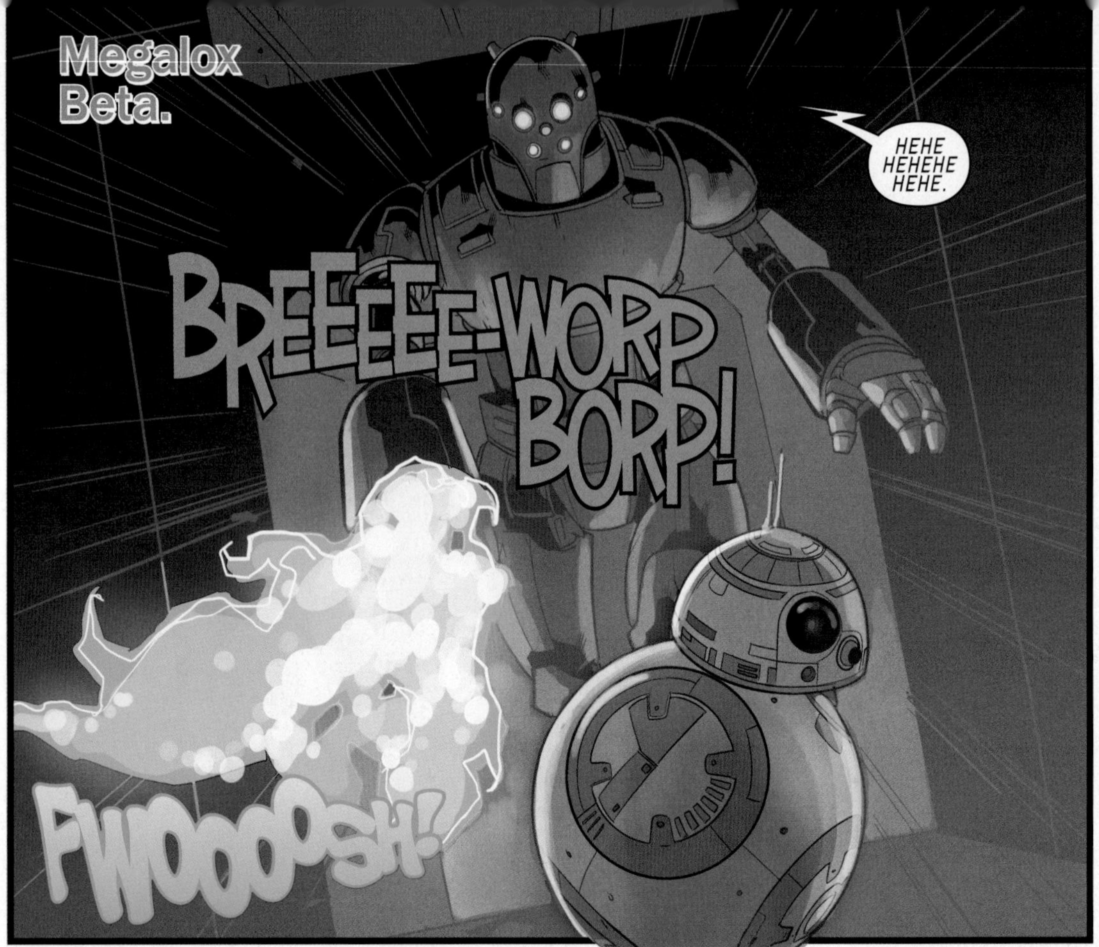
Megalox Beta.
HEHE HEHEHE HEHE.
BREEEEE-WORP BORP!
FWOOOOSH!

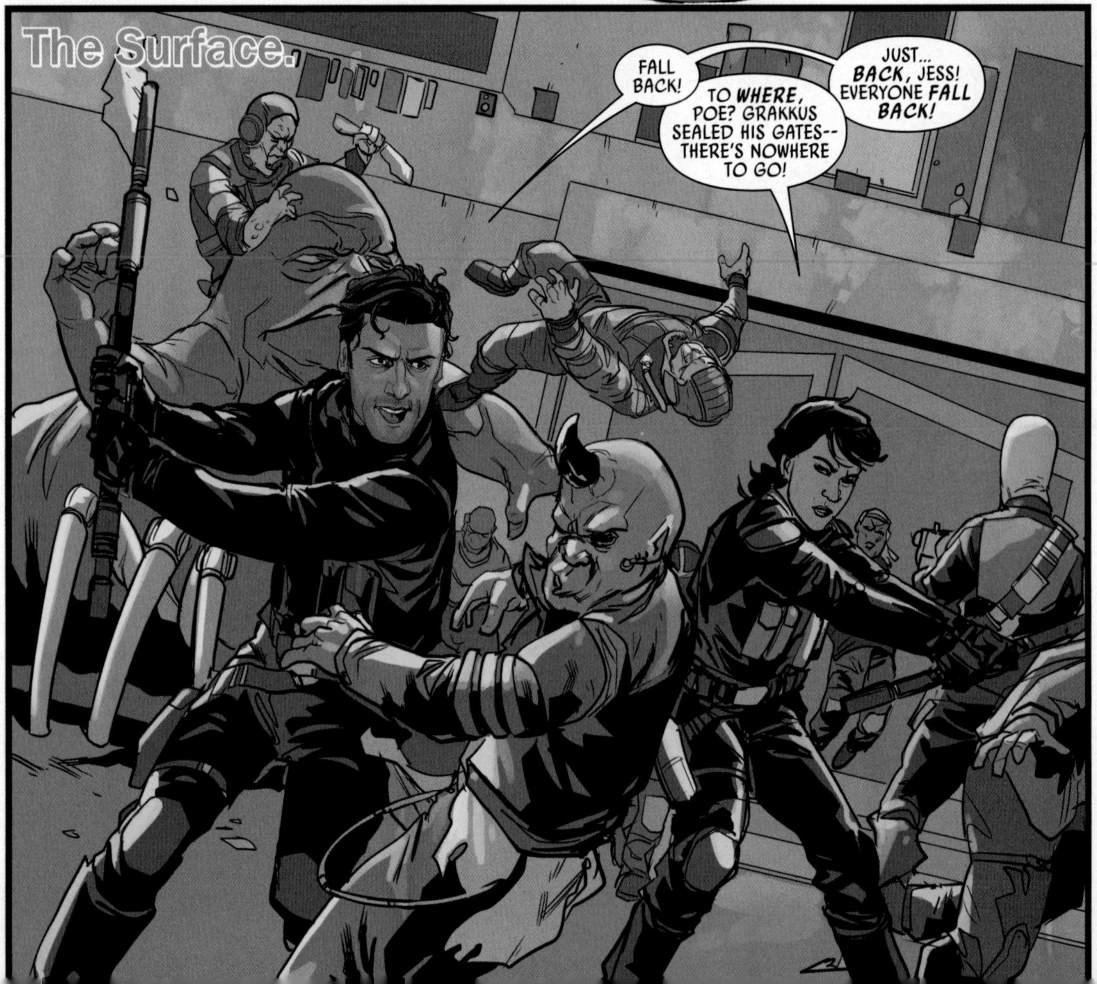
The Surface.
FALL BACK!
TO WHERE, POE? GRAKKUS SEALED HIS GATES-- THERE'S NOWHERE TO GO!
JUST... BACK, JESS! EVERYONE FALL BACK!

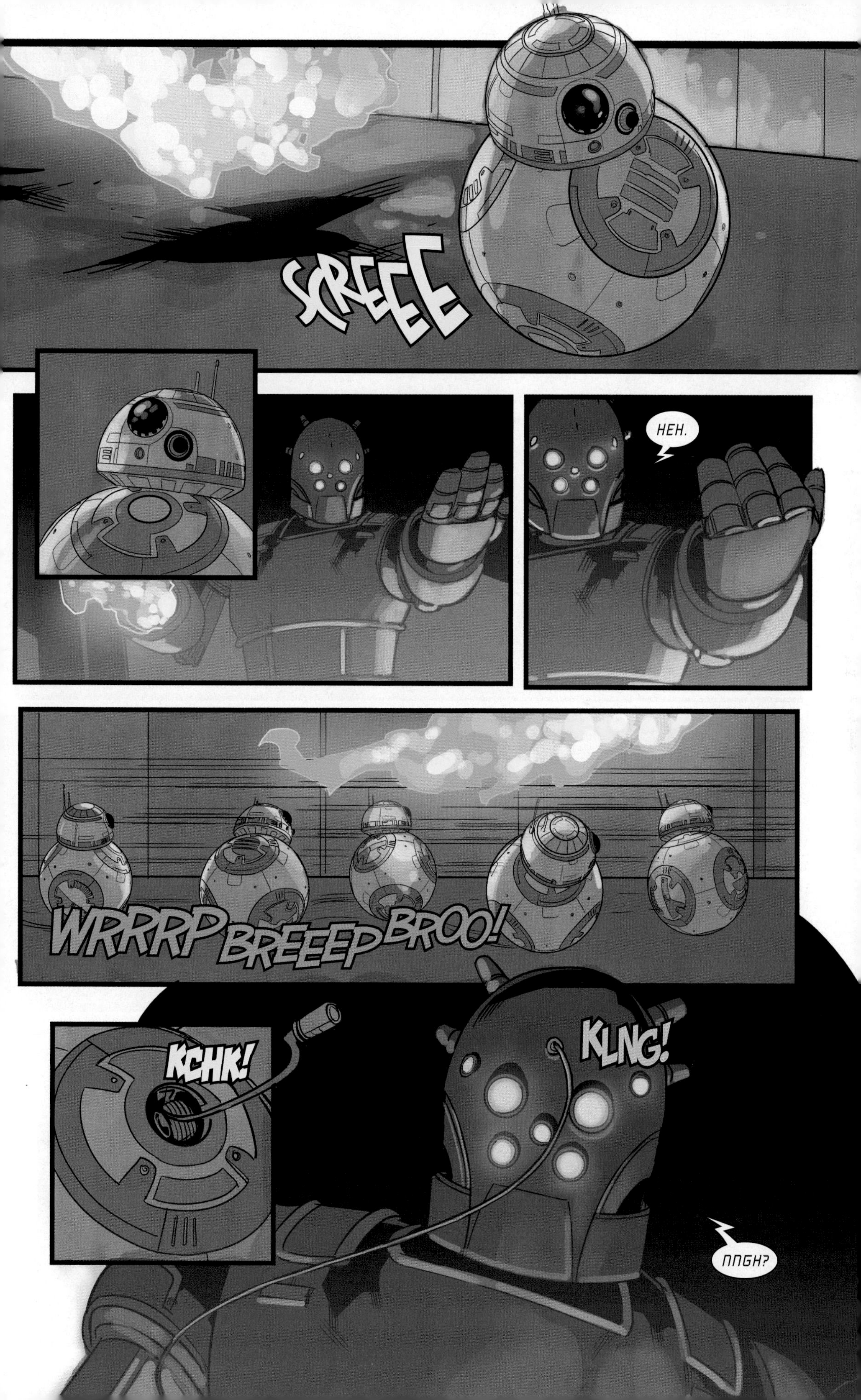
SCREEEE
HEH.
WRRRP BREEEEP BROO!
KCHK!
KLNG!
NNGH?

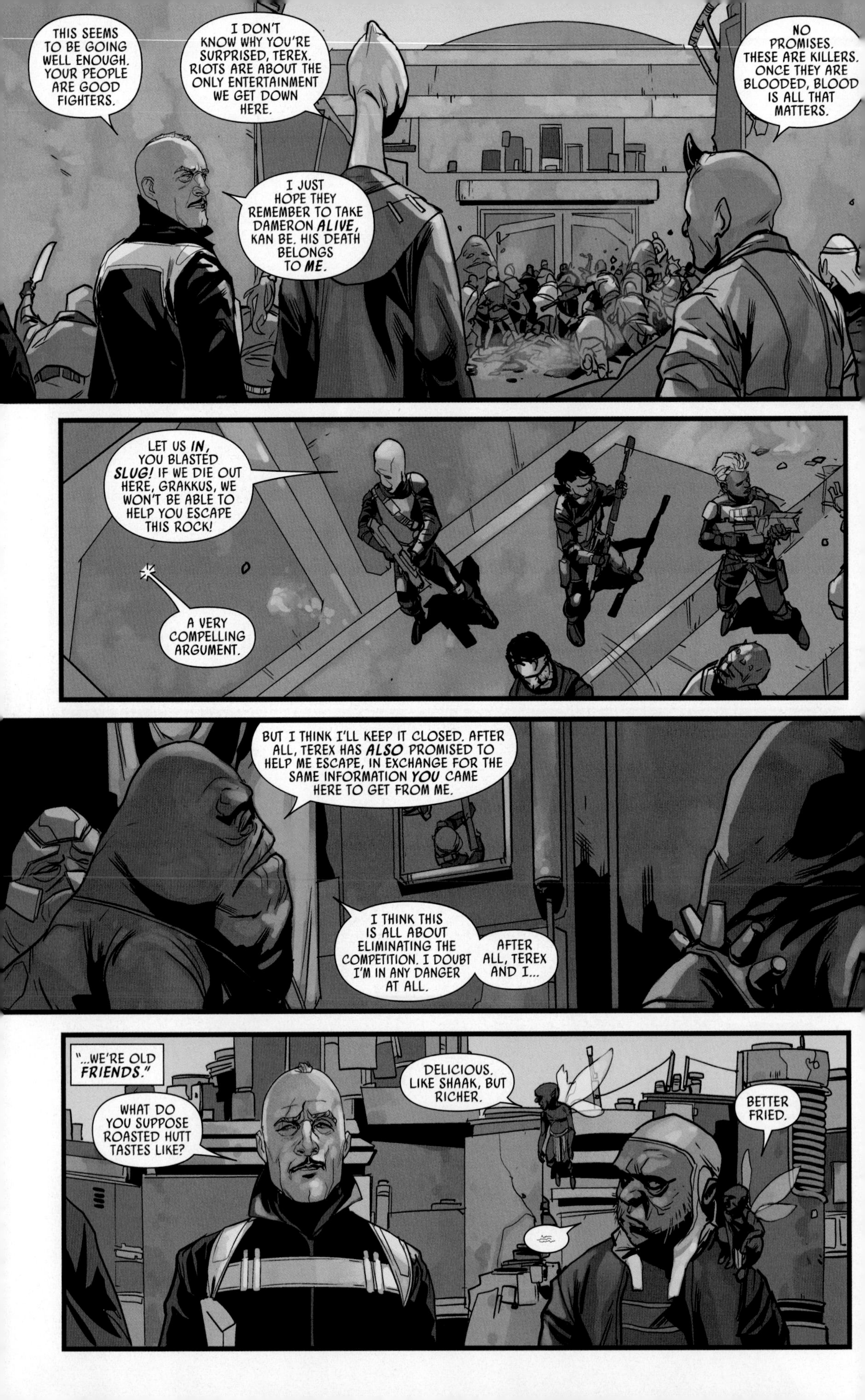

THIS SEEMS TO BE GOING WELL ENOUGH. YOUR PEOPLE ARE GOOD FIGHTERS.
I DON'T KNOW WHY YOU'RE SURPRISED, TEREX. RIOTS ARE ABOUT THE ONLY ENTERTAINMENT WE GET DOWN HERE.
NO PROMISES. THESE ARE KILLERS. ONCE THEY ARE BLOODED, BLOOD IS ALL THAT MATTERS.
I JUST HOPE THEY REMEMBER TO TAKE DAMERON *ALIVE*, KAN BE. HIS DEATH BELONGS TO *ME*.
LET US *IN*, YOU BLASTED *SLUG!* IF WE DIE OUT HERE, GRAKKUS, WE WON'T BE ABLE TO HELP YOU ESCAPE THIS ROCK!
A VERY COMPELLING ARGUMENT.
BUT I THINK I'LL KEEP IT CLOSED. AFTER ALL, TEREX HAS *ALSO* PROMISED TO HELP ME ESCAPE, IN EXCHANGE FOR THE SAME INFORMATION *YOU* CAME HERE TO GET FROM ME.
I THINK THIS IS ALL ABOUT ELIMINATING THE COMPETITION. I DOUBT I'M IN ANY DANGER AT ALL.
AFTER ALL, TEREX AND I...
"...WE'RE OLD *FRIENDS*."
WHAT DO YOU SUPPOSE ROASTED HUTT TASTES LIKE?
DELICIOUS. LIKE SHAAK, BUT RICHER.
BETTER FRIED.

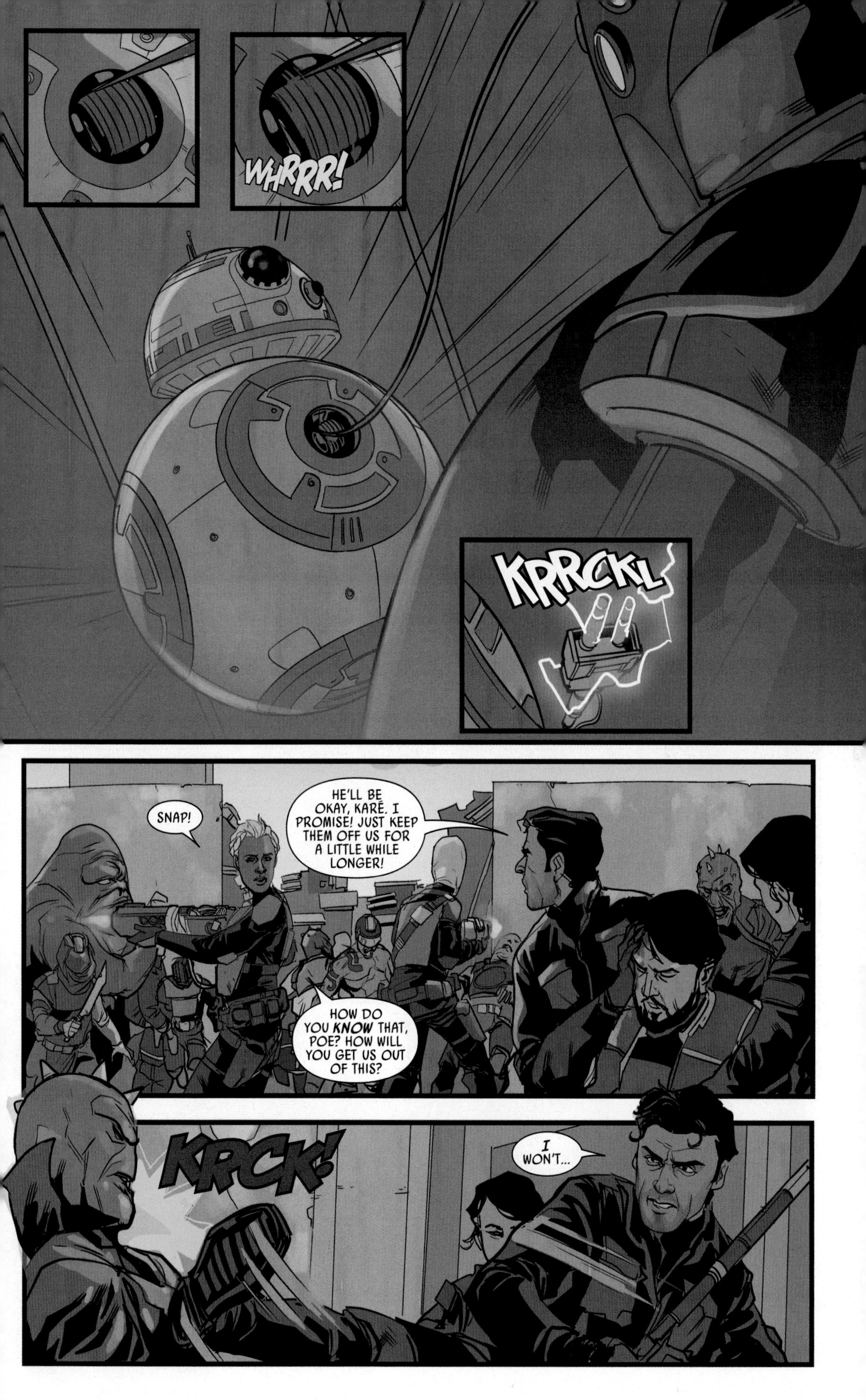
WHRRR!
KRRCKL
SNAP!
HE'LL BE OKAY, KARÉ. I PROMISE! JUST KEEP THEM OFF US FOR A LITTLE WHILE LONGER!
HOW DO YOU KNOW THAT, POE? HOW WILL YOU GET US OUT OF THIS?
KRCK!
I WON'T...

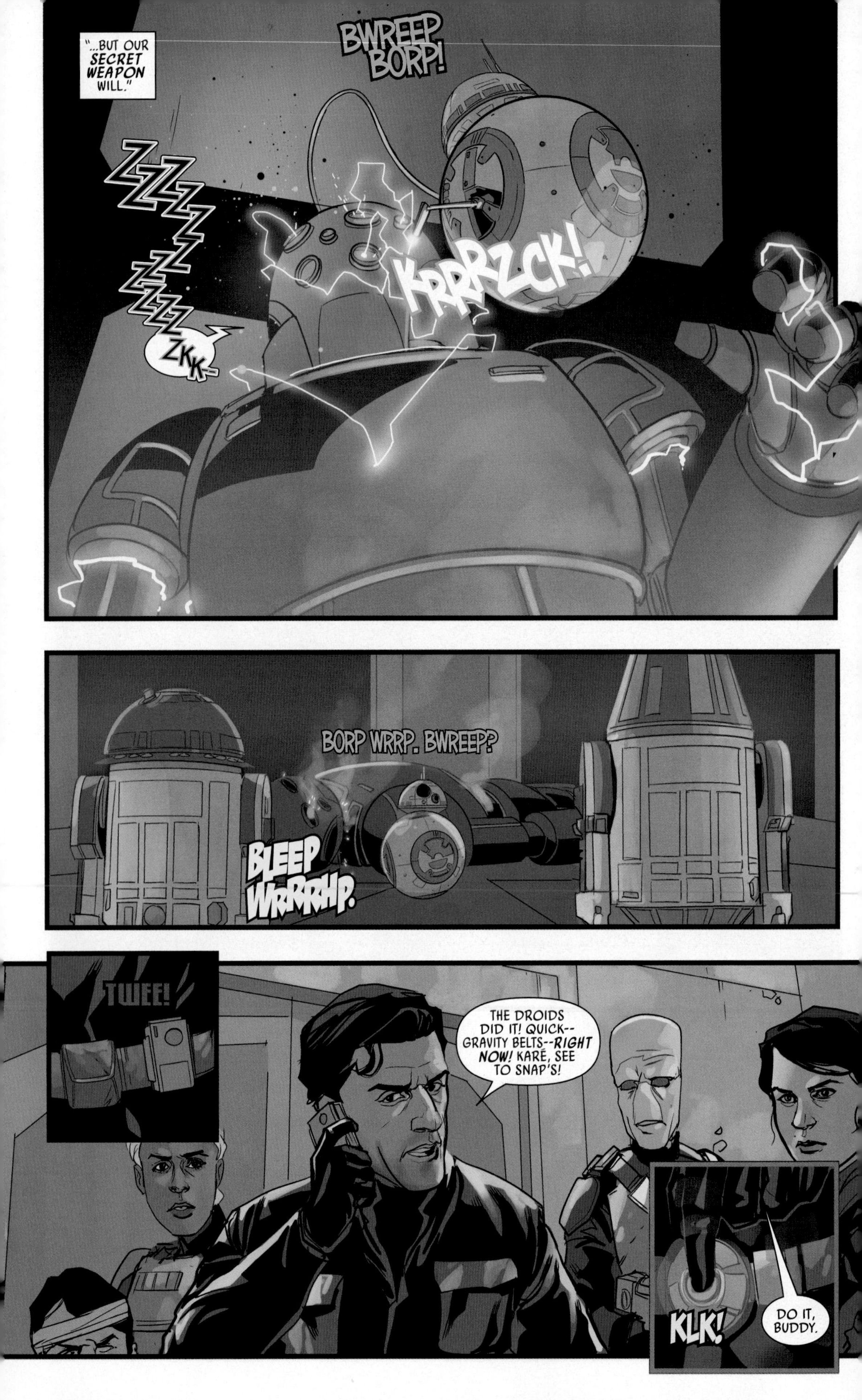

"...BUT OUR SECRET WEAPON WILL."
BWREEP BORP!
ZZZZZZZZ
KRRRZCK!
ZKK-
BORP WRRP. BWREEP?
BLEEP WRRRHP.
TWEE!
THE DROIDS DID IT! QUICK--GRAVITY BELTS--RIGHT NOW! KARÉ, SEE TO SNAP'S!
KLK!
DO IT, BUDDY.

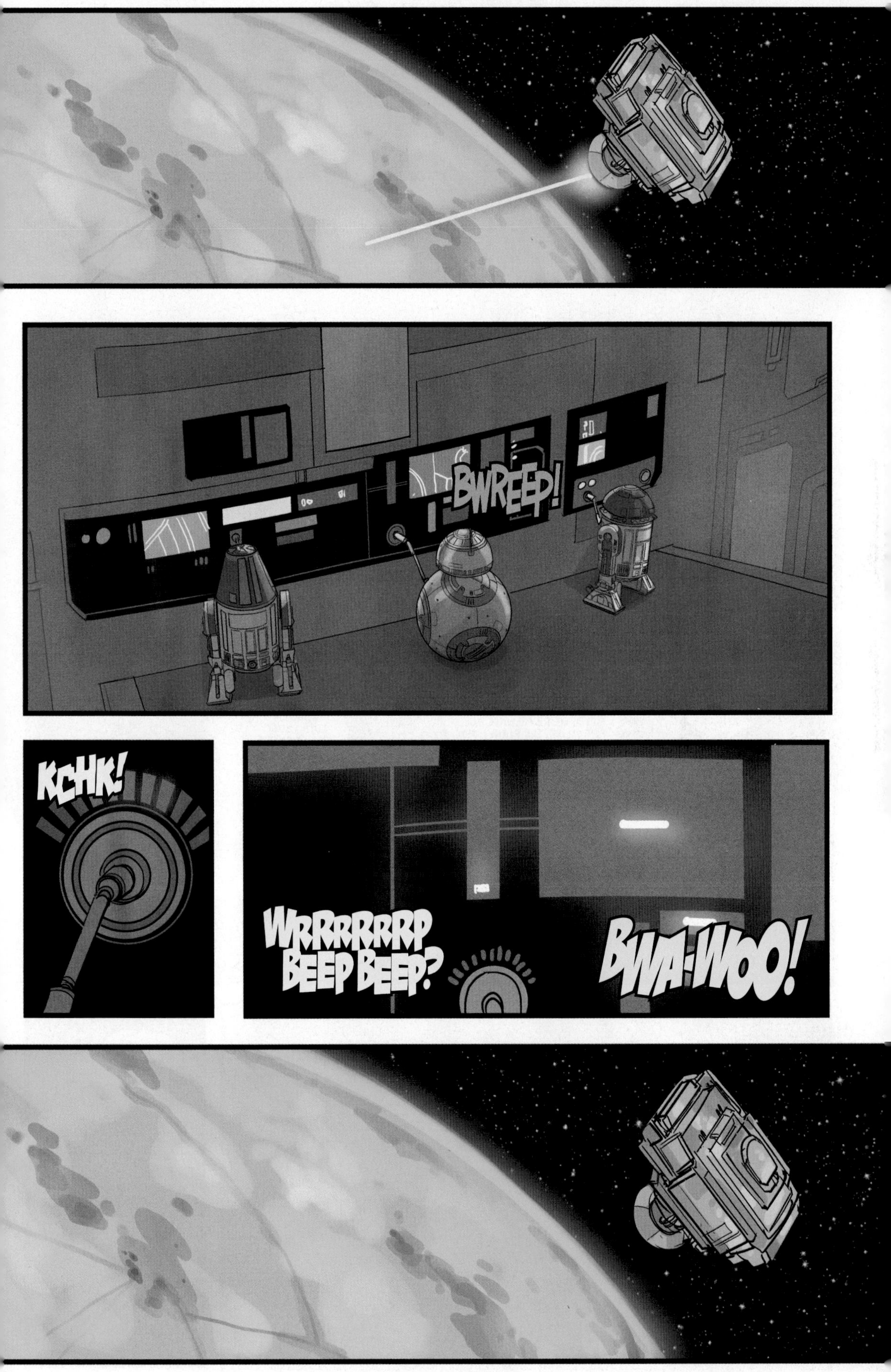
BWREEP!
KCHK!
WRRRRRRP BEEP BEEP?
BWA-WOO!

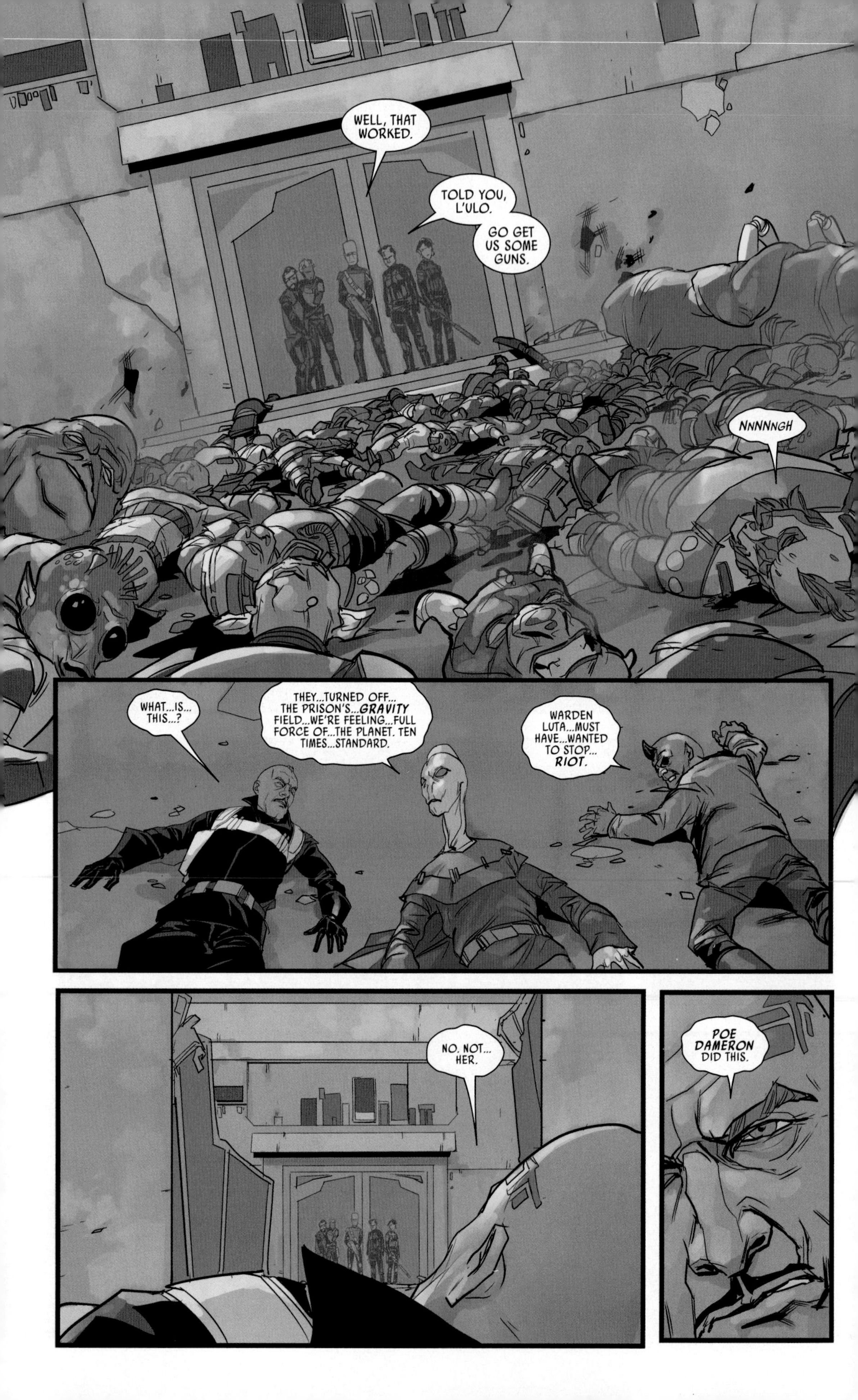
WELL, THAT WORKED.
TOLD YOU, L'ULO.
GO GET US SOME GUNS.
NNNNNGH
WHAT...IS... THIS...?
THEY...TURNED OFF... THE PRISON'S...GRAVITY FIELD...WE'RE FEELING...FULL FORCE OF...THE PLANET. TEN TIMES...STANDARD.
WARDEN LUTA...MUST HAVE...WANTED TO STOP... RIOT.
NO. NOT... HER.
POE DAMERON DID THIS.

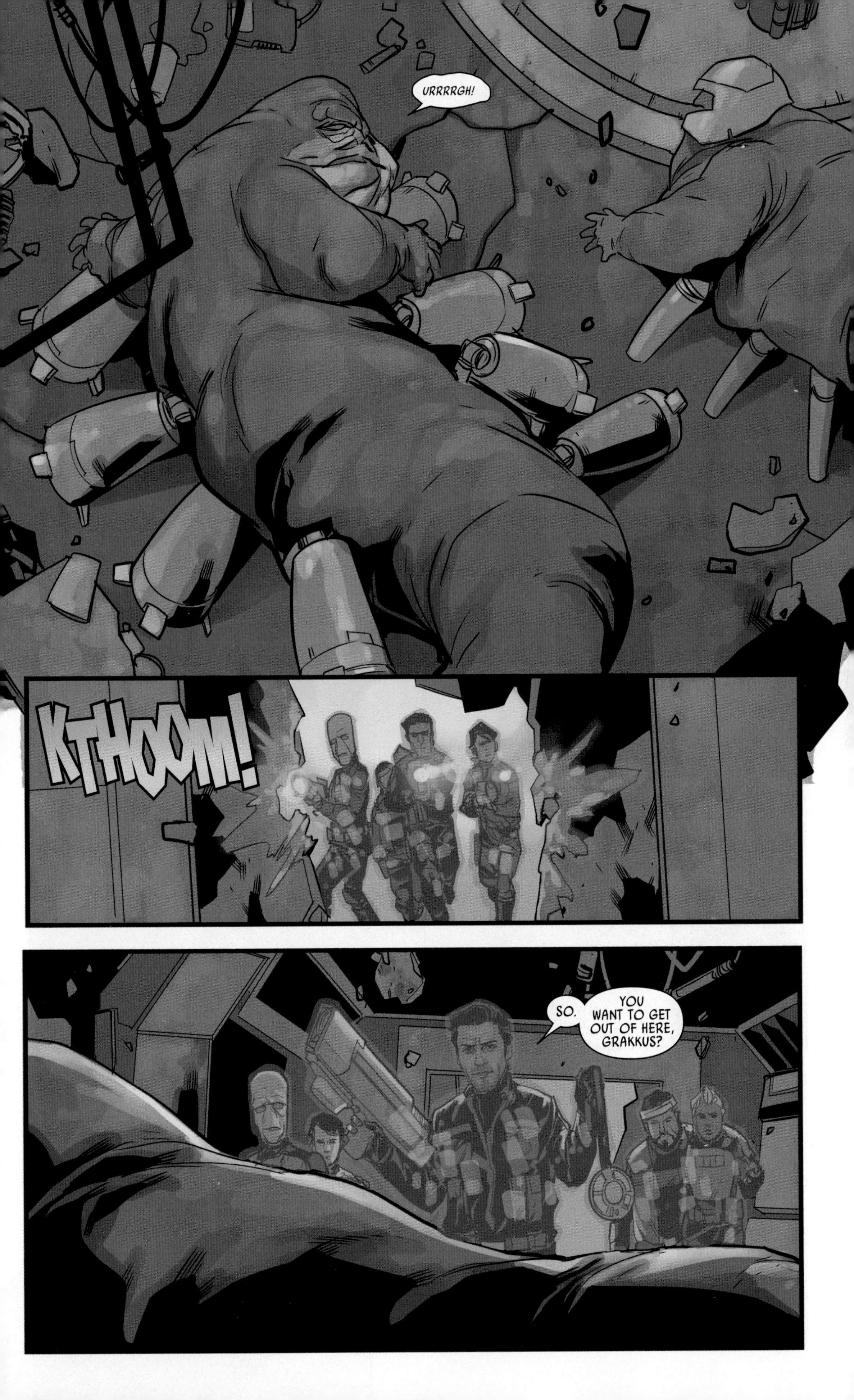
URRRRGH!
KTHOOM!
SO.
YOU WANT TO GET OUT OF HERE, GRAKKUS?

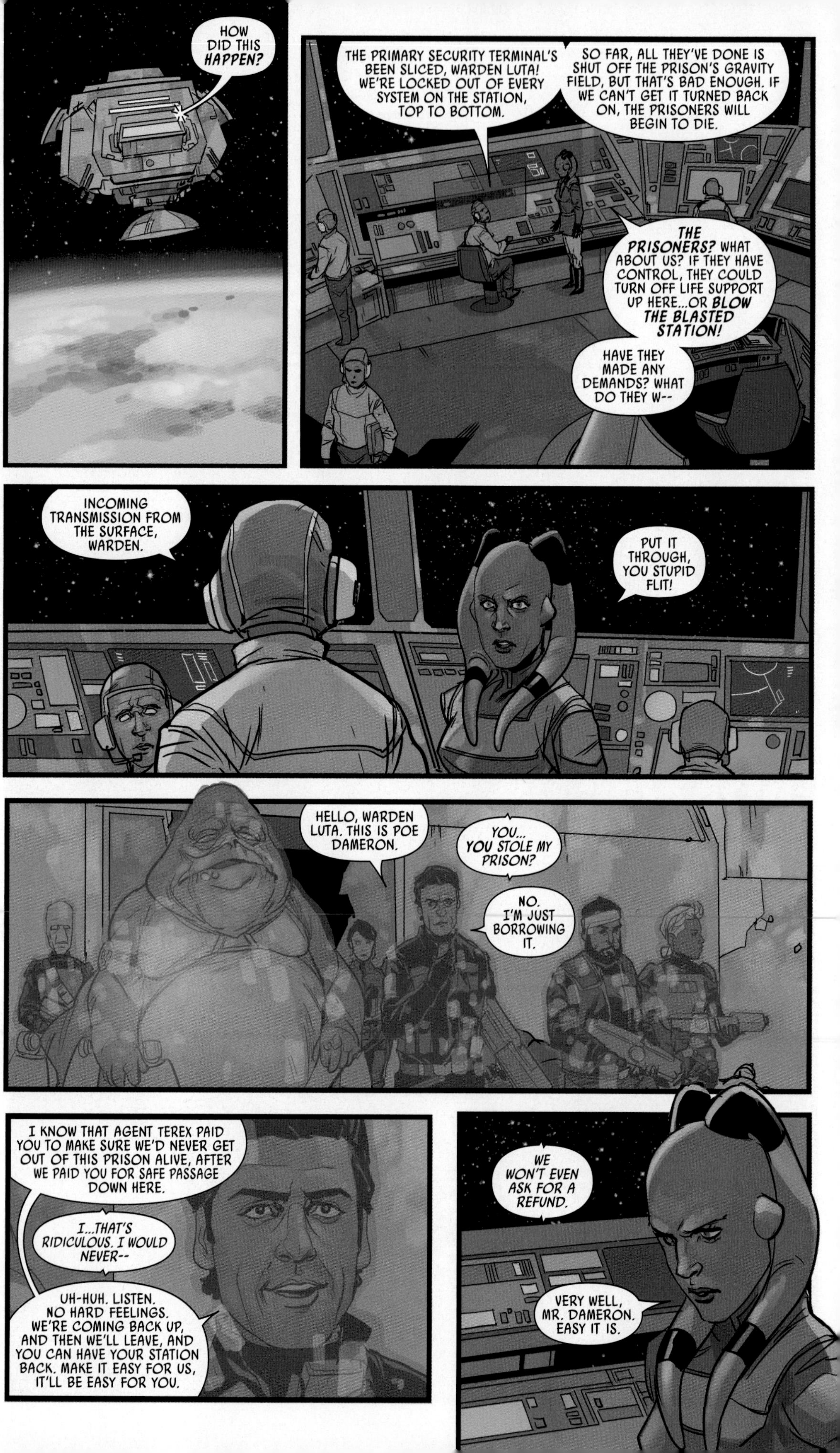

HOW DID THIS *HAPPEN?*
THE PRIMARY SECURITY TERMINAL'S BEEN SLICED, WARDEN LUTA! WE'RE LOCKED OUT OF EVERY SYSTEM ON THE STATION, TOP TO BOTTOM.
SO FAR, ALL THEY'VE DONE IS SHUT OFF THE PRISON'S GRAVITY FIELD, BUT THAT'S BAD ENOUGH. IF WE CAN'T GET IT TURNED BACK ON, THE PRISONERS WILL BEGIN TO DIE.
THE PRISONERS? WHAT ABOUT US? IF THEY HAVE CONTROL, THEY COULD TURN OFF LIFE SUPPORT UP HERE...OR ***BLOW THE BLASTED STATION!***
HAVE THEY MADE ANY DEMANDS? WHAT DO THEY W--
INCOMING TRANSMISSION FROM THE SURFACE, WARDEN.
PUT IT THROUGH, YOU STUPID FLIT!
HELLO, WARDEN LUTA. THIS IS POE DAMERON.
*YOU... **YOU** STOLE MY PRISON?*
NO. I'M JUST BORROWING IT.
I KNOW THAT AGENT TEREX PAID YOU TO MAKE SURE WE'D NEVER GET OUT OF THIS PRISON ALIVE, AFTER WE PAID YOU FOR SAFE PASSAGE DOWN HERE.
I...THAT'S RIDICULOUS. I WOULD NEVER--
UH-HUH. LISTEN. NO HARD FEELINGS. WE'RE COMING BACK UP, AND THEN WE'LL LEAVE, AND YOU CAN HAVE YOUR STATION BACK. MAKE IT EASY FOR US, IT'LL BE EASY FOR YOU.
WE WON'T EVEN ASK FOR A REFUND.
VERY WELL, MR. DAMERON. EASY IT IS.

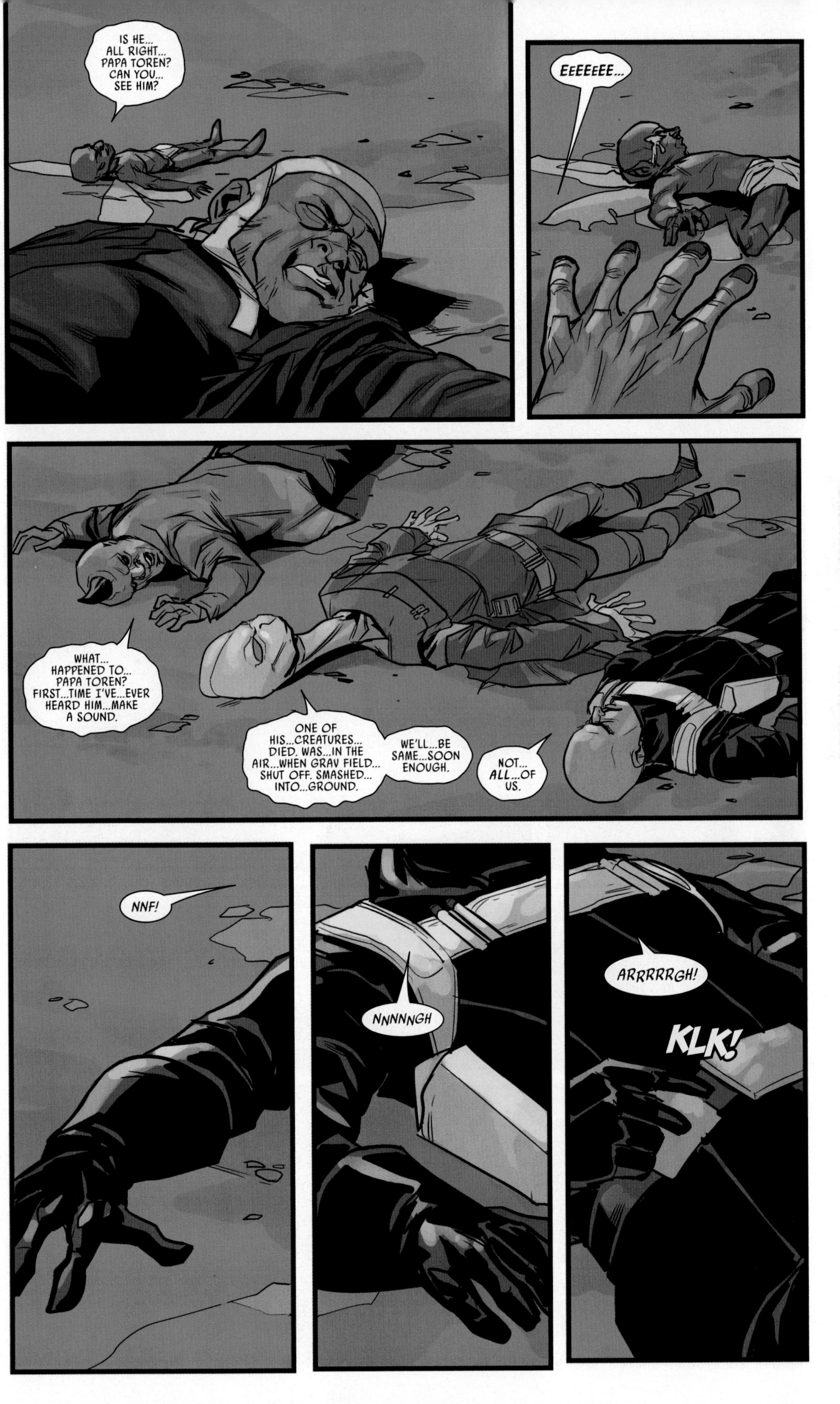
IS HE... ALL RIGHT... PAPA TOREN? CAN YOU... SEE HIM?
EEEEEEE...
WHAT... HAPPENED TO... PAPA TOREN? FIRST...TIME I'VE...EVER HEARD HIM...MAKE A SOUND.
ONE OF HIS...CREATURES... DIED. WAS...IN THE AIR...WHEN GRAV FIELD... SHUT OFF. SMASHED... INTO...GROUND.
WE'LL...BE SAME...SOON ENOUGH.
NOT... ALL...OF US.
NNF!
NNNNNGH
ARRRRRGH!
KLK!

HELLO... BEAUTIFUL.

KRRNCH

KRRR

WHERE... ARE YOU...GOING? YOU...PROMISED TO... TAKE US OUT OF HERE... IF WE HELPED...WITH GRAKKUS.

DID I?

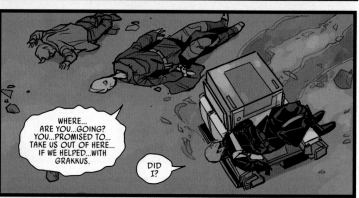

AH, THAT'S BETTER. THE *SPIKE* HAS ITS OWN GRAVITY FIELD, OF COURSE. WHY, I FEEL A THOUSAND KILOS LIGHTER.

AS I REMEMBER IT, GENTLEMEN, I AGREED TO HELP YOU ESCAPE IF YOU KILLED GRAKKUS, POE DAMERON, AND HIS SQUADRON.

THEY'RE ALL STILL *ALIVE*, WHICH MEANS I OWE YOU...

NO! PLEASE!

YOU...WILL *DIE*...FOR THIS... TEREX! ISIN WILL... COME...FOR YOU!

...NOTHING.

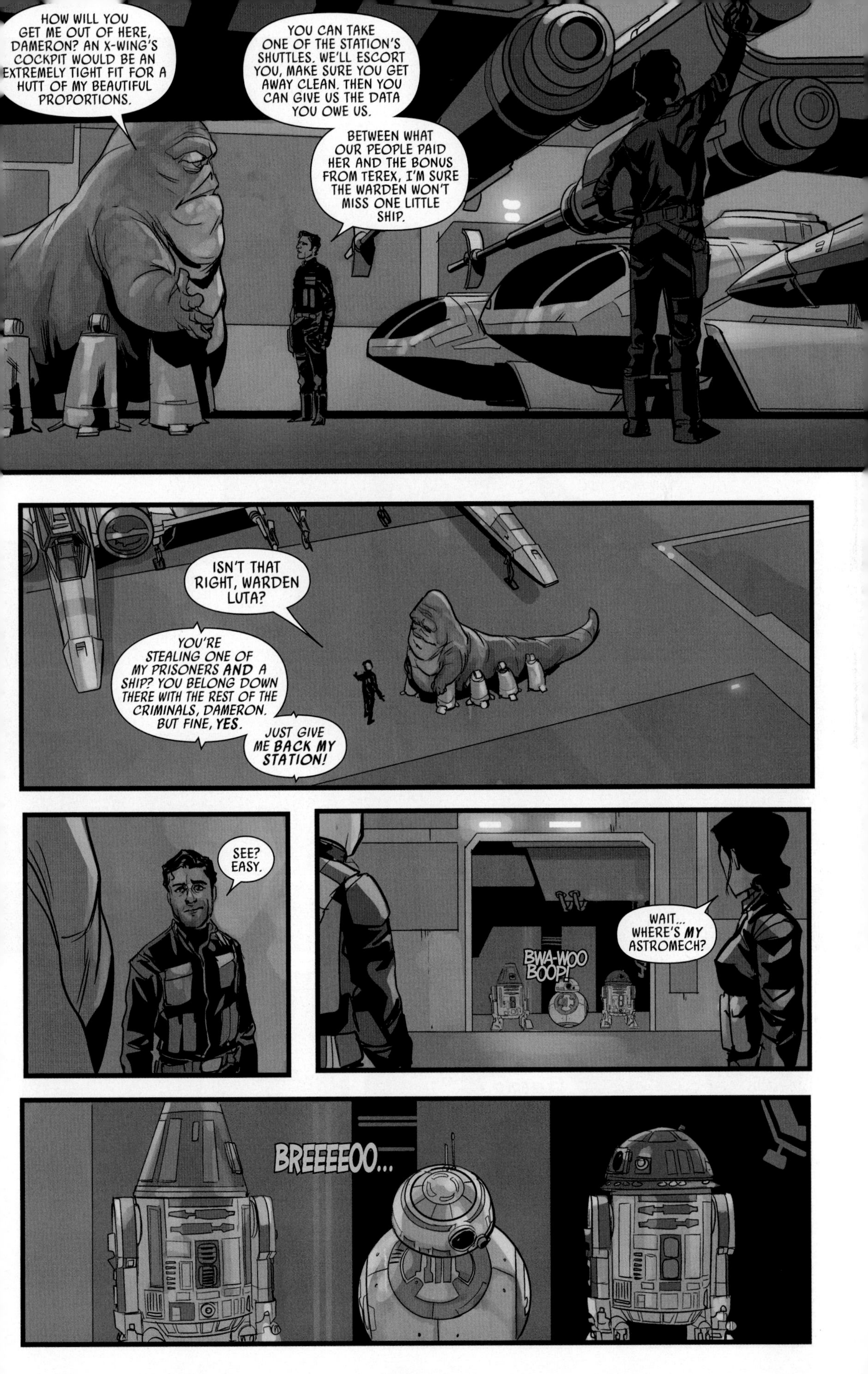
HOW WILL YOU GET ME OUT OF HERE, DAMERON? AN X-WING'S COCKPIT WOULD BE AN EXTREMELY TIGHT FIT FOR A HUTT OF MY BEAUTIFUL PROPORTIONS.
YOU CAN TAKE ONE OF THE STATION'S SHUTTLES. WE'LL ESCORT YOU, MAKE SURE YOU GET AWAY CLEAN. THEN YOU CAN GIVE US THE DATA YOU OWE US.
BETWEEN WHAT OUR PEOPLE PAID HER AND THE BONUS FROM TEREX, I'M SURE THE WARDEN WON'T MISS ONE LITTLE SHIP.
ISN'T THAT RIGHT, WARDEN LUTA?
YOU'RE STEALING ONE OF MY PRISONERS AND A SHIP? YOU BELONG DOWN THERE WITH THE REST OF THE CRIMINALS, DAMERON. BUT FINE, YES.
JUST GIVE ME BACK MY STATION!
SEE? EASY.
WAIT... WHERE'S MY ASTROMECH?
BWA-WOO BOOP!
BREEEEOO...

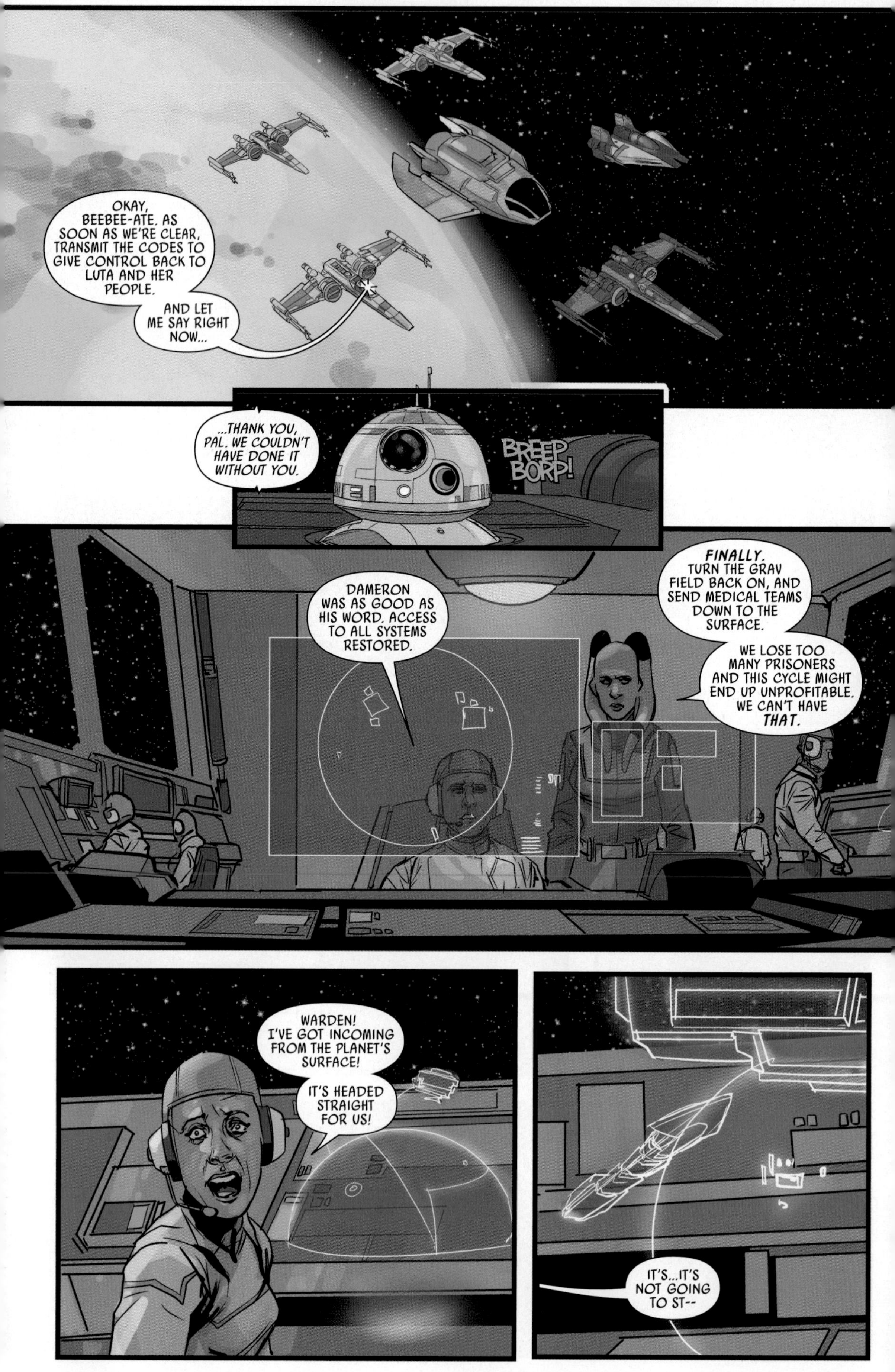
OKAY, BEEBEE-ATE. AS SOON AS WE'RE CLEAR, TRANSMIT THE CODES TO GIVE CONTROL BACK TO LUTA AND HER PEOPLE.
AND LET ME SAY RIGHT NOW...
...THANK YOU, PAL. WE COULDN'T HAVE DONE IT WITHOUT YOU.
BREEP BORP!
DAMERON WAS AS GOOD AS HIS WORD. ACCESS TO ALL SYSTEMS RESTORED.
FINALLY. TURN THE GRAV FIELD BACK ON, AND SEND MEDICAL TEAMS DOWN TO THE SURFACE.
WE LOSE TOO MANY PRISONERS AND THIS CYCLE MIGHT END UP UNPROFITABLE. WE CAN'T HAVE THAT.
WARDEN! I'VE GOT INCOMING FROM THE PLANET'S SURFACE!
IT'S HEADED STRAIGHT FOR US!
IT'S...IT'S NOT GOING TO ST--

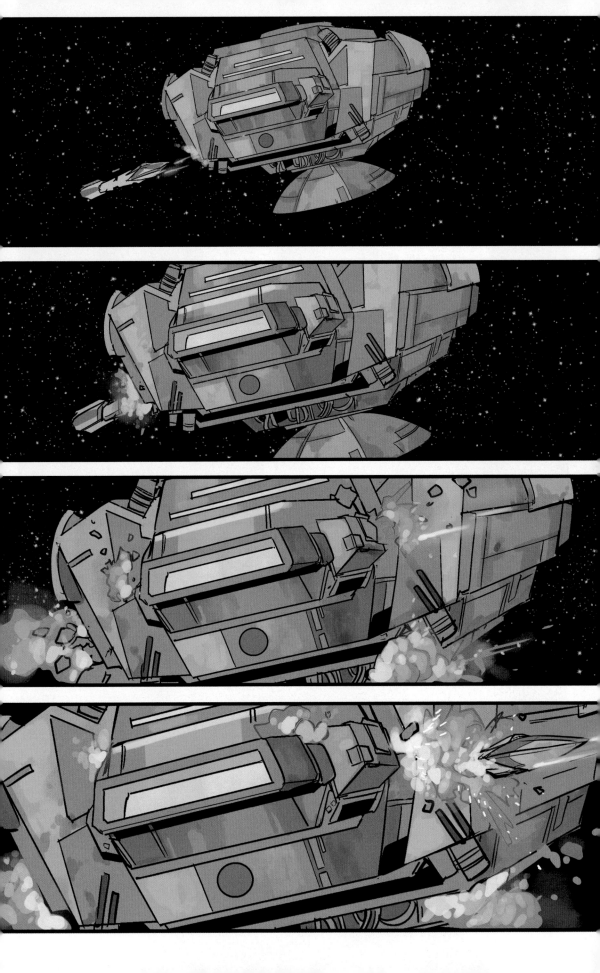

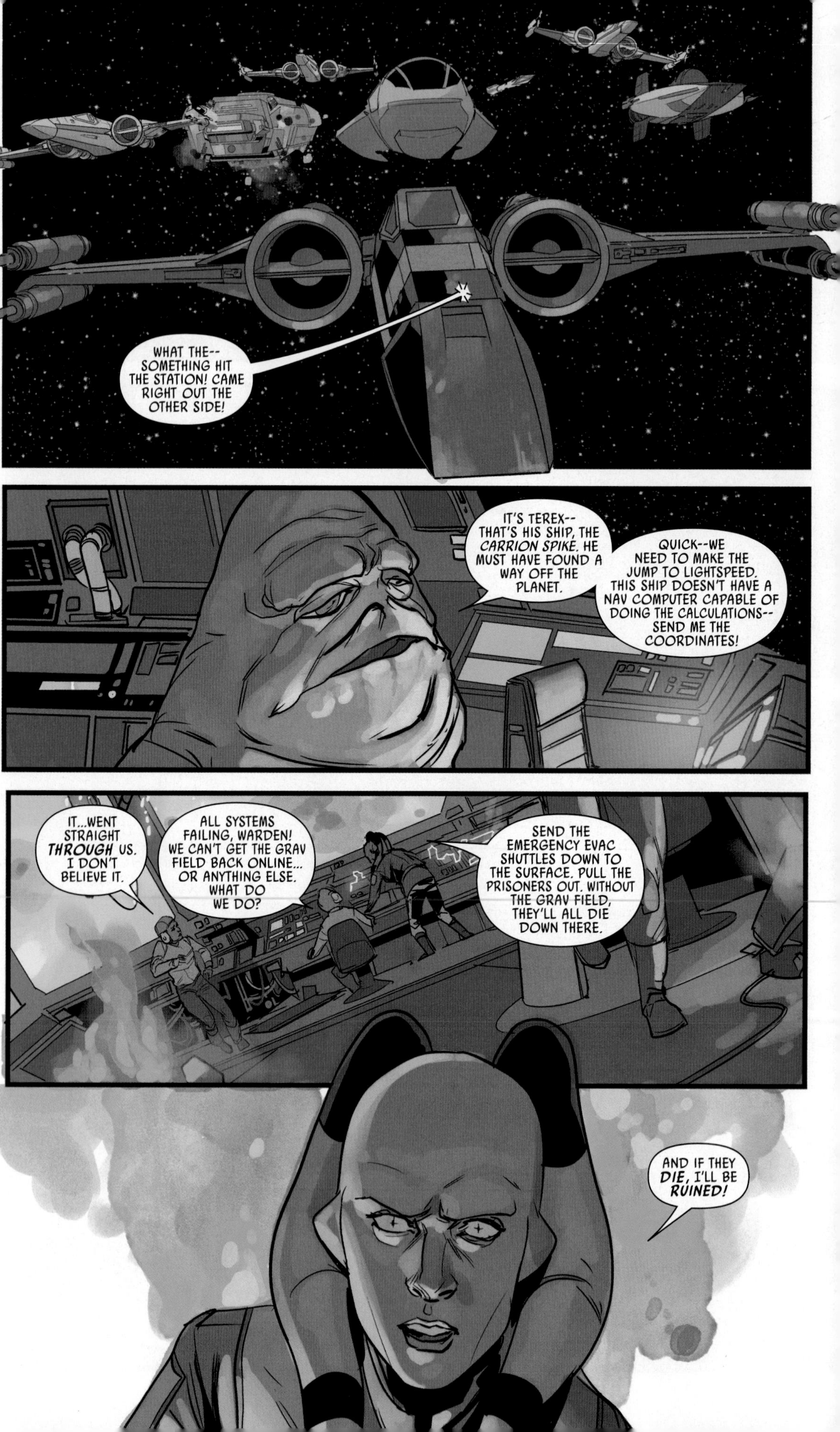
WHAT THE-- SOMETHING HIT THE STATION! CAME RIGHT OUT THE OTHER SIDE!
IT'S TEREX-- THAT'S HIS SHIP, THE *CARRION SPIKE.* HE MUST HAVE FOUND A WAY OFF THE PLANET.
QUICK--WE NEED TO MAKE THE JUMP TO LIGHTSPEED. THIS SHIP DOESN'T HAVE A NAV COMPUTER CAPABLE OF DOING THE CALCULATIONS-- SEND ME THE COORDINATES!
IT...WENT STRAIGHT ***THROUGH*** US. I DON'T BELIEVE IT.
ALL SYSTEMS FAILING, WARDEN! WE CAN'T GET THE GRAV FIELD BACK ONLINE... OR ANYTHING ELSE. WHAT DO WE DO?
SEND THE EMERGENCY EVAC SHUTTLES DOWN TO THE SURFACE. PULL THE PRISONERS OUT. WITHOUT THE GRAV FIELD, THEY'LL ALL DIE DOWN THERE.
AND IF THEY ***DIE***, I'LL BE ***RUINED!***

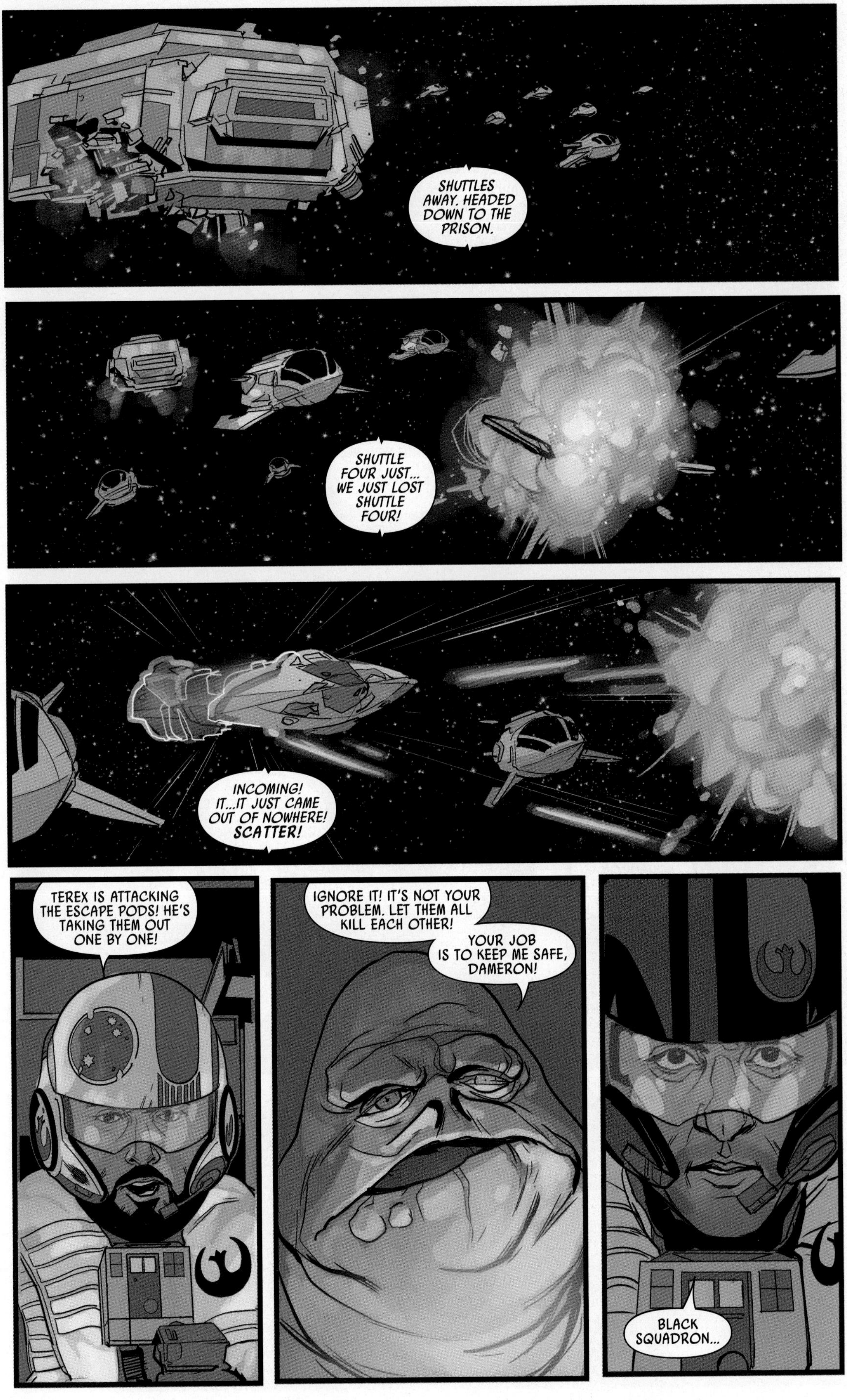
SHUTTLES AWAY. HEADED DOWN TO THE PRISON.
SHUTTLE FOUR JUST... WE JUST LOST SHUTTLE FOUR!
INCOMING! IT...IT JUST CAME OUT OF NOWHERE! SCATTER!
TEREX IS ATTACKING THE ESCAPE PODS! HE'S TAKING THEM OUT ONE BY ONE!
IGNORE IT! IT'S NOT YOUR PROBLEM. LET THEM ALL KILL EACH OTHER!
YOUR JOB IS TO KEEP ME SAFE, DAMERON!
BLACK SQUADRON...

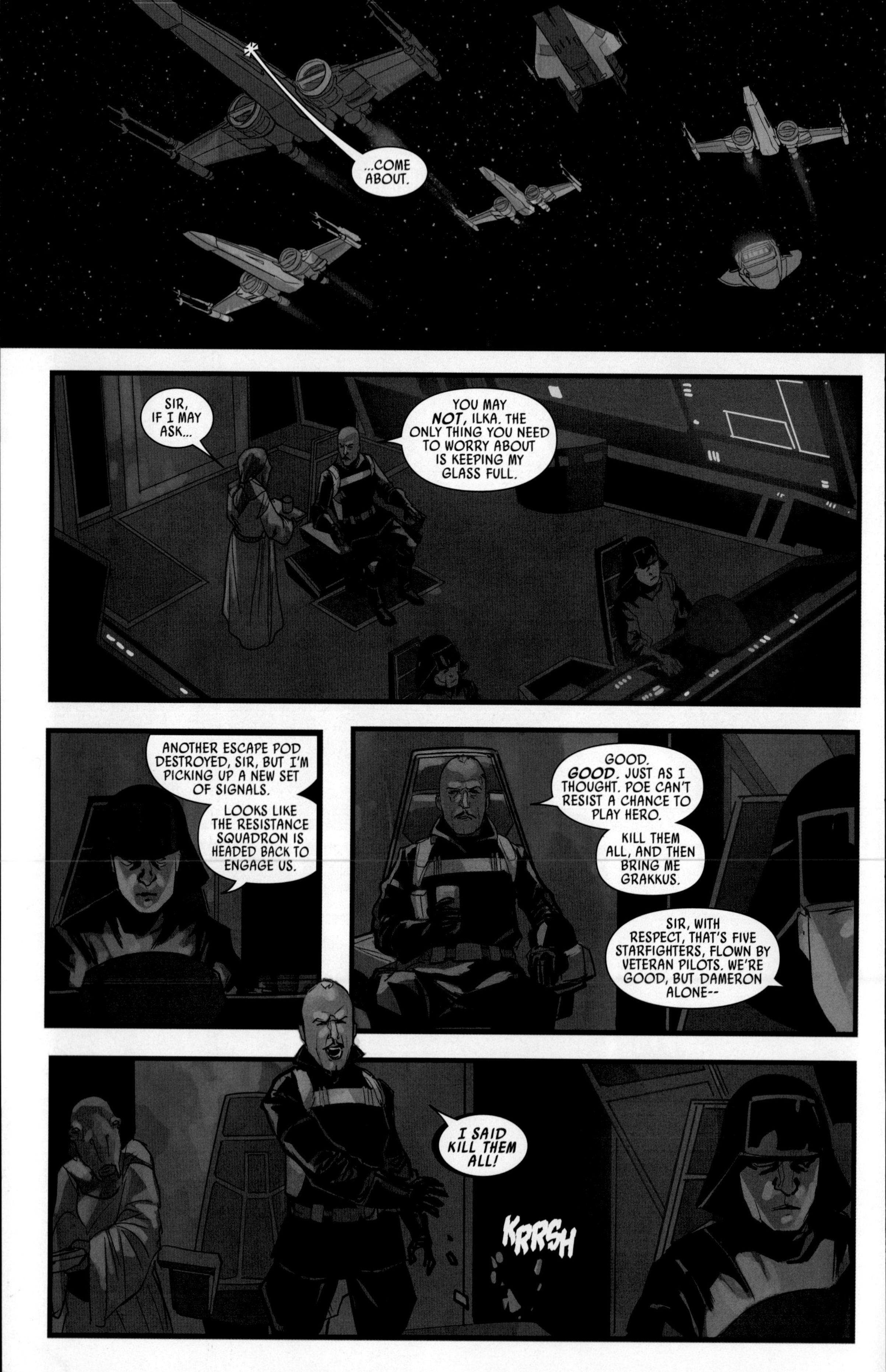
...COME ABOUT.
SIR, IF I MAY ASK...
YOU MAY NOT, ILKA. THE ONLY THING YOU NEED TO WORRY ABOUT IS KEEPING MY GLASS FULL.
ANOTHER ESCAPE POD DESTROYED, SIR, BUT I'M PICKING UP A NEW SET OF SIGNALS.
LOOKS LIKE THE RESISTANCE SQUADRON IS HEADED BACK TO ENGAGE US.
GOOD. GOOD. JUST AS I THOUGHT. POE CAN'T RESIST A CHANCE TO PLAY HERO.
KILL THEM ALL, AND THEN BRING ME GRAKKUS.
SIR, WITH RESPECT, THAT'S FIVE STARFIGHTERS, FLOWN BY VETERAN PILOTS. WE'RE GOOD, BUT DAMERON ALONE--
I SAID KILL THEM ALL!
KRRSH

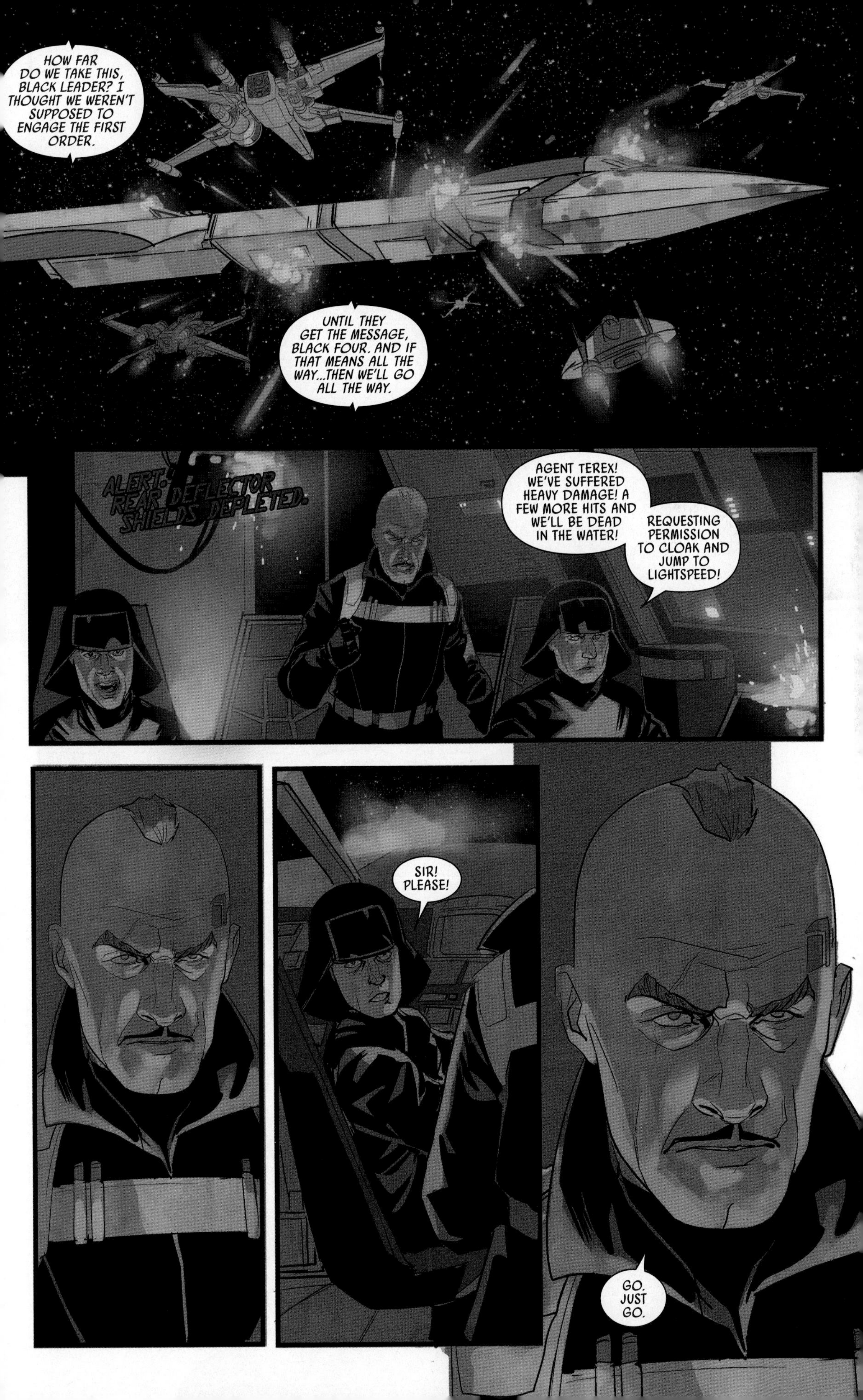
HOW FAR DO WE TAKE THIS, BLACK LEADER? I THOUGHT WE WEREN'T SUPPOSED TO ENGAGE THE FIRST ORDER.
UNTIL THEY GET THE MESSAGE, BLACK FOUR. AND IF THAT MEANS ALL THE WAY...THEN WE'LL GO ALL THE WAY.
ALERT: REAR DEFLECTOR SHIELDS DEPLETED.
AGENT TEREX! WE'VE SUFFERED HEAVY DAMAGE! A FEW MORE HITS AND WE'LL BE DEAD IN THE WATER!
REQUESTING PERMISSION TO CLOAK AND JUMP TO LIGHTSPEED!
SIR! PLEASE!
GO. JUST GO.

D'Qar.
Secret
Resistance
Base.

THIS IS EVERYTHING GRAKKUS GAVE YOU?

YES, GENERAL ORGANA. HE NEEDED US TO RUN HYPERSPACE CALCULATIONS FOR HIM, AND WE WOULDN'T DO *THAT* UNTIL HE GAVE UP HIS INFO ABOUT LOR SAN TEKKA.

DOES IT LOOK LEGIT?

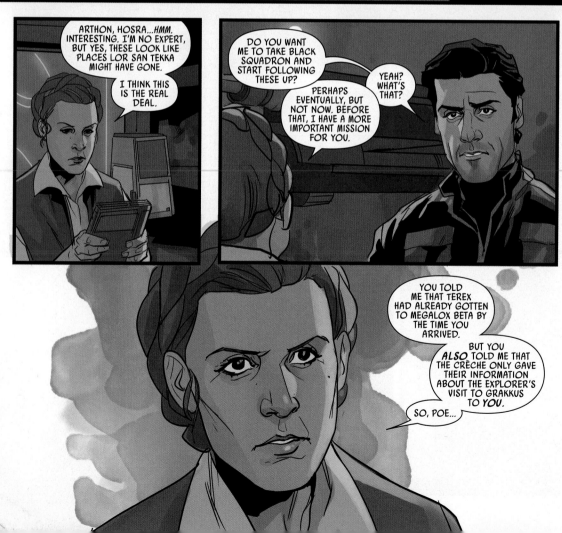

ARTHON, HOSRA...HMM. INTERESTING. I'M NO EXPERT, BUT YES, THESE LOOK LIKE PLACES LOR SAN TEKKA MIGHT HAVE GONE.

I THINK THIS IS THE REAL DEAL.

DO YOU WANT ME TO TAKE BLACK SQUADRON AND START FOLLOWING THESE UP?

PERHAPS EVENTUALLY, BUT NOT NOW. BEFORE THAT, I HAVE A MORE IMPORTANT MISSION FOR YOU.

YEAH? WHAT'S THAT?

YOU TOLD ME THAT TEREX HAD ALREADY GOTTEN TO MEGALOX BETA BY THE TIME YOU ARRIVED.

BUT YOU *ALSO* TOLD ME THAT THE CRÈCHE ONLY GAVE THEIR INFORMATION ABOUT THE EXPLORER'S VISIT TO GRAKKUS TO *YOU.*

SO, POE...

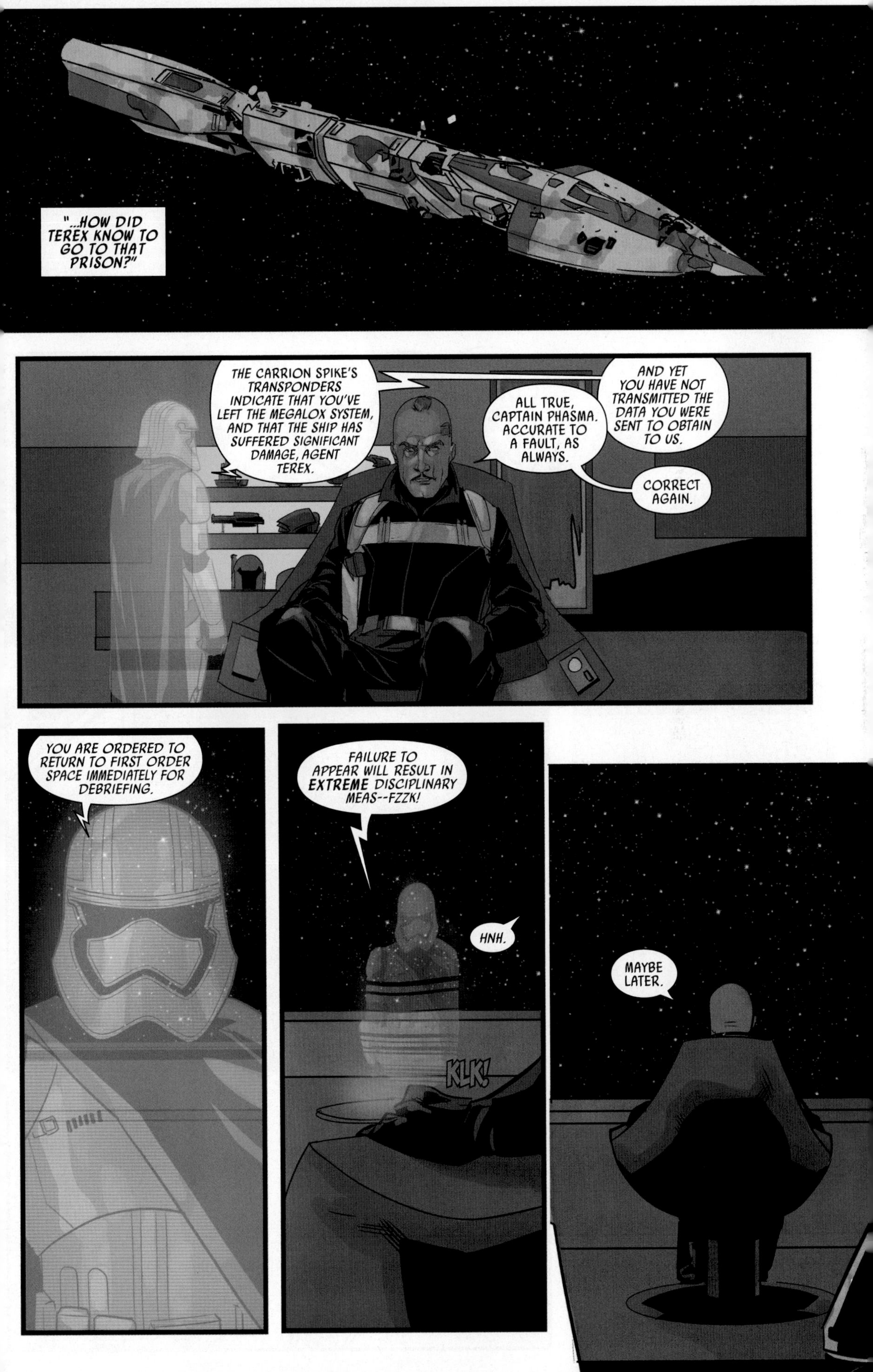
"...HOW DID TEREX KNOW TO GO TO THAT PRISON?"
THE CARRION SPIKE'S TRANSPONDERS INDICATE THAT YOU'VE LEFT THE MEGALOX SYSTEM, AND THAT THE SHIP HAS SUFFERED SIGNIFICANT DAMAGE, AGENT TEREX.
ALL TRUE, CAPTAIN PHASMA. ACCURATE TO A FAULT, AS ALWAYS.
AND YET YOU HAVE NOT TRANSMITTED THE DATA YOU WERE SENT TO OBTAIN TO US.
CORRECT AGAIN.
YOU ARE ORDERED TO RETURN TO FIRST ORDER SPACE IMMEDIATELY FOR DEBRIEFING.
FAILURE TO APPEAR WILL RESULT IN EXTREME DISCIPLINARY MEAS--FZZK!
HNH.
KLIK!
MAYBE LATER.

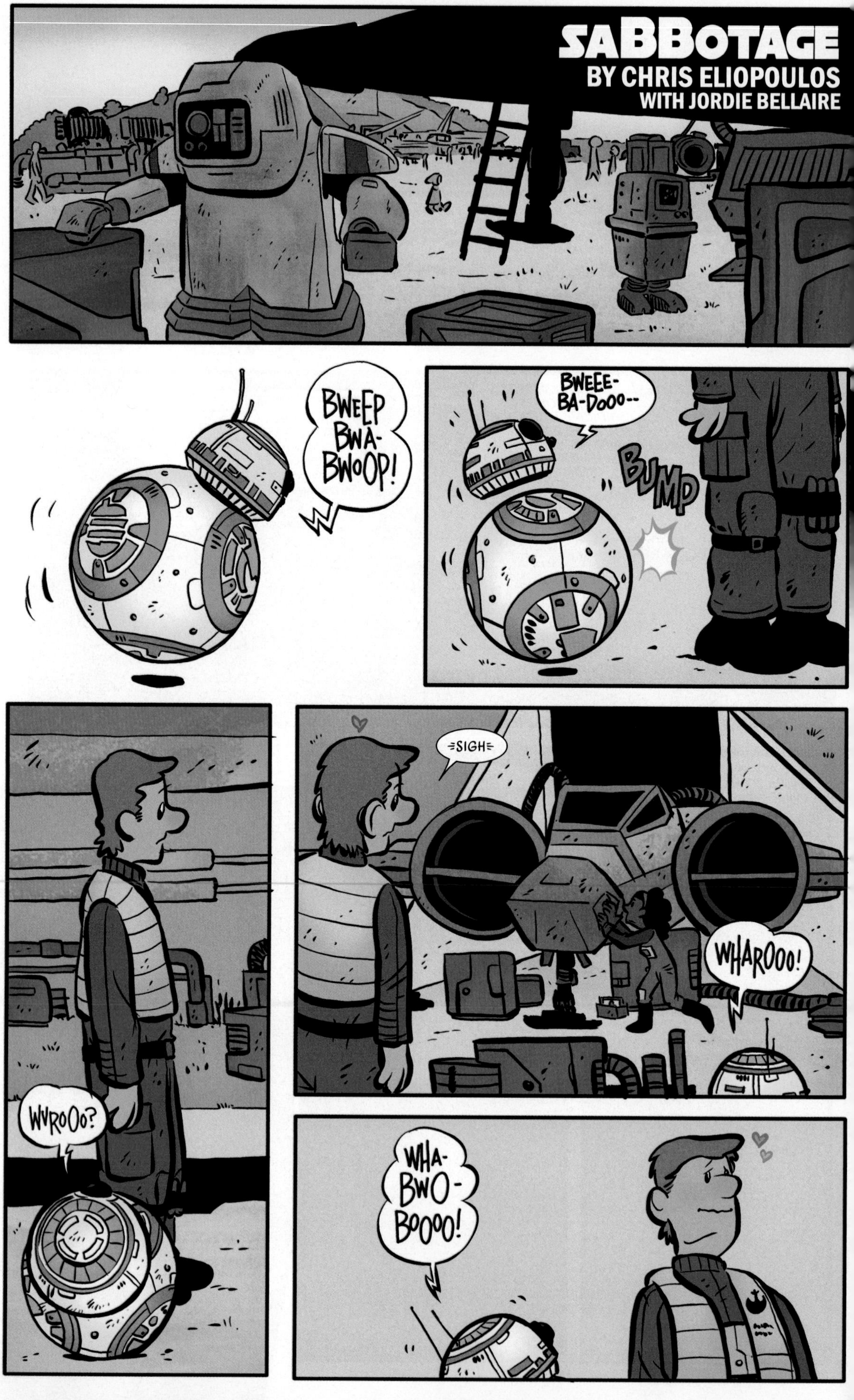
SaBBotage
BY CHRIS ELIOPOULOS
WITH JORDIE BELLAIRE
BWEEP BWA-BWOOP!
BWEEE-BA-DOOO--
BUMP
WVROOO?
SIGH
WHAROOO!
WHA-BWO-BOOOO!

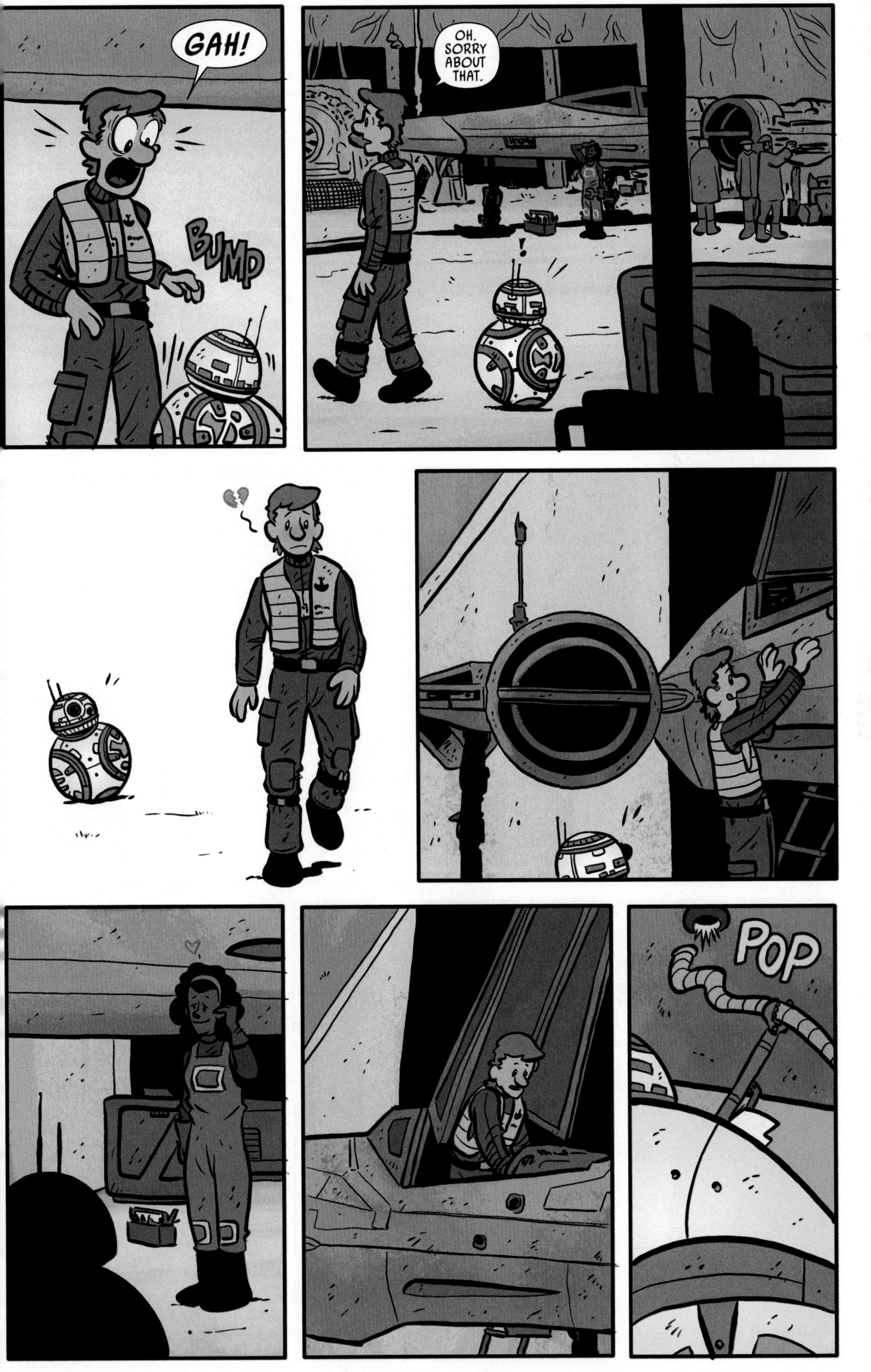
GAH!
BUMP
OH. SORRY ABOUT THAT.
POP

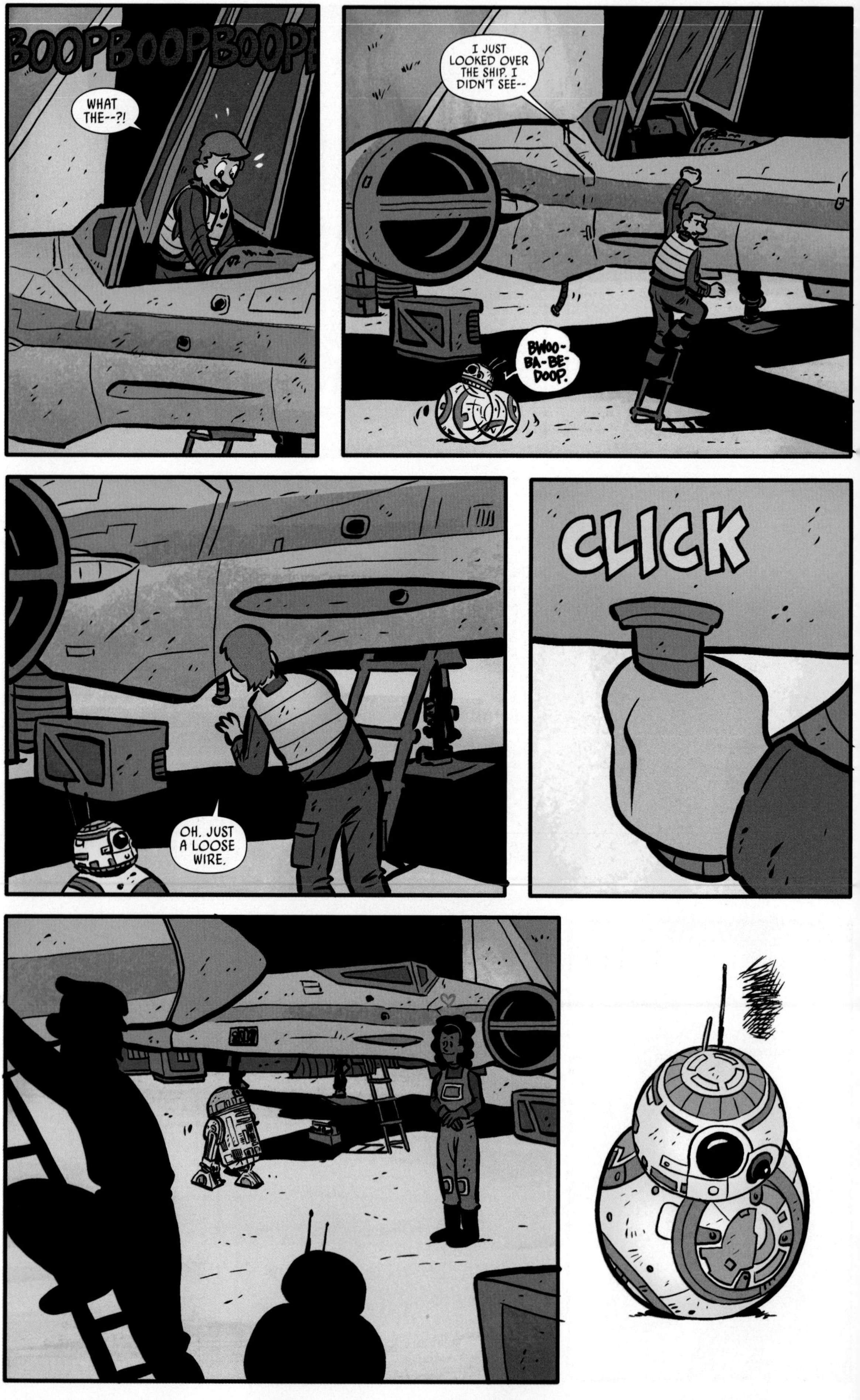

BOOPBOOPBOOPB
WHAT THE--?!
I JUST LOOKED OVER THE SHIP. I DIDN'T SEE--
BWOO-BA-BE-DOOP.
OH. JUST A LOOSE WIRE.
CLICK

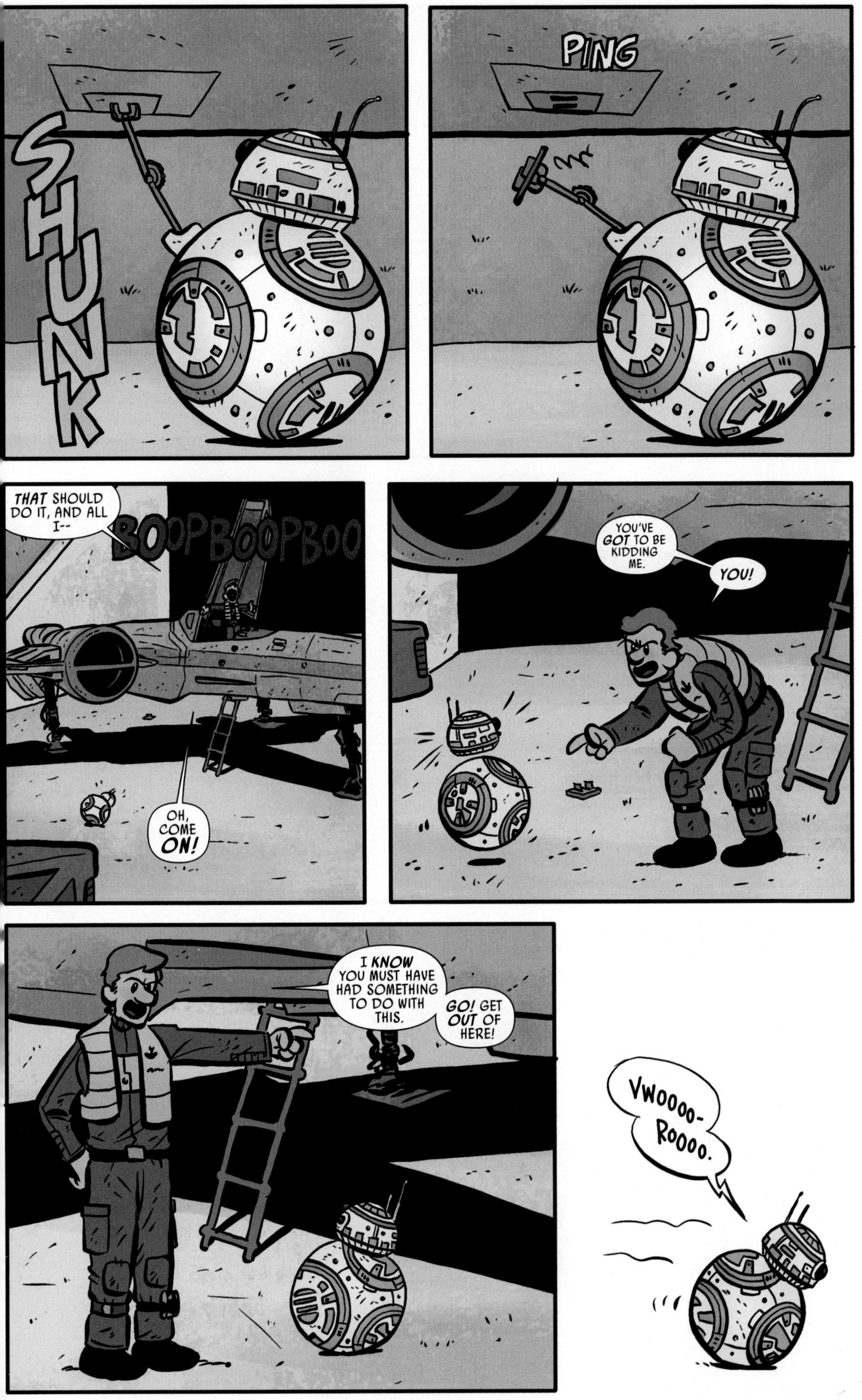
SHUNK
PING
THAT SHOULD DO IT, AND ALL I--
BOOPBOOPBOO
OH, COME ON!
YOU'VE GOT TO BE KIDDING ME.
YOU!
I KNOW YOU MUST HAVE HAD SOMETHING TO DO WITH THIS.
GO! GET OUT OF HERE!
VWOOOO-ROOOO.

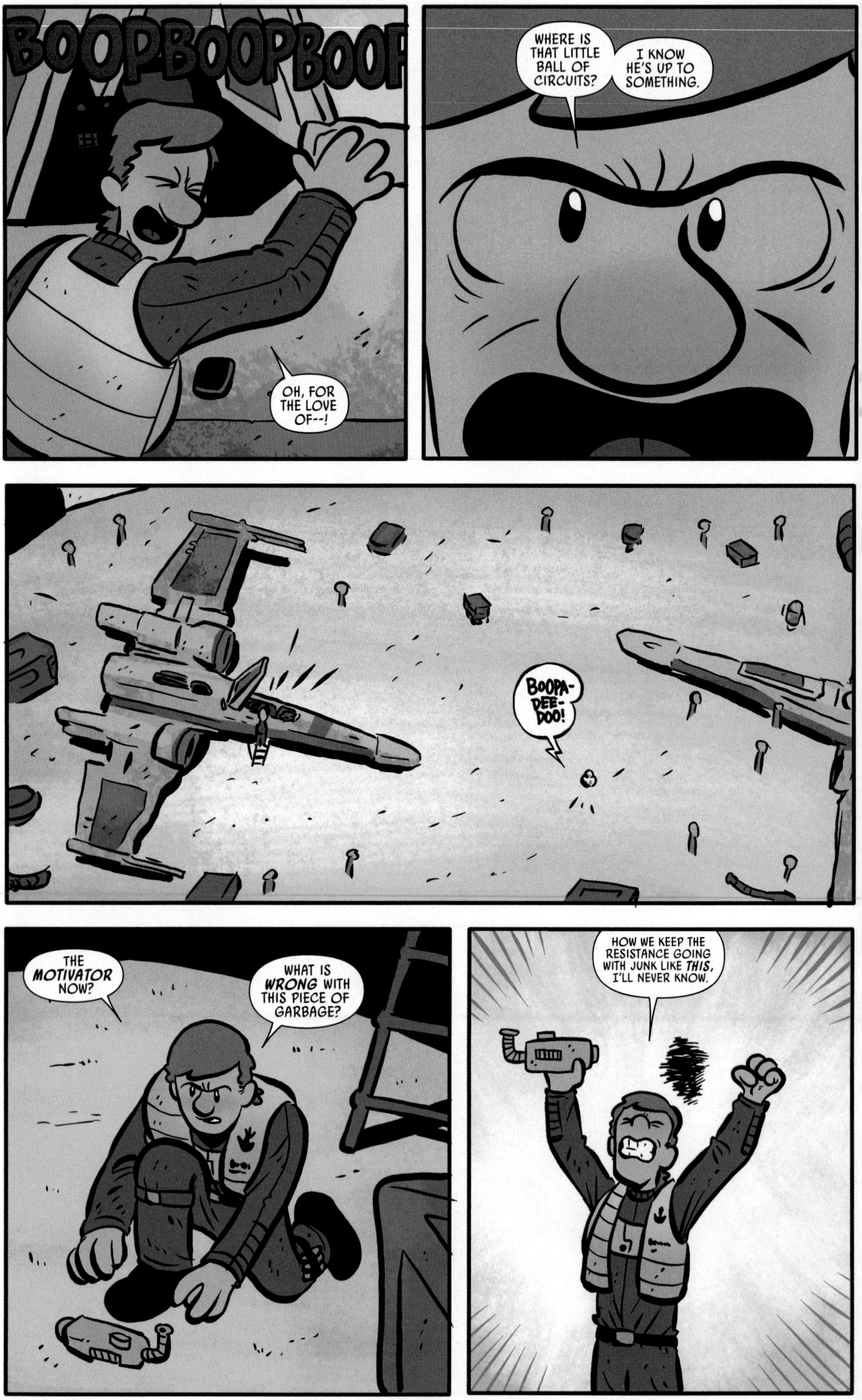
BOOPBOOPBOOP
OH, FOR THE LOVE OF--!
WHERE IS THAT LITTLE BALL OF CIRCUITS?
I KNOW HE'S UP TO SOMETHING.
BOOPA-DEE-DOO!
THE *MOTIVATOR* NOW?
WHAT IS *WRONG* WITH THIS PIECE OF GARBAGE?
HOW WE KEEP THE RESISTANCE GOING WITH JUNK LIKE *THIS*, I'LL NEVER KNOW.

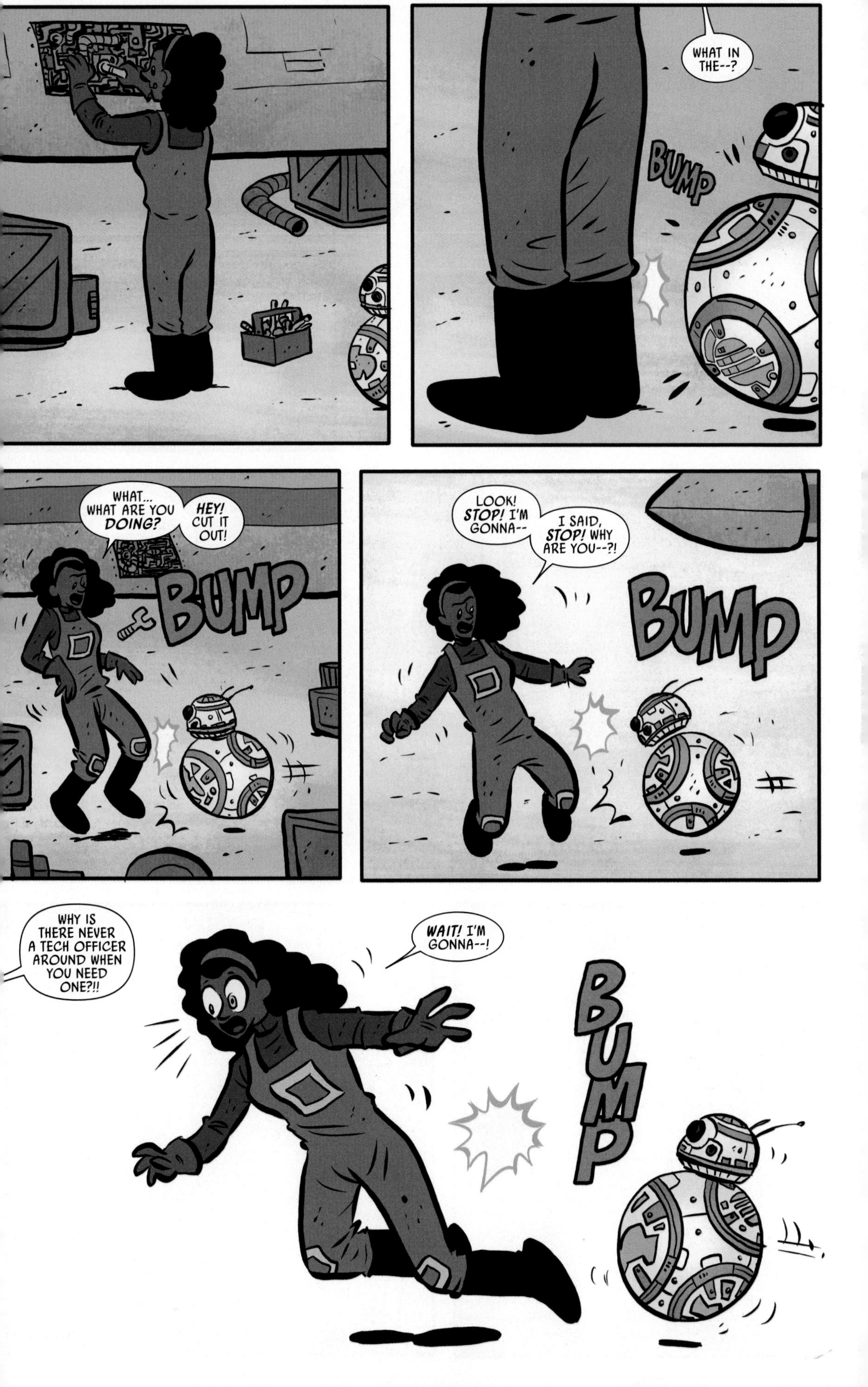

WHAT IN THE--?
BUMP
WHAT... WHAT ARE YOU DOING?
HEY! CUT IT OUT!
BUMP
LOOK! STOP! I'M GONNA--
I SAID, STOP! WHY ARE YOU--?!
BUMP
WHY IS THERE NEVER A TECH OFFICER AROUND WHEN YOU NEED ONE?!!
WAIT! I'M GONNA--!
BUMP

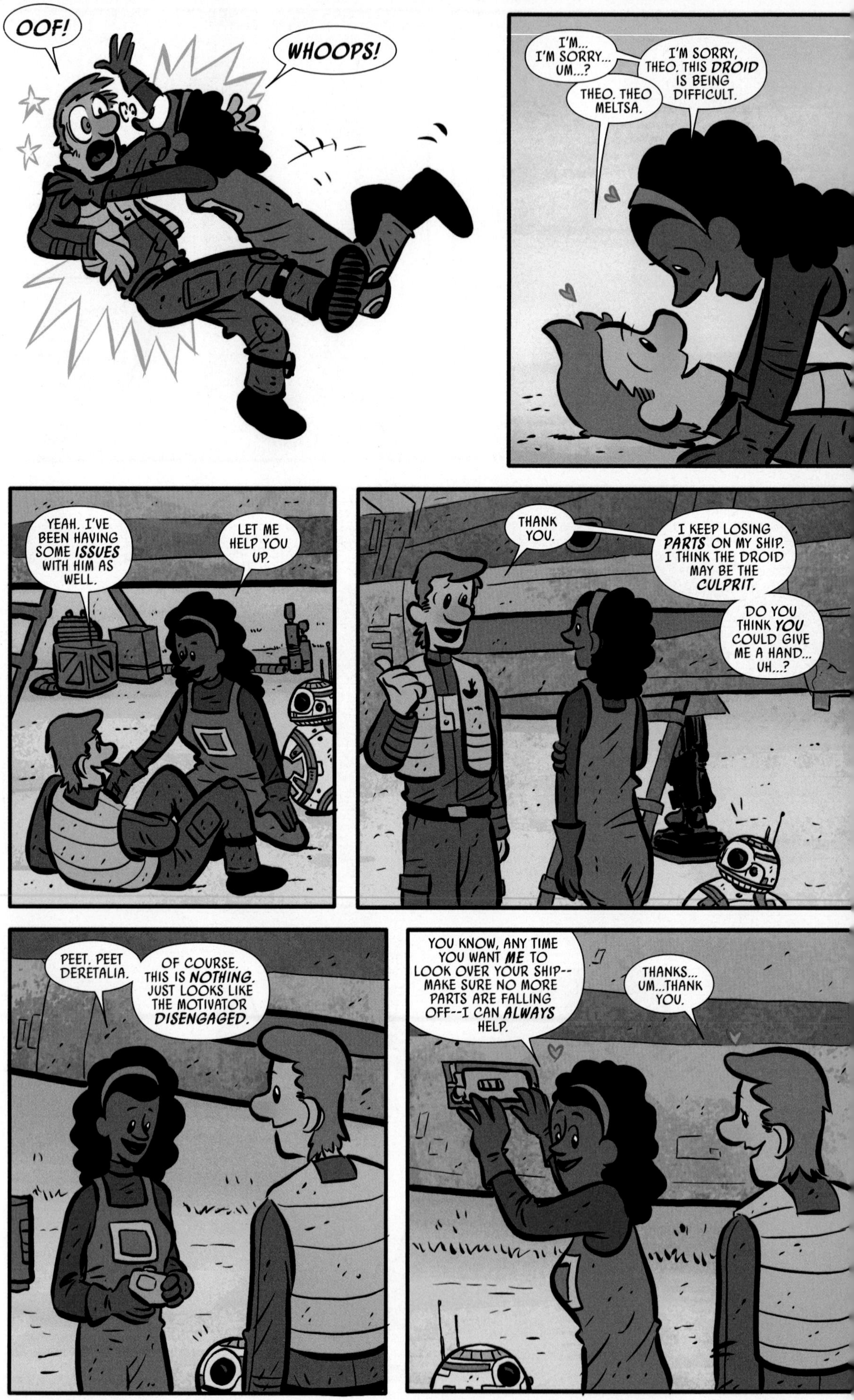

OOF!
WHOOPS!
I'M... I'M SORRY... UM...?
THEO. THEO MELTSA.
I'M SORRY, THEO. THIS DROID IS BEING DIFFICULT.
YEAH. I'VE BEEN HAVING SOME ISSUES WITH HIM AS WELL.
LET ME HELP YOU UP.
THANK YOU.
I KEEP LOSING PARTS ON MY SHIP. I THINK THE DROID MAY BE THE CULPRIT.
DO YOU THINK YOU COULD GIVE ME A HAND... UH...?
PEET. PEET DERETALIA.
OF COURSE. THIS IS NOTHING. JUST LOOKS LIKE THE MOTIVATOR DISENGAGED.
YOU KNOW, ANY TIME YOU WANT ME TO LOOK OVER YOUR SHIP--MAKE SURE NO MORE PARTS ARE FALLING OFF--I CAN ALWAYS HELP.
THANKS... UM...THANK YOU.

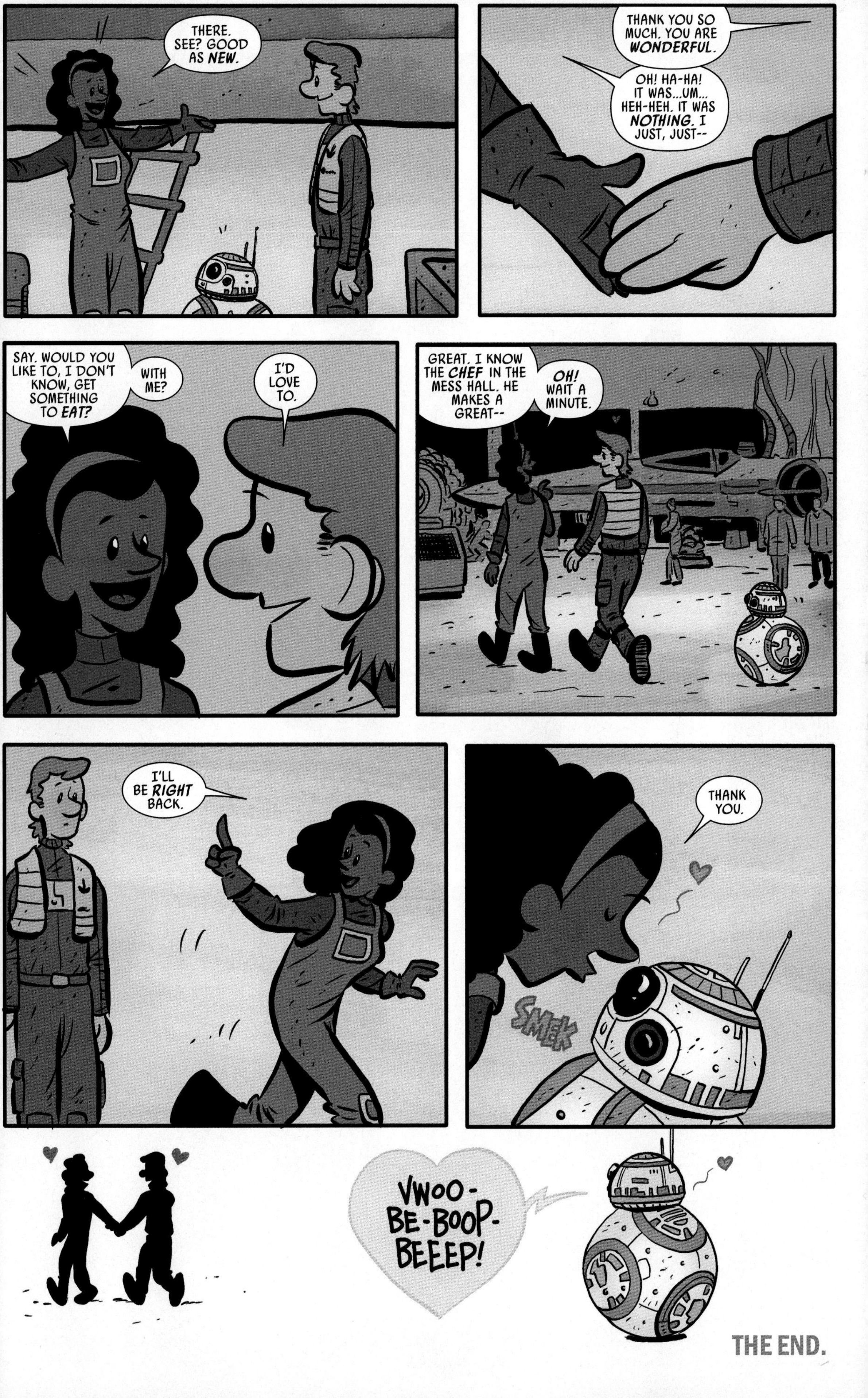
THERE. SEE? GOOD AS NEW.
THANK YOU SO MUCH. YOU ARE WONDERFUL.
OH! HA-HA! IT WAS...UM... HEH-HEH. IT WAS NOTHING. I JUST, JUST--
SAY. WOULD YOU LIKE TO, I DON'T KNOW, GET SOMETHING TO EAT?
WITH ME?
I'D LOVE TO.
GREAT. I KNOW THE CHEF IN THE MESS HALL. HE MAKES A GREAT--
OH! WAIT A MINUTE.
I'LL BE RIGHT BACK.
THANK YOU.
SMEK
VWOO-BE-BOOP-BEEEP!
THE END.

CHARACTERS YOU KNOW.
STORIES YOU DON'T.

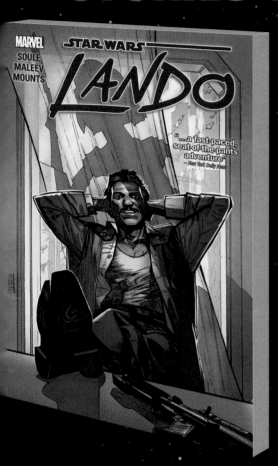

STAR WARS: LANDO TPB
978-0-7851-9319-7 • $16.99

STAR WARS: CHEWBACCA TPB
978-0-7851-9320-3 • $16.99

ON SALE NOW
IN PRINT & DIGITAL WHEREVER BOOKS ARE SOLD.